Leadership Style Finder

How Your Personality Defines Your Leadership Style

PETER BUROW

The material contained in this book is not intended as medical advice. If you have a medical issue or illness, consult a qualified physician.

Leadership Style Finder

Published by;

Copernicus Publishing Pty Ltd
www.copernicusproductions.com

Proofing by Amanda Banhidi
Desktop Publishing by Wade McFarlane

Copyright (c) 2014 Copernicus Publishing Pty Ltd, Edition 1.0.1 2014.

All rights reserved. No part of this publication may be reproduced, stored in a retrieval system, transmitted in any form or by any means, electronic, mechanical, photocopying, recording or otherwise, without the prior written permission of the publisher.

Readers' Comments

"I've used the insight from the Leadership Style Finder to build high performance teams that have exceeded all expectations. Filled with practical applications you can use immediately, Leadership Style Finder both educates and inspires."

Markus Von Der Luehe,
Country Manager, AdParlor
(Germany, Austria, Switzerland)

My reaction to the Leadership Style Finder is that it has the strengths of many of the other personality systems, and almost none of the weaknesses. It is accurate, it is flexible, it points to a capacity in human beings to develop, and it makes allowances for the fact that our responses are state specific so it enables one to see the interaction between oneself and others.

My hunch is that this is cutting edge technology in the realm of personality, and this whole area, and that in 30 years time this will be a very well known, taken-for-granted baseline system. I have great hope for it and I think it will become much more comprehensive. My sense is that we are going to be as indebted to the NeuroPower Framework 30-50 years down the track as we are now to the mid-20th Century Ego-psychologists who picked up from Jung, Freud and Adler.

It is as important as that.

Dr. Daniele Viliunas
Senior Psychiatrist
Brisbane, Queensland

Leadership Style Finder enables people to get a better understanding of their personality at a deeper level. It also helps people understand the underside or shadow of their personality. I think that is one of the critical differences.

Ricky Burgess
President
Australian Institute of Management
Western Australia

Within a week of having our leadership group exposed to Leadership Style Finder, we found that a number of people in our group were already using it to help them understand more about their individual attributes and how this affects other people. As an organization we are very keen to use the system as a way to galvanize our business together.

Garry Downes
Senior Executive
Forest Products Commission
Western Australia

Leadership Style Finder has certainly been an eye-opener for me because when you are dealing with people, sometimes you don't realize why everybody is different and to be able to do that is really beneficial.

Paul Neiderer
General Manager
Infomedia Fulfillment Services
Gold Coast, Queensland

How to Use this Book

This book has three distinct sections.

SECTION 1: YOUR FIRST STEP IN YOUR LIFE QUEST

The first section explores the mind's six thinking functions. These are used to solve the problems we face and the issues we need to think through on a daily basis. We introduce you to each function, its strength, weakness, opportunity and threat and how you can best use it in daily life.

SECTION 2: CHARACTER PROFILES

The second section introduces readers to the universal personalities that emerge when the six functions are combined in eight different ways.

This is a fascinating section that enables you to discover your own personality.

SECTION 3: THE QUEST FOR PERSONAL FOCUS

The third section examines how each of us can successfully use our leadership style in our daily life. It is a practical hands-on guide for applying the insight from the first two sections.

Contents

SECTION 1 — 1

Your First Step In Your Life Quest — 1

Chapter 1 — 5

We all laugh at different things and each one of us is motivated in different ways — 5

Introducing the six core functions or critical elements — 6

The soul, willpower and spirit — 7

Let's imagine you donate your brain to science — 7

C2 - Creative Vision — 8

C1 - Creative ingenuity — 8

I1 - Factual Information Gathering — 9

I2 - Qualitative information gathering — 9

P2 - Processing through values and beliefs — 10

P1 - Processing through logic — 11

The one dominant function — 11

Now, if your house burnt down and you used only your C1 function, what would you do when you arrived at the scene? — 12

What would happen if you accessed just your C2 thinking function after your house burnt down? — 12

What would happen if you accessed only your P1 function? — 12

Now what would happen if you used the P2 function, and nothing else? — 12

What happens if you access just your I1 function once your house has burnt down? — 13

What happens if you access your I2 function only? — 13

As you make your way through life, you access a combination of these functions — 13

Chapter 2 — 15

Creativity: The Song of the Soul — 15

So let's have a closer look at this creativity — 16

Looking deeper at the two distinctly different types of creativity - C1 and C2	17

Chapter 3 — 19

The First Kind of Creativity - C1 - Lateral Thinking — 19

Your greatest strength is your greatest weakness	20
The C1 function and relationships	21
Some challenges for the C1 function	21
A few comments about C1 and management	21
C1 and communication	22
Identifying C1 in another person	22

Chapter 4 — 25

The Second Kind of Creativity - C2 - Imagination — 25

C2 - your greatest strength is your greatest weakness	25
How does C2 apply to work and to relationships?	26
The impractical nature of the C2 function	26
The C2 function and management	26
The C2 function and communication	27
How do you identify a C2-dominant mind?	28

Chapter 5 — 31

Processing: The Act of Willpower — 31

P1 Logic and P2 Values and Beliefs	31

Chapter 6 — 33

Systematic Willpower - P1 — 33

Your greatest strength is your greatest weakness	33
The P1 function and relationships	34
The P1 function's challenges	34
The P1 function and management	35
The P1 function and communication	35
The P1 function likes frameworks	36

Chapter 7 — 39

Passion and Enthusiasm-Based Willpower - P2 — 39

- The P2 function's greatest strength is its greatest weakness — 39
- What's great about P2? — 40
- The P2 function's challenges — 40
- How does P2 affect communication? — 40

Chapter 8 — 43

The Human Spirit's Search for Information, The Mind's Search for Wisdom — 43

Chapter 9 — 45

Factual Data and Wisdom - I1 — 45

- The I1 function's greatest strength is its greatest weakness — 46
- So how does this apply to relationships and work? — 46
- What are your weaknesses? — 46
- So how does the I1 function affect management? — 46
- If you naturally access your I1 function, how will you communicate? — 47
- How can you identify someone who naturally accesses their I1 function? — 47

Chapter 10 — 49

Qualitative Earthly Wisdom - I2 — 49

- The I2 function's greatest strength is its greatest weakness — 49
- How does that relate to relationships at work? — 50
- The I2 function: broad themes or trends and management — 50
- The challenges for the I2 function — 51

Chapter 11 — 55

Putting it Together to Form a Leadership Style — 55

SECTION 2 — 59

Leadership Styles — 59

Chapter 12 — 61

The Crusader — 61

- The Crusader Profile — 62
- Overview — 62
- Focus of Attention — 62
- Key Character Drivers — 63
- The Subtypes — 63
- Leadership styles Related to the Crusader — 66
- Children's Stories/Nursery Rhymes — 66
- The Mirror — 66
- Understanding Crusaders — 67
- When negotiating with Crusaders — 68
- Famous Crusaders — 70
- Crusaders at Work — 71
- Leadership Style of the Crusader — 72
- School of Strategic Thought — 76
- The Genius of the Crusader – Pathfinding — 76

Chapter 13 — 77

The Coach — 77

- The Coach Profile — 78
- Overview — 78
- Focus of Attention — 79
- Key Character Drivers — 79
- The Subtypes — 80
- Leadership styles Related to the Coach — 82
- Children's Stories/Nursery Rhymes — 82
- The Mirror — 82
- Understanding Coaches — 83
- When negotiating with Coaches — 85
- Famous Coaches — 87
- Coaches at Work — 87

The Leadership Style of the Coach	88
School of Strategic Thought	91
The Genius of the Coach – Assigning Meaning	91

Chapter 14 — 93

The Diplomat — 93

The Diplomat Profile	94
Overview	94
Focus of Attention	95
Key Character Drivers	95
The Subtypes	96
Leadership styles Related to the Diplomat	97
Children's Stories	97
The Mirror	97
Understanding Diplomats	98
When Negotiating with Diplomats	100
Famous Diplomats	101
Diplomats at Work	101
The Diplomat's Mirror in the Workplace	103
The Leadership Style of the Diplomat	103
School of Strategic Thought	106
The Genius of the Diplomat – Building Bridges	107

Chapter 15 — 109

The Innovator — 109

The Innovator Profile	110
Overview	110
Focus of Attention	111
Key Character Drivers	111
The Subtypes	111
Leadership styles Related to the Innovator	113
Children's Stories/Nursery Rhymes	113

The Mirror	113
Understanding Innovators	114
When Negotiating with Innovators	116
Famous Innovators	118
The Innovator at Work	118
Leadership Style of the Innovator	119
School of Strategic Thought	122
The Genius of the Innovator – Problem-Solving	122

Chapter 16 — 123

The Change Agent — 123

The Change Agent Profile	124
Overview	124
Focus of Attention	125
Key Character Drivers	125
The Subtypes	125
Leadership styles Related to the Change Agent	127
Children's Stories	127
The Mirror	127
Understanding Change Agents	128
When Negotiating with Change Agents	130
Famous Change Agents	132
Change Agents at Work	132
The Change Agent's Mirror in the Workplace	134
Leadership Style of the Change Agent	134
School of Strategic Thought	136
The Genius of the Change Agent – Seeing Congruence	137

Chapter 17 — 139

The Planner — 139

The Planner Profile	140
Overview	140

Focus of Attention	140
Key Character Drivers	141
The Subtypes	141
Leadership styles Related to the Planner	142
Children's Stories/Characters	142
The Mirror	143
Understanding Planners	144
When Negotiating with Planners	146
Famous Planners	147
Planners at Work	147
The Planner's Mirror in the Workplace	149
The Leadership Style of the Planner	149
School of Strategic Thought	152
The Genius of the Planner – Planning	152
Chapter 18	**153**
The Analyzer	**153**
The Analyzer Profile	154
Overview	154
Focus of Attention	154
Key Character Drivers	154
The Subtypes	155
Leadership styles Related to the Analyzer	155
Children's Stories/Characters	156
The Mirror	156
Understanding Analyzers	157
When Negotiating with Analyzers	159
Famous Analyzers	160
Analyzers at Work	161
The Analyzer's Mirror in the Workplace	163
Leadership Style of the Analyzer	163
School of Strategic Thought	164

The Genius of the Analyzer – Creating Order	165
Chapter 19	**167**
The Energizer	**167**
Overview	168
Focus of Attention	168
Key Character Drivers	169
The Subtypes	169
Leadership styles Related to the Energizer	170
Children's Stories/Nursery Rhymes	170
The Mirror	171
Understanding Energizers	171
When Negotiating with Energizers	173
Famous Energizers	175
The Energizer at Work	175
Leadership Style of the Energizer	175
School of Strategic Thought	178
The Genius of the Energizer – Energizing and turning talk into action	178

SECTION 3   179

**The Quest For
Personal Focus**   179

Chapter 20	**183**
F: Fight The Good Fight	**183**
The million dollar answer	183
But, how does a master become a master?	185
But why would I bother making the second transition from awakening to focus? 185	
You will never reach your full potential by yourself	186
The first step is always the hardest	187
Let's do this thing	187
Your mission if you choose to accept it	187

Meet the most powerful strategist of all time	188
Sun-Tzu was a brilliant strategist who can help you fight the good fight	188
Barbara's Mirror ran her life!	189
Exploring the Master and Mirror	190
The role of the Master (what you want)	191
The role of the Mirror (what you need)	191
How empowered is your Master? (what you want)	192
How satisfied is your Mirror? (what you need)	192
Applying the insight from the capacity matrix at work	192
Applying the insight from the capacity matrix in life	192
The law of averages	196
Sun-Tzu's preparation phase	197

Chapter 21 — 203

O: Operationalize Your Attributes — 203

Develop your personal code of conduct	203
You must now learn how to manage your energy	211

Chapter 22 — 215

C: Courageously Examine Your Life — 215

Analyze your personal characteristics and external trends	215
Keep the upper hand	216
Understand the power of the seasons and learn how to work with them rather than fight them and fail!	217
Applying product life cycle analysis to your life (the BCG of life)	217
Analyze where your effort in life goes	219
Let me explain	220
Give yourself a round of applause	220

Chapter 23 — 223

U: Use A Master's Strategy — 223

But what is strategy?	223

Even the simplest task requires the implementation of a strategy or plan of attack	224
Refining the strategy	224
Ignore the nagging question to your own peril!	224
Ask the million-dollar question	225
Sun-Tzu's five basic strategies for life	225
How many of these strategies do you use?	226
Becoming a master	227
Your outcome is only as good as your strategy for action	227
But how do you know a strategy will work for you?	228
The power of a metaphor	228
The building blocks of creating a master strategy	228
If only masters realized that they are unconscious competents!	229
Here's a bonus ... strategies are 100 per cent transferable	230

Chapter 24 — 233

The Six Keys to Unlocking Your Own Master Strategy — 233

Step 1 - Notice how you prepare for the task	233
Step 2 - Notice the meaning you are making	234
Step 3 - Notice the sequence	234
Step 4 - Notice where you place your attention; on what do you focus?	234
Step 5 - Realize that you do nothing by accident	235
Step 6 - Tidy everything up	236
A strategy is like a personal road map	236
Individual strategies for learning	237
The author's learning strategy	238

Chapter 25 — 243

S: Strive to Manage Your Energy — 243

How well do you manage your energy levels?	243
There are five keys to personal energy	243
How much of your life are you doing things that empower you and how much of your life are you doing things that drain you of energy?	244

We feel good when we're doing tasks that give us energy, so why not structure your life accordingly?	244
Here's how to boost your P1 And P2 functions	245
Here's how to boost your I1 And I2 functions	245
Here's how to boost your C2 vision	245
How to boost your C1 function	246
Manage your energy level	246
Using Sun-Tzu's strategies to boost your energy	246
Frontal attack	247
Fragment attack	247
Flanking strategy	247
The defend strategy	247
The seasons of life and how they affect your energy levels	247
The cycle of life*	248
Energy in the Question Mark Phase	249
Energy in the Rising Star phase	249
Energy in the Cash Cow phase	250
Using the BCG matrix for strategic insight	250
What happens in the Dog phase?	250
Applying the BCG matrix to your relationships	252
Questions people sometimes ask	252
Use the principles of time management to energize you	254
Your destiny is shaped by your decisions, so use the NeuroPower thinking technology to make powerful decisions	254
Have instant access to all your thinking functions with the following exercises	255
Learn from the experiences of other masters — find their master strategies	256

A Final Word	**259**
Appendix One	**261**
Discover Your Strength or Unique Gift	**261**
The awakening — understanding the nature of human differences	262
Introducing the eight leadership styles	264

Appendix Two — 265
Compatibility Matrix — 265

Appendix Three — 267
Capacity Matrix
(Exploring the Mirror) — 267
   The four quadrants explained — 268

Appendix Four — 271
Leadership Style Inventory — 271
   Select two paragraphs that sound most like you — 273

Bibliography — 279

About the Author — 281

Acknowledgements

In writing this book I'd like to thank a number of people for their generous support and assistance. Firstly, I'd like to thank the thousands of people who so generously and openly shared their stories in our workshops and conferences, and have helped define and refine the Personalities.

I'd like to thank Leonel Chevez, Nana Chica and the Maya Lenca people for their significant contribution to the six thinking functions, the leadership styles and the Master/Mirror.

I also wish to thank Murray Jorgensen and Liz Ellis for constantly challenging me on the usefulness of this book and working with me to make sure it had practical applications.

I'd also like to thank Andrew Burow for his constant support and for the thoroughness of his proofing and editing and my mother Irene Burow for her decades of work with gifted, talented and special needs students, and her insights into personality, learning and creativity that have been included in this edition.

Finally I'd like to thank Anna Byrne for her editing, synthesising and refining of this edition.

Peter L. Burow
February 2014

SECTION 1

Your First Step In Your Life Quest

Your First Step in Your Life Quest

*To the dull mind all nature is leaden. To the illuminated mind,
the whole world burns and sparkles with light.*

Ralph Waldo Emerson

Your First Step in Your Life Quest

Chapter 1

*It's not enough to have a good mind,
the main thing is to use it well.*

Descartes

It becomes obvious early in life that everyone is different in the way they use their mind, and how well they use it. Humor, for example, is a complex mental process which varies from person to person depending on how their mind ticks.

We all have a different sense of humor. This I know because for a short period of time I was a stand-up comic, and I found very early in my career that we all laugh at different things. I quickly discovered that about three quarters of the group would love puns, or 'the switch'. They'd like the humor in TV programs like, *Two and a Half Men, The Simpsons, Yes Prime Minister,* or *The Nanny*. The other quarter would like smut and anything that's taboo. They'd enjoy programs like *South Park, Absolutely Fabulous and The Young Ones*. Whatever thrilled the first group would bore the second group, and whatever thrilled the second group would offend the first.

As the comic, my challenge was to make sure that by the end of the night no one wanted their money back!

WE ALL LAUGH AT DIFFERENT THINGS AND EACH ONE OF US IS MOTIVATED IN DIFFERENT WAYS

Have you ever tried to motivate someone and found it didn't work? If you are a high-energy, passionate type of person trying to motivate a low-energy, low passionate type, have you found that your approach actually demoralizes or even angers them? The fact is we do have different senses of humor, different motivations, and different preferences on everything from the ideal job to the ideal partner in life.

And just to make things complicated we are often inconsistent. Sometimes we agree with someone on one topic and then fiercely disagree with that same person on another five minutes later.

Often, people we enjoy working with are people we wouldn't invite to our home, or vice versa. And we can change in an instant, acting and feeling one way around one person, and then being completely different with somebody else.

Why is it that we can appear fluent, convincing, charming, sincere and powerful in one meeting, and yet at the next, become inarticulate and appear to be lacking credibility? Why do we all live, laugh, learn and love so differently? These are just some of the questions you can answer if you understand the way your mind works and appreciate its strengths, its weaknesses and its leadership style.

This section will help you understand how your mind works

The NeuroPower framework, on which this book is based, explains how decision-making is a constant internal battle between different parts of your mind, as they jostle for priority. It gives you the ability to recognize and understand the inner conversations you have with yourself, the inner conflicts you experience, and the formula for accessing your mind's full potential.

This powerful personality system can explain why some people seem to have boundless energy and others none at all; why some people appear cold and others warm; why some love to offend and others enjoy being offended; and why some people are refreshingly crazy and others are refreshingly sane.

All these variables are determined by just one simple process: the way the mind solves problems with the benefit of modern neuroscience, we now have a much better understanding of how our brains work and determine our thoughts, feelings and actions. These insights enable us to respond consciously as we move through life, rather than react habitually. After all as Anthony Robbins says, "It's in your moments of decision that your destiny is shaped." Yet how often have you seriously thought about the way you make decisions?

The NeuroPower Framework enables you to study seriously the way you make decisions and so shape your destiny. The way you do this is unlike any other person in the world. It's your thinking fingerprint. Your decision-making profile is your primary identity. It's the you that you recognize. When using your mind's natural strengths, you'll be fluent. When using your mind's weaknesses, your ability to articulate subsides to the point that both you and others will see you at best as insincere and at worst as very stupid.

INTRODUCING THE SIX CORE FUNCTIONS OR CRITICAL ELEMENTS

In total there are six functions used by the mind when solving a problem. Each one is a critical element in making a powerful and balanced decision. These six critical elements or natural programs are:

C1 - *The creative ingenuity function*

C2 - *The creative vision function*

P1 - The processing with logic function

P2 - The processing through values and beliefs function

I1 - The factual information gathering function, and

I2 - The qualitative information gathering function

So to understand the thing educators call metacognition (the science of thinking about thinking), we simply need to fully understand these six functions[1].

THE SOUL, WILLPOWER AND SPIRIT

These six functions can then be grouped into three subgroups: creativity, willpower and wisdom.

Creativity comes in two forms: There's C1, which is the function related to lateral thinking and ingenuity, and there's the C2 function, which enables us to have imagination. Willpower we segment into either P1 (logic) or P2 (values and beliefs).

Finally, there are two kinds of wisdom. We learn in one of two ways: either through the I1 function, which collects factual information or hard data, or through the I2 function which collects emotional information or soft data.

By nature you'll be strong in some of these functions and weak in others. If we understand how to access these six functions we can begin to use them in everyday life and experience the enormous power of our mind.

LET'S IMAGINE YOU DONATE YOUR BRAIN TO SCIENCE

For the purposes of explaining how your mind creates, processes and absorbs information, we'll use a graphic illustration. Even though the metaphor may seem unorthodox (the creative types amongst you won't mind), the story enables us to dissect the way the mind solves problems. Imagine for a moment that you've donated your brain for use in a scientific experiment. The researchers take your brain out of your body and place it in a little tank full of brain fluid. You don't have any eyes. In fact, you don't have any external senses and you have no ability to communicate with the outside world. All you have is your brain sitting in brain fluid. In this state you can still imagine who you are, the roles you play and the people you know. You can use your imagination to dream ideas. This ability to use your imagination is independent of your life experience.

---

1 These six dimensions of personality are described in *NeuroPower: Leading with NeuroIntelligence, Third Edition, Peter Burow, 2013* as Six Social Cognitive Needs and are charted back to clear functional networks within the brain. They develop in a particular order not reflected in this book, namely, P1, C1, P2, I2, I1 and C2. The way we've described them in this text is focused only on the 'thinking' aspect for the six dimensions of personality. The other two aspects of each dimension, the 'somatic' aspect and the 'feeling' aspect, are outlined in detail in the *NeuroPower: Leading with NeuroIntelligence* text.

You can even imagine things you know nothing about as if you are tapping into another source, from another place.

This is what we call your C2 function. The C's stand for **CREATIVITY**. The pure C2 function refers to your mind's ability to tap into creative vision, which is often described as a stream of ideas. It is an uncontrolled, unbridled, dreaming part of your mind.

When Martin Luther King said, "I have a dream", he was expressing his C2 function.

C2 - CREATIVE VISION

'Inspirational' is a word that comes to mind when describing the C2 function. This function enables people to make great inspirational speeches because they can totally ignore mundane reality and think of ideas that no one else has ever thought of before.

While C2 is a very high-energy part of the mind, it is also very fragile. Without an outlet, the C2 function will feel squashed, undervalued and unmotivated. Because the C2 function visualizes well, it enjoys being able to communicate this vision to other people who are keen to listen. The C2 function is great at breaking new territory because it is the source for a touch of something brilliant - Mozart and Leonardo da Vinci are two examples of people with minds that accessed the C2 function.

The other type of creativity is less dreamy and more practical and is known as the C1 function. It enables ingenuity or lateral thinking. The C1 function spontaneously breaks the mind out of thinking ruts.

C1 - CREATIVE INGENUITY

The C1 function likes to challenge everything, including the good and bad. For this reason people with a mind dominated by the C1 function can often get themselves into trouble by brainstorming ideas and intellectually freewheeling at any opportunity rather than getting on with the job.

C1 is a high-energy function of the mind. It makes for witty and funny conversationalists. George Bernard Shaw, Oscar Wilde, Barry Humphries and Clive James are people who have minds with a very high C1 influence.

Meanwhile back at the laboratory, your brain is still floating in the tank and is able to both visualize concepts using C2 and think spontaneously using C1. But it's not solving problems. It's just generating ideas. It's certainly not in touch with reality because it doesn't have information entering from the outside world.

Now we will add the ability to see and read (visual communication). For the sake of the exercise we'll imagine they attach a pair of eyes to your brain floating in the tank. If a newspaper is placed in front of the tank this enables your mind to absorb factual information through your eyes. This absorption of factual data is referred to as the I1 function. The I's stand for **INFORMATION**.

I1 - FACTUAL INFORMATION GATHERING

When making a decision the I1 function will always be looking for the facts. This function of your brain will search every nook and cranny for all relevant factual information.

People with minds dominated by this I1 function tend to study a specific topic in close detail as revealed in how they approach their hobbies. A client of mine with a very high I1, is a train enthusiast. He knows every conceivable fact about trains built over a 15-year period, down to the name of the designer and the number of bolts used in each loco.

Remember that the I1 function enables you to process factual data. When reading books, for example, rather than deciding if they agree or disagree with what is being said, minds dominated by I1 will enjoy categorizing the information and cross-referencing it with other information from other books they have read. They may not necessarily do anything else with the information.

People who naturally use the I1 function usually take in information through the eyes; they are mostly visual communicators and visual learners. They are usually excellent spellers, remember phone numbers and are usually good writers.

Because most of their communication involves the exchange of facts, conversations between I1 minds usually take the form of information trading. The I1 function enables you to remember the petrol prices in the area, area codes for different geographical areas and all the right dates for past events. The I1 function also loves collecting information about all aspects of the world in which the person lives. The search for this information can involve adventure, physical activity and action. In education, the Western world focuses on training and evaluating the I1 function. The majority of people with brains dominated by I1 excelled at school and enjoy further studies.

Returning to the laboratory, let's imagine they now attach a pair of ears and a nose and they let you look around the laboratory giving you the ability to pick up intuitively what is happening in the room.

I2 - QUALITATIVE INFORMATION GATHERING

With access to your I2 function you can start to pick up the feelings of people in the laboratory. You begin feeling strange emotions for no reason and you notice that you have picked up feelings from a technician who is upset. Like a child, each of us has the ability to intuitively transmit and receive emotional information. The I2 function gives us access to this empathetic ability. The information is qualitative rather than quantitative.

People who naturally use the I2 function are sensitive because the I2 program enables them to access their feeling antenna and they can pick up the 'vibes' in the room from all the different people.

When your mind accesses I2 you will have a wonderful way of knowing just what to do or what to say in most sensitive or diplomatic situations. So while the I1 reads the factual data on the lines, I2 reads the emotional information between the lines. Females tend to describe I2 as intuition. Males tend to describe I2 as gut reaction.

In 1997, an Australian university conducted a study which analyzed the process for awarding contracts of $10 million plus in the building industry. They wanted to understand how boards made multi-million dollar decisions. What they expected to find was a structured and impartial process. What they discovered was that 95 per cent of these multimillion-dollar decisions were made by 'gut reaction'. Now that's male code for intuition. Isn't that fascinating? At the end of the day even large public companies go with what 'feels' right. These groups used their I2 function because it deals well with complex tasks and can assess many variables simultaneously. So while the decision may not be structured and logical it may still be the best decision because it draws on the vast experience that's held in the subconscious I2 function.

So far we've explored four of the six thinking functions or critical elements C1, C2, I1, I2. But as yet we haven't discussed the deciding part of your mind. You can have creative juices flowing and information coming into the mind, but there will be no action until a decision is made. If your mind consisted only of these four critical elements you would have no views and opinions and you would have no desire to act. The C1, C2, I1 and I2 parts of the mind are the being parts. (We are human *beings* after all.) But the *doing* parts of your mind are P1 and P2. The P's stand for **PROCESSING**.

You process what you know in one of two ways. You process it according to either what is right and wrong, or what is logical. So the last two functions, P1 and P2, refer to the mind's preferred style of processing the information. For example, the P2 function sifts ideas through a set of values and beliefs. This function lets us judge what is right and wrong. When your mind uses the P2 function you will have an amazing ability to show commitment to, and passion for, a cause.

P2 - PROCESSING THROUGH VALUES AND BELIEFS

The P2 function enables you to feel concerned about moral and justice issues. This function is a very high-energy part of the mind and drives people to achieve amazing things. Politics, religion, excellence - anything that is related to passion will be related to the P2 function. P2 is used for selling, negotiating, buying or convincing. Often many of the world's most powerful and inspirational leaders are experts at using their mind's P2 function.

> ***Prove to yourself that you can do it. Prove that you were always who you thought you were, not who they said you had to be.***
>
> Rachel Snyder

P1 - PROCESSING THROUGH LOGIC

Alternatively, the P1 function enables the mind to access reasoning and logic. P1 has an enormous need not to be subjective, but instead to be very objective, carefully sifting the information and sorting it into some sense of logic or progression. P1 gives your mind the ability to work through one project at a time, preferably systematically in a controlled environment. People who by nature use their P1 function prefer order and systemisation and usually work well in structured environments. The most demotivating event to befall a mind dominated by P1 is to have the system changed mid-flight through a project.

THE ONE DOMINANT FUNCTION

So in total there are six different thinking functions or critical elements in the problem-solving process. Most brains are, however, dominated by just one function, which often rules over the other less dominant functions. This dominant function alone decides what problems the brain will tackle and to what extent it will solve them. **The evolved mind, however, is able to move away from this natural inclination to just use one of these functions and instead use the right one or combination for the right job.**

So in summary, we can use:

- C1 and C2 for creating new opportunities and responding creatively to situations;
- I1 and I2 for collecting information, and
- P1 and P2 for processing those creative thoughts and the collected information. Pretty simple really!

NOW, IF YOUR HOUSE BURNT DOWN AND YOU USED ONLY YOUR C1 FUNCTION, WHAT WOULD YOU DO WHEN YOU ARRIVED AT THE SCENE?

Let's imagine for a moment that your brain could use only the C1 thinking function, and let's imagine for a moment that your house burnt down. What would you do? Well, you would probably start thinking of all the possible reasons the house burnt down. Was it the iron? Was it electrical? Perhaps I should have spent more money on that circuit breaker? Oh, I wonder whether I left the iron on this morning? You'll think laterally about all the possibilities.

Now because C1 is a function that creates energy, people who are watching you may think that there's something a bit strange about someone who seems to be energized rather than upset about the situation.

WHAT WOULD HAPPEN IF YOU ACCESSED JUST YOUR C2 THINKING FUNCTION AFTER YOUR HOUSE BURNT DOWN?

Well, you would probably think to yourself, 'Hmm! That house was good, but the next one will be even better.' You would start visioning what the new house would look like, because vision is future-centered. So you'd be dreaming, 'Tomorrow we'll build a new and even better home.' C2 would give you the ability to see that house as clearly in your mind as if it were already built.

WHAT WOULD HAPPEN IF YOU ACCESSED ONLY YOUR P1 FUNCTION?

The P1 function always asks, 'What's the next action step?' So you'd ask, 'Have we rung the insurance people? Where are we going to stay tonight? Do we have money for tonight's accommodation?' To others you may appear disconnected, detached, or unfeeling and uncaring, but they would have to admit that you took action and it was the logical thing to do.

NOW WHAT WOULD HAPPEN IF YOU USED THE P2 FUNCTION, AND NOTHING ELSE?

What would you do when you arrive? P2 decides whether it's right or wrong, good or bad. You'd probably decide, 'This is not good.' And you may search for the meaning that you should derive from this event, because everything in the P2 world happens for a reason. You may also seek to define where the responsibility for this disaster lies to discover whose fault it is, and to see to it that justice is done.

WHAT HAPPENS IF YOU ACCESS JUST YOUR I1 FUNCTION ONCE YOUR HOUSE HAS BURNT DOWN?

You would conduct a fact-finding mission. What exactly was the time the fire started? How long did it take the fire brigade to get here? What was the name of the person who took the phone call? What is the exact number of our insurance policy? How many people saw it? How long did it take to put out the fire? You would collect all the factual information, write it down, and possibly even file it for future reference.

WHAT HAPPENS IF YOU ACCESS YOUR I2 FUNCTION ONLY?

I2 is interested in picking up energy through emotion. The I2 function would be interested in how people are feeling. Do we need to have a hug as a family? How am I feeling? Do I need to have a hug? How are the neighbors? Is anybody really angry with us? Is somebody upset? Is everyone OK? How are the fire brigade men feeling? You will focus on tapping into everyone's emotional response.

As you can see, each one of these six functions has a different way of interpreting and dealing with the world.

AS YOU MAKE YOUR WAY THROUGH LIFE, YOU ACCESS A COMBINATION OF THESE FUNCTIONS

As you are reading this book, for example, if you are accessing your P1 you will be logically thinking of any inconsistencies you detect in the way it is written.

If you are accessing your P2 you may be wondering whether you believe it is right or wrong, and whether this is the best possible use of your time.

If you are accessing your I1 you will be noticing the grammar and the punctuation and the spelling and even the font we have used.

If you are accessing your I2 you will probably be pausing every now and then just to remember different situations in your life and recall the emotions created by that situation. You may even be thinking, 'I feel this is right' or 'Something about this doesn't feel right.'

If you are accessing your C2 you may be visualizing situations relevant to the book's content. Of course C2 could also mean you could be thinking of completely unrelated images.

If you are accessing your C1 you will be thinking of all the different ways you can use the information in this book in different situations at home and at work or in relationships. For the C1 function, every second word will also trigger a whole plethora of unrelated thoughts, which will flood your mind.

In a nutshell

There are six thinking functions (critical elements) used by our mind to solve problems.

By nature, we use some of our six thinking functions more than others.

The thinking functions we naturally use, create patterns of behavior that we recognize as being 'us'. These preferred thinking functions combine to create our unique thinking profile - or personality profile.

To take Descartes' advice and use our minds well, we need to fully understand each of these six thinking functions and how and when to use them.

Chapter 2

Creativity: The Song of the Soul

We've looked globally at how the mind works, but now let's spend some time focusing on creativity. We're going to explore creativity because if you can access the creative functions, you will be able to recreate your life so that it's the kind of life you want. Sadly when we lose touch with our soul's creativity, we lose touch with the spontaneity, fun and joy of life.

Now creativity is one of those strange things that everybody's heard about but very few people understand. Ralph Waldo Emerson once said, "To the dull mind, all nature is leaden. To the illuminated mind, the whole world sparkles with light." George Bernard Shaw said, "Some men see things as they are and say Why? I dream of things that never were and say, Why not?"

"Imagination," says Albert Einstein, "is more important than knowledge." Can you believe Einstein saying that? Science teaches that you start with a premise and use logic to find the answer. The myth is that logic can solve every problem. Well, here's the exception to the rule. Albert Einstein failed school. He failed institutional thinking processes. Einstein failed because he would use creativity to find the answer and then use logic to justify it. He died before he managed to logically justify some of his answers.

For centuries, science has underestimated the power and truth of creativity.

It often fascinates me that it's been creativity that's given rise to thousands of brilliant ideas that have changed our lives in the past 2000 years! It's been inspired creativity that's made many corporations, their executives and their shareholders wealthy. With this track record, you'd think that the ability to inspire and motivate the creative flair in people would be a well-honed skill held by team leaders worldwide.

Surprisingly, exactly the opposite holds true. While there have been many studies conducted on creativity, most show that creative people remain misunderstood. Within organizations, the creative people are often ostracized or even expelled from the group. In group work, the creatives are often the hardest to manage, and so they're often excluded from the very activity to which they could make the best contribution. At school, they usually fail.

In advertising, one industry that sells creativity, the problem is solved by isolating the 'creatives'. If you were to visit a major ad agency, you'd find that they break their employees into two distinct groups - the 'creatives' and the 'suits'. The 'creatives' grow their hair to the floor, wear the most extraordinary clothes and use language you'd prefer not to be used in the right circles. The 'suits', on the other hand, are beautifully manicured, with extraordinary dress sense, and they have the political talent to say exactly what you'd expect to be said in all the right circles.

The only way agencies prevent the 'creatives' from offending the clients is by hiding them. And so an environment is created where the outside world relates to a 'suit', and the 'suit' plucks up the courage to deal with the 'creatives'.

This system humidicribs the creative people by creating a barrier between them and the outside world. For the creative people, it means isolation, which usually leads to crummy ideas and premature burnout. Yet in the advertising industry, just like the rest of business, it's the creative genius, it's that new idea, that catapults us from the familiar solution to the brilliant new paradigm that solves the problem so much better than before.

Oliver Wendell Holmes says, "Man's mind, stretched to a new idea, never goes back to its original dimensions." He's right, but after that flash of brilliance often the creative person is cast to one side. Once they've got the idea, business tends to exclude the creative person because many managers subscribe to the notion that creativity is an optional extra.

The paradigm in the West is that if we simply apply logic, everything will slowly improve. Now, I have nothing against accessing the mind's logical function, but I can tell you from my personal experience that if you apply logic in isolation, everything eventually grinds to a halt. If you look at most of the great breakthroughs, they've been as a result of creativity - a creative flash, not a logical flash! Look at your life. Whether you're an accountant, an engineer or somebody who holds logic as your greatest strength, you will have experienced a creative flash any number of times in your life. You may call it 'flying by the seat of your pants'. You may not publicly acknowledge that it has happened, but I can almost guarantee you that if you recall some of your greatest achievements they will have resulted from creative flashes of brilliance. Everybody's had them - it's when we're most alive.

As the Tibetans would say, 'Creativity is the song of the soul.'

SO LET'S HAVE A CLOSER LOOK AT THIS CREATIVITY

First of all, what creativity isn't is polite, civil, conformist or realistic. It's often zany - it's out of the box. The process of making a creative leap is about disregarding all the precedents and preconceptions, and instead it's about thinking on the edge. Creativity is freewheeling, unstructured, and challenges the status quo, even to the point of being rude. It's fresh, it's new, it's spontaneous and untried. It's risky.

But individuals and teams need to be organized, structured and disciplined to keep on track and on time to perform. Both at work and at home we have these two competing influences. On the one hand, we need efficiency and organization; and on the other, we need to access the potentially very disruptive brilliance of creativity. The *wrong* kind of personal discipline squeezes the creativity out. The *right* kind of discipline lets it grow to contribute and flourish.

LOOKING DEEPER AT THE TWO DISTINCTLY DIFFERENT TYPES OF CREATIVITY - C1 AND C2

To understand this weird, powerful, dynamic thing called creativity, we must remember that there are two distinctly different types of creativity. The first is highly practical - that's C1. The second is dreamy - that's C2. In 1937 Napoleon Hill (the Grandfather of the personal development movement in the US) wrote - that the imaginative faculty functions in two forms. One he called 'synthetic imagination' - we'd call that C1; the other he called 'creative imagination' - we'd call that C2. Here is his definition of C1, or synthetic imagination: 'Through this faculty, one may arrange old concepts, ideas or plans into new combinations. This faculty creates nothing, it merely works with the material of experience, education and observation with which it is fed. It is the faculty used most by the inventor, with the exception of the genius, who draws upon the creative imagination when he cannot solve his problems through synthetic imagination.'

What we call C2 Hill calls 'creative imagination'. 'Through the faculty of creative imagination, the finite mind of man has direct communication with infinite intelligence [one of his terms]. It's this faculty through which hunches and inspirations are received. It's by this faculty that all new ideas are handed over to man. The great leaders of business, industry, finance, and the great artists, musicians, poets and writers become great because they've developed the faculty of creative imagination' (*Think and Grow Rich*, by Napoleon Hill, written in 1937). And I can say it no better today over sixty years later.

Your First Step in Your Life Quest

Chapter 3

The First Kind of Creativity - C1 - Lateral Thinking

Thomas Edison, who was very high in C1, once said, "I'm not discouraged, because every wrong attempt discarded, is another step forward." Have you ever seen one of those child's wind up toy cars? The ones I have in mind, you put them on the ground and they run along the floor. When one hits a wall, it backs up and changes direction and runs forward until it hits something else, then it backs up, changes direction and it moves again and again until it is out of energy. That's one way to describe your C1 function. Whenever you hit a wall, your C1 function will come up with a creative way to move around it.

The C1 function gives you access to the ingenious and creative part of the mind. Approximately 75 per cent of the population naturally favor their C1 function. C1 is an indication of the ability to think laterally. When you access your C1, your strength is ingenuity or being able to think laterally. Your C1 function gives you the capability of thinking of new ways to approach old issues. The C1 function creates interest in the new and the different. It identifies resourcefulness and innovation and gives you the ability to enjoy continual change.

If you enjoy using this C1, your productivity and energy are at their highest when your mind is brainstorming. C1 never ever tires of new discoveries or applications. Levels of motivation and conscientiousness are at their peak when new ideas and solutions are being sought. Interest diminishes when an idea has been adopted. C1 is used by the mind when it is under pressure or stress and needs to quickly think of a lateral, practical solution. It likes to challenge everything. It's the part of the mind that won't like to accept anything until it's had first-hand experience; it's very hands-on.

Those minds that naturally access the C1 function tend to be conversational rabbits. So if you use this function a lot you'll tend to jump from one topic to another, savoring the flavor, and thinking about many things at the same time or in rapid succession. This can be frustrating for minds who don't naturally access the C1 function and who like to keep to the one topic and stay focused.

I have a friend who naturally accesses her C1 function and my brother doesn't. Sometimes they get together and she'll want to talk about something for about seven or ten seconds, then she'll want to move on to the next topic. This really frustrates my brother. He'll say, 'Hey, let's resolve this first issue.'

Meanwhile she'll be bouncing around in a dozen different directions, trying to solve the problem from 101 different angles. My brother will tell you that C1 can be very frustrating for people who do not access it by their nature.

Those who enjoy using C1 and foster using this function at the exclusion of the other five can experience a sense of not achieving, because they move from one idea, project, or activity to the next, without becoming involved in the task of implementation. C1 is one of the very high-energy functions of the mind. It makes for witty conversationalists. What's amazing about C1, is that it doesn't change much from when you're seven to when you're seventy. People who have had a stroke can still naturally use their C1 function because it is timeless. First thing in the morning, when you're waking up, you can be half asleep and the C1 function of your mind almost seems to work separately from you. It's a strange thing that if you naturally use this function you can say witty, or funny things, and turn a comment around even when you're half asleep - later you may not even remember the conversation.

YOUR GREATEST STRENGTH IS YOUR GREATEST WEAKNESS

Your greatest strength is your greatest weakness and amazingly, your greatest weakness can become your greatest strength! If you naturally use your C1 function, your great strength is that you love anything new. Your greatest weakness is that you *only* love anything new. Your greatest opportunity for personal development is to become discerning - to realize that 'new' does not equal 'better'. Your greatest threat to your balance and success is that you could become addicted to constant, new activity.

Now, if you take nothing else away from this whole C1 discussion and you believe you naturally use you C1 function, absorb this truth and it will change you forever. This pattern of 'new is better' will apply to everything in your life. You can buy a house and renovate it but you'll become tired of it because something else that is new will catch your attention.

I've known people very high in C1 who have renovated a house and when it's finished, even though it has cost an enormous effort, they look back at where they started and think, 'Now, the way it was before we started wasn't so bad, after all.' Whatever is newest or different is assumed to be best. They always want to go for the newest thing, the newest fashion, the newest trend or the newest idea. Whenever they see something new, they get a buzz. It gives them energy.

We're all energy addicts. We all move towards that which provides us with energy. If you're high in C1 you love to have the new, whatever it is. But what happens when the new is not better than the old and you have lost the ability to discern that?

THE C1 FUNCTION AND RELATIONSHIPS

Let's apply some of this understanding of C1 function to relationships both at work and at home. A great strength the C1 function gives you is the ability to think fast on your feet and create energy. It also gives you the ability to quickly absorb new ideas, approaches, and paradigms.

Another strength is that you can adapt to different concepts and quickly change your opinion. If somebody walks in with a new idea, you're not going to be closed to that idea; instead you'll be open to it. This makes you very appealing to everyone else high in C1, because you'll be able to jump from one topic to another very quickly, you'll be excellent at lateral thinking, and you'll have a quick and witty sense of humor - just like them.

Now, sometimes people who are high in C1 don't recognize these attributes in themselves. They may even say, 'Oh, that doesn't sound like me.' But their friends say, 'Yes, it is, it is. Yes, you're very quick.' If you are high in C1 you can also juggle many activities, so that means that you'll always have a new idea or a new approach, and you can always lighten a situation by changing the topic.

SOME CHALLENGES FOR THE C1 FUNCTION

Now, what about your weaknesses? When accessing your C1 function you will speak before you think. This can lead to some embarrassing situations. In C1 you will keep adopting and creating rather than applying, so people may suspect you are all talk and no action. You can confuse people in your conversations as you jump from one topic to another. Sometimes listeners feel as though you're trying to 'snow' them or confuse them, or that you're totally 'scatty', illogical and disorganized. Your ideas can be so new that they're totally untried. People can feel as though you're flying by the seat of your pants. And you have so many new ideas that people can feel overwhelmed with the sheer volume of the content.

A FEW COMMENTS ABOUT C1 AND MANAGEMENT

C1 managers have a potpourri of practical ideas for solving problems. They are also a sucker for the very latest idea, tool or solution. I have a friend who discovered early in her career that as a manager high in C1, one of the quickest ways she could erode the enthusiasm of her team was to constantly change her mind. After a while, people would say, 'Here she goes again. This is her latest idea. We won't get started on it, because we know that tomorrow she'll come in with yet another one.' The first time she presented a new idea, they said, 'This is fantastic. We needed somebody with a new approach. Isn't this exciting,' and they started getting it implemented that day. They came back in the next day to show some of their work and sure enough, as a C1 manager, she said, 'I'm not so convinced about that idea now. What about this?' Of course, everybody moaned, 'What about all this work we've already done?' 'Well,' she explained, 'I've got a new idea, a better idea.' You can almost hear the echo of their groans today just thinking about it.

Now it's true, leaders need to be creative. It's absolutely impossible to be a powerful and effective leader if you don't access your creative functions. But if you don't manage it, it will end up burning out your team and they'll become cynical and zapped of energy. The constant stream of new ideas will frustrate staff low in the C1 function and you will end up spending enormous organizational resources chasing the latest idea, just for the sake of it. This will energize you but at the expense of the team.

C1 AND COMMUNICATION

In conversation, C1 is witty and humorous and loves puns, will hop from topic to topic, loves brainstorming, often seems highly motivated is often smiling, doesn't talk to a time limit, and spends a lot of time trying to enthuse people about the latest idea, the latest thought.

IDENTIFYING C1 IN ANOTHER PERSON

How do you identify a person who's high in C1, without a test? Of course, all of us are high in C1 at times but sometimes you may want to be able to identify when a person's natural C1 function is strong. Here are some hints. Firstly, they will be interested in all the latest ideas. When you look in their home, they'll have all the latest gadgets, all the latest ideas, and a grab bag of different colors, mementos and keepsakes. They will be eclectic. C1 doesn't mature over life, so you'll find a child who's high in C1 - at seven may have the same sense of humor as they have in their 70s. Therefore, children who are high in C1 may sometimes appear to be more mature than the average kid and seventy year olds seem eternally young.

Another characteristic of C1, is their ability to multi-task. Someone high in C1 will watch TV and read a book, and be talking to you all at the same time.

If you were to walk into a room looking for someone high in C1, the first thing that you'd notice is that they're enthusiastic and they love anything novel, different or quirky. The way you capture their attention is by using words and phrases like 'new', 'fresh', 'never been tried before', 'brand new', 'revolutionary'. To turn off a C1 use words and phrases like, 'tried and tested', 'been tried before', 'track record', 'background', 'due process'. They want to be at the cutting edge and they'll tend to have short conversations. Their physical movements will tend to be a little bit jerky as they constantly scan the room for new people, objects, ideas and experiences.

In a nutshell

C1 is valuable for lightening the atmosphere, injecting fun into a situation and for generating practical new ideas when there is a problem to solve.

Access your C1 by relaxing into a playful mood and playing with ideas. If you need to increase your pace, it helps to do something physical like a brisk walk.

Then relax your judgements and controlling impulses, focus on the problem ready to have fun, and see where it leads.

STRENGTH	WEAKNESS
Loves anything new	Only loves anything new

OPPORTUNITY	THREAT
To become discerning - new doesn't equal better	Becomes addicted to constant new activity

C1 and Management

- Great for adapting concepts and designs.
- Has excellent ideas – although these are sometimes lost to newer, not necessarily better ideas.
- Can frustrate staff low in C1 because every day there is a new 'pet idea'.
- Good tension releaser (if sensitive).
- Time with the C1 can be spent covering an enormous diversity of topics and not necessarily resolving anything.
- Can spend organizational resources chasing new ideas for the sake of it.

C1 and Communication

- Witty and humorous - loves puns.
- Can conversation/topic hop.
- Loves brainstorming.
- Often seen as highly motivated and smiling.
- Doesn't talk to a time limit.
- Spends a lot of time trying to enthuse people about the latest idea.

Chapter 4

The Second Kind of Creativity - C2 - Imagination

Joseph Conrad once said, "Only in men's imagination does every truth find an effective and undeniable existence. Imagination, not invention, is the supreme master of art as of life." Proverbs 29:18 says, 'Where there is no vision, the people perish.' Donald Curtis once said, "We are what and where we are, because we first imagined it."

C2 is the creative function we use when we want the ability to visualize. C2 refers to the mind's ability to generate new and often abstract ideas and thoughts. C2 is creative vision. C2 is the part of the mind that can paint pictures of brand new concepts or ideas. It can be an absolutely fascinating area of the mind, because it's so uncontrollable. People who naturally access their C2 function describe these thoughts as coming from somewhere outside themselves or descending on them. These thoughts can often be completely unrelated to what they're doing or thinking at the time. C2-dominant people often amaze themselves with some of the perverse thoughts that seem to come spontaneously into their mind. The way they respond to these thoughts depends on how they use their other functions.

Any person can choose to learn about and harness the C2 function. People who can tap into C2 can make great inspirational speakers, because they can totally ignore reality and create a new world in their imagination. However, while C2 is powerful, it is also incredibly fragile. Without the opportunity to express themselves, most C2-dominant minds feel confined, undervalued and unmotivated. Minds dominated by the C2 function need a clear vision at all times. This vision could be, for example, how the organization, their family, or a project will look in the future. This function visualizes brilliantly. It enjoys being able to dream something and then watch that dream become reality.

C2 - YOUR GREATEST STRENGTH IS YOUR GREATEST WEAKNESS

If your mind is dominated by the C2 function your greatest strength is the ability to see the future! Your greatest weakness is that you're able to see the future. Your opportunity for personal development is to learn how to use this information to prepare. Your greatest threat to your personal happiness and success is to let this information overwhelm you. If you take nothing else away with you these four insights can change your life. Let's look at applying them.

HOW DOES C2 APPLY TO WORK AND TO RELATIONSHIPS?

First of all, the C2 function is future-centered. This is excellent because it gives your mind the ability to give a client or someone you're working with a clear vision of how the project could end up. You can paint pictures of the future with words. You're able to see the way forward when all is bleak. Isn't that a central quality we are looking for in a leader?

As a leader you need to access the C2 function to have a clear vision of where you're going. This enables you to make connections with how the current activity links into the future and answers the question, 'Why are we doing this?' C2 also gives you the ability to think in terms of models, abstract concepts, and ideas.

THE IMPRACTICAL NATURE OF THE C2 FUNCTION

If you naturally access and express your C2 function many will see you as impractical because most people (remember only 25 per cent are future-centered) are focused on the here and now. They may make comments like, 'Well that's all very exciting about the future, but where are we now?' Some may even see you as being unwilling to deal with the present. And because you start with the vision in mind and work backwards, and they don't, they simply will not understand what on earth you're talking about.

THE C2 FUNCTION AND MANAGEMENT

C2 managers are great at painting a new vision and transmitting this vision to others. They motivate others by drawing them towards the vision. But here's the drawback - C2 is the most fragile part of the profile, so it's sensitive and often reluctant to share. C2-dominated minds create people who are usually introverts. The reason for this is simple. The vision of the future can be incredibly clear in the C2 function, and yet still relatively loose, for a logical, structured person. For example while C2 can see clearly what the house will look like, the vision is broad and conceptual, not practical and precise.

Often the C2 function will express the vision of the future to the team as clearly as possible. But the more grounded members will say, 'Well that doesn't make sense. I can't see that working.' They are saying this because they look at what is, rather than what is possible. They see reality by examining the details. The C2 function sees the big picture and then works backwards. All the other functions see the small picture and piece together the big picture. So the implication of this is simple. Often, senior leaders know exactly where they're going but are reluctant to express it because they torn down for their vague notions. Rather than express their ideas, these C2 leaders just shut up.

Remember that if you're a trainer, a counsellor or a leader who by nature accesses the C2 function, you'll tend to see students, participants, and employees as they could be rather than as they are. C2 leaders often overpay their employees because they confuse their current skills. If you're an art teacher who is C2-dominant, be aware of your tendency not only to see the pictures students draw, but also to simultaneously see the potential of what they *could* draw. If they're writers you won't necessarily see what they're writing; you'll see what they could be writing. You will see their potential. So your C2 function transports you to the future and does not ground you in present reality. In fact, many would agree that you see things as the universe sees them, that is; in terms of their potential rather than just the immediate reality.

THE C2 FUNCTION AND COMMUNICATION

C2 talks enthusiastically about the latest vision. If you are C2-dominated you'll see things as they could be rather than as they are, and this is incredibly relevant to relationships. If you meet somebody, in the courting stage for example, your C2 function won't see them as they are, it will see a future vision of them. This creates some real challenges. It's a bit like somebody who says, 'That dog has the potential to be a perfect pet' and when the dog bites, the person just can't understand it. Just because the dog has the potential not to bite, it doesn't mean that it won't and doesn't bite *now*. I've worked extensively with people in caring professions. If you're a counsellor and you're high in the C2 function and you're dealing with difficult people, odds are you won't see that thief as a criminal; you'll see them as the ideal citizen that they could be. But the great danger is that you could end up losing your TV, your CD player and your household contents if your potentially ideal citizen steals them! Probably, at the time they are being counselled, they're not that person you can see in your C2 function; they're actually still a thief.

There is great hope in seeing the potential in people but there is also great danger in losing touch with who they are now.

Here is an interesting question for you. If you're a person who's high in C2, how in touch with current reality are you? Are you constantly projecting forward and imagining things as they could be, rather than as they are? The C2 function can become very tunnel-focused on its vision.

If you're high in C2 you may see this vision as part of your self-identity; that is, 'I'm the vision-creator.' I've seen visionaries become so umbilically attached to a particular vision that to criticize the vision is to criticize the person. At this point their ego gets involved. This is a major potential flaw for someone high in C2. We must all constantly remind ourselves that this is just one vision and that other visions (that are just as valid) will come. If somebody criticizes the vision, it's not a criticism of you; it's a criticism of the vision and what is more, it could be a very valid criticism. Don't take it personally. Finally, if the C2 function is attacked it will lose all focus and vanish.

HOW DO YOU IDENTIFY A C2-DOMINANT MIND?

Often C2 people are considered to be dreamy, on another planet, or constantly thinking about something else. In point of fact, if they're most dominant in C2 their reality often will be somewhere else. If you know someone who is quiet and shy and every now and then comes up with odd sorts of vague and conceptual ideas, it could be that they're naturally high in the C2 function. C2 minds will tend to come up with their own alternative, dreamed-up reality which they prefer to the real world. This can be a mighty force, for example, when structuring a new company. The C2 function enables you to totally ignore where the company is at present and instead imagine where you want that company or organization to be in the future.

This C2 lets you create a picture so keenly in your mind's eye that when you implant the vision in the minds of a team of logical or passionate people, virtually anything can be achieved. C2, therefore, can be a very strong asset. It's also a very delicate, sensitive part of the mind. We need to learn as a society how to nurture these people because they will be our future leaders.

In the next chapter we are going to be talking about willpower (P1 and P2), because at the end of the day, you can be incredibly creative and have the best creative ideas, but it doesn't amount to a hill of beans if you don't do something about it.

STRENGTH	WEAKNESS
Able to see the future	Attachment to a particular future
OPPORTUNITY	**THREAT**
Able to prepare	May become overwhelmed

C2 and Management
- Great at painting a new vision and transmitting this vision to others.
- Great at motivating others by drawing them towards the vision.
- Sensitive and often reluctant to share.
- Can accurately anticipate difficulties further down the track.

C2 and Communication
- Talks enthusiastically about the latest vision.
- Sees things as they could be rather than as they are.
- Can be very task oriented if vision is firmly in mind.
- Can be so focused they can become tunnel visioned.
- Will instantly lose all enthusiasm if attacked.

Your First Step in Your Life Quest

Chapter 5

Processing: The Act of Willpower

P1 LOGIC AND P2 VALUES AND BELIEFS

In this chapter we are going to be looking at the two functions which give our minds access to personal power - specifically, your willpower. Benjamin Disraeli says, 'Nothing can resist the human will, that will stake even its existence on the stated purpose.' Power, the 'P' in P1 and P2, represents the mind's ability to process information and create action. This is the power of the human will. Willpower is behind all achievement.

The P scores measure the kind of focus the mind prefers. Effectively there are two kinds of focus. One is systematic and detached. The other is enthusiastic and attached. Both are incredibly powerful. When a person is described as powerful, that will be a measure of their P function. A person high in the P functions will want issues and details tidied up and resolved. Their motto is often 'Fire, ready, aim!' The focused P1 mind will win the endurance award for keeping up the activity until there is resolution and the P2 mind will win the award for blasting through obstacles. These are two opposite applications of willpower.

Willpower is something we all know quite a bit about. If there is one thing that the West specializes in, it is willpower! If you are going to achieve anything in life, you need to have mastered your own ability to harness your own willpower.

Once again Napoleon Hill speaks about harnessing willpower (*Think and Grow Rich,* Napoleon Hill, 1937). He talks about six ways to turn desires into gold. He suggests a method by which great desire for riches can be transmuted into a real and great financial equivalent, which consists of six definite, practical steps. This is his formula for increasing your willpower.

First, he suggests that you fix in your mind the exact outcome you desire. It is not sufficient merely to say, 'I want plenty of money.' Be definite as to the amount. Second, determine exactly what you intend to give in return for the outcome you want. There is no such reality as *something for nothing*.

Third, establish a definite date when you intend to achieve this outcome. Fourth, create a definite plan for carrying out your desire, and begin at once, whether you're ready or not, to put this plan into action. Fifth, write out a clear, concise statement of the specific outcome you want, name the time limit for its acquisition, state what you intend to give in return for it, and describe clearly the plan you intend to use. Sixth, read your written statement aloud twice daily, once just before retiring at night and once after arising in the morning. As you read, begin to see, feel and believe yourself already having achieved your desired outcome.

It is important, he says, that you follow the instructions described in these six steps. It is especially important that you observe and follow the instruction in the sixth step. You may complain that it is impossible for you to see yourself having achieved this before you actually have it. Here is where the burning desire will come to your aid. If you truly desire the outcome so keenly that your desire is an obsession, you will have no difficulty in convincing yourself that you will acquire it.

"The object is to want this to happen and to become so determined to have it, that you convince yourself you will have it." You can see this approach amplifies personal focus. It is a process to harness your willpower.

Persistence, he says, is a state of mind; therefore it can be cultivated. "Like all states of mind, persistence is based upon definite causes. Among them having a definite purpose is most important. Knowing what one wants is the first and perhaps the most important step forward towards the development of persistence. A strong motive forces one to surmount many difficulties. As well as purpose," he says, "one needs desire. It is comparatively easy to acquire and maintain persistence in pursuing the object of intense desire. Further," he says, "one needs self-reliance. Believing in one's ability to carry out a plan encourages one to follow the plan through with persistence."

Definiteness of plans will encourage persistence. Willpower, the habit of concentrating one's thoughts upon the building of plans for the attainment of a definite purpose, leads to persistence. His final ingredient is habit. "Persistence is the direct result of habit. The mind absorbs and becomes a part of the daily experiences upon which it feeds. Fear, the worst of all enemies, can be effectively cured by forced repetition of acts of courage." Just reading this description of willpower written by Napoleon Hill will have the effect of increasing your mind's strength and desire to use the P1 and P2 functions. (*Think and Grow Rich*, Napoleon Hill, 1937).

Chapter 6

Systematic Willpower - P1

The P1 function gives your mind access to reasoning or logical analysis. P1-dominant minds are often described as being 'rational' or 'intellectual'. The P1 function prefers to be very analytical. P1-dominant minds are often described as being objective, carefully sifting information and sorting it into some sense of logic or progression and comparing apples with apples. The greatest strength of the P1 function is to work through one project at a time. It prefers to do this in a systematic, controlled environment. P1-dominant minds like order and systemisation and may experience difficulty when the system with which they are familiar changes.

Tight or rushed deadlines can be very stressful to a P1-dominant mind. If there are a number of critical deadlines in a particular project, and quality control may be impacted in any way, P1-dominant minds will express their total disapproval with the specified deadline. However, P1-dominant minds work well in a crisis as long is there is a precedent or a logical set of procedures to be followed. If this cannot be done, often the P1 function will assume the task cannot be achieved.

YOUR GREATEST STRENGTH IS YOUR GREATEST WEAKNESS

The greatest strength for those who naturally access the P1 function is their ability to be consistent and stable, taking one step at a time! What is P1's greatest weakness? Consistency, stability and taking one step at a time. Why is it a weakness to take one step at a time? Because sometimes you need to be able to skip a step or cut corners, and failure awaits those without this flexibility. Sometimes, consistency and stability will not produce the energy you require to get a project under way. Instead, some projects require creative brilliance or passion to be successful.

Remember when describing C1 we were picturing how, when the wind-up toy car hits the wall, it reverses back and tries again and again? If you can imagine, the P1 function is the opposite in that it hits the wall and stalls! One TV advert, which shows this P1 function in action, shows a child's mechanical walking bunny. The point of the advertisement is to show that the advertised battery lasts longer than any other brand of battery. Imagine a walking toy hitting a wall and not repositioning, but instead just keeping on walking, with its feet running in the same spot. One of the reasons that projects managed by the P1 function often hit walls and fall behind schedule is because (unless the project manager also has access to the C1 function), they cannot reposition and so find a way around the particular obstacle.

The P1 function works well in a crisis as long as there is a precedent because it is looking for a structured process to follow. The opportunity for P1 minds to develop is to practise not falling into a rut and instead to try new tactics. If you naturally use the P1 function, you may experience an impasse in a relationship, at work or with a hobby. You will tend to go on trying the same approach time and time again, rather than trying different tactics.

What is the threat to happiness and success? You can lack prioritization and enthusiasm and so can appear disorganized and disinterested. Why is that? If you naturally use the P1 function you'll tend to get drawn into what is *urgent*, rather than what's *important*. P1-dominant minds must learn to complete the important tasks and non-urgent tasks, rather than just focus on the urgent and often unimportant tasks.

THE P1 FUNCTION AND RELATIONSHIPS

So if you naturally access your P1, how does this apply to relationships? Well, the P1 function is stable, which is reassuring because people find you predictable and consistent. The P1 function is balanced, considered, systematic, reliable, and likes to be planned. You will like structure, organization and process, and you will take on all projects one step at a time. You are accomplished at analyzing a situation and deciding on the next move. This means that you will not overwhelm your partner, colleagues or friends.

THE P1 FUNCTION'S CHALLENGES

The P1 function can be low in energy. It can take a long time to change track and can get bogged down when it hits a brick wall. You can be seen as plodding when speed is required. You can get overwhelmed with too much activity or information and can find managing time a challenge, so if you are not careful you can break deadlines.

Another interesting observation about P1 minds is that they are often not very good personal time managers, in that they cannot see the *end* point; they can only see the *next* point.

If you are a P1-dominated mind, you may find that if you sit down at a computer at 8 o'clock at night and think that the task will only take you an hour to complete, it may end up taking you something like five hours. (The P1 function loves computers because logic is at the heart of programming.)

For those of you who have read about or studied neuro-linguistic programming (NLP), you'll know about 'meta-programs'. Meta-programs refer to specific ways we interact with and understand the world. According to NLP there are two ways to see time. There are those who are 'in time' and those who are 'through time'. If you are 'in time', it means that you are so involved in the project that the time limit can come and go and it goes unnoticed. 'In time' people are usually late and they usually do not finish projects when they think they will, but instead get totally absorbed in the project and just work at their own pace straight through deadlines. The P1 function lives in this 'in time' paradigm.

(The P2 'through time' function helicopters above time and has a 'through time' paradigm, so from that point of view they will tend to be very cognisant of how long things take and how much time they should spend on a project.)

So if you naturally access the P1 function, odds are you are going to have an 'in time' meta-program, an 'in time' way of seeing things. That is why logical P1 computer programmers, accountants and engineers inexplicably break deadlines. Whereas the P2 function will tend to allocate timeframes and work faster, the P1 function works longer. So a weakness of P1 is that it finds managing time a challenge and often breaks deadlines and appointments, running at a constant speed rather than speeding up and slowing down. If you put a P1 person under an enormous amount of stress they will not work faster; they will work longer. It does not work to threaten a P1 mind if your desired outcome is that they will work faster.

THE P1 FUNCTION AND MANAGEMENT

Firstly, those who naturally access the P1 function will be very ordered and logical with an organized desk, coffee breaks, and morning and afternoon tea. They like everything that is important to them to be neat and tidy. If information about a topic does not fit with their framework it is ignored. They complete projects one step at a time in an ordered and unflustered way. If you are a P1-dominant manager, you need to learn to be flexible and understand that 50 per cent of the population will consider your natural style to be dull and controlling.

THE P1 FUNCTION AND COMMUNICATION

The P1 function often feels frustrated if others take the discussion off track, even if it is beneficial to the discussion. The P1 function makes for a good impartial chairperson or mediator although it can appear to lack sympathy at times. P1-dominant minded people will logically provide clarification when they speak. They will listen for a lack of logic and draw attention to it. They will have great difficulty understanding why people are irrationally angry or moody, and will tend to plough through discussions regardless of the hidden agenda of others.

THE P1 FUNCTION LIKES FRAMEWORKS

"As the fletcher whittles and makes straight his arrows, so the master directs his straying thoughts," says the Buddha. And this is so true of the P1 function. The teachings of Buddha are very compatible with the P1 function.

P1-dominated minds will not like to start on something new until they finish what they are doing or learning at the moment. They will like to have things written down, organized, and put in a structure with straight lines. They love grids and they love charts.

In a nutshell

If you naturally access your P1 function you will appear calm and approach your work in a methodical, step-by-step fashion. Your challenge is to not get lost 'in time' when there is a deadline, but to monitor your time management.

When a job needs to be completed efficiently, without fuss, you can access your P1 function to keep you on track. To do this, plant your feet firmly on the ground, forget the past and the future, and ask yourself calmly, 'What is the procedure here?' Or 'What is the next step?' Stay in the present and your P1 will get the job done.

STRENGTH	WEAKNESS
Consistent and stable. Takes one step at a time.	Consistent and stable. Takes one step at a time.
OPPORTUNITY	**THREAT**
To practise not getting bogged down or paralyzed by obstacles.	Can lack prioritization and enthusiasm and so is seen to be disorganized and disinterested.

P1 and Management

- Very ordered and logical.
- Organized desk and coffee breaks/morning and afternoon tea.
- Very diary conscious often keeps one for work and one for home.
- Likes everything neat and tidy.
- If information doesn't fit into the structure, it is ignored.
- Completes projects one step at a time.

P1 and Communication

- Often feels frustrated if others take the discussion off track even if it's a beneficial discussion.
- Makes a good impartial chairperson or mediator.
- Can appear to lack sympathy at times.
- Will logically clarify when people speak.
- Will listen for a lack of logic and draw attention to it.
- Will not understand why people are irrationally angry or moody.
- Tends to plough through agendas and discussions regardless of the hidden agendas.

Your First Step in Your Life Quest

Chapter 7

Passion and Enthusiasm-Based Willpower - P2

Our second type of willpower is P2. Andre Gide says, "The belief that becomes truth for me is that which allows me the best use of my strength, the best means of putting my virtues into action." The P2 function gives the mind the ability to filter ideas through a set of values and beliefs. P2-dominant minds will immediately judge what is right and wrong. They have an extraordinary ability to show commitment and passion to a cause. P2 is a very high-energy function and drives people to do remarkable things. Politics, religion, morals and race anything that is linked to passion is P2-oriented. P2-dominant minds are ideal for energizing, striving, convincing and debating.

Many of the world's most powerful leaders are P2-dominant. P2-dominant minds make decisions very quickly. Sometimes this makes the P2 mind appear very opinionated. Fervid arguments occur between P2 minds who disagree. In this situation, both have passion and believe they are right. They also believe it's their right and obligation not to let the other mind leave unconvinced. The P2-dominant mind is that of a moral person, eager to succeed and gain the admiration of their seniors and their peers. The P2 function loves to over-perform.

THE P2 FUNCTION'S GREATEST STRENGTH IS ITS GREATEST WEAKNESS

Let us have a look at this P2 element. Remember, your mind's greatest strength is your greatest weakness. The strength of the P2 function is that it is committed, focused and attached to doing whatever it takes to achieve the outcome. P2-dominant minded people's greatest weakness is that they are committed, focused and attached to whatever it will take to achieve the outcome, even if that means half-killing themselves and half-killing their team!

The P2-dominant mind's opportunity for personal development is to detach and to rejuvenate. The great threat to happiness and success is to burn out because the pace can't be maintained. If your mind is totally dominated by P2, you will notice that you have periods of high, intense activity, and then periods of recuperation. Periods of being highly positive and then periods of being highly negative. Periods of being as high as a kite and periods of being depressed. The degree to which you move up is the degree to which you move down. So, whereas P1 is stable and consistent, P2 is passionate and dynamic.

WHAT'S GREAT ABOUT P2?

If you are most dominant in P2, what are your strengths? Well, you have passion and energy. You focus on *results*, rather than *process*. (Remember, P1 focuses on process rather than results.) P2 shows a commitment to getting a task done and you will enjoy exceeding expectations. You talk confidently and passionately and you do what it takes to delight your chosen people in a given situation.

THE P2 FUNCTION'S CHALLENGES

P2-dominated minds will sometimes cut corners to get the job done. This can be negative if you leave the wrong bit out! Your passion can become argumentative if someone is standing in your way. You may take a personal dislike to those who *do* stand in the way, and often you will drive yourself to the point of becoming inhumane.

At what point does a leader stop being a great savior and start being the enemy? When they stop seeing people as people and start seeing them only as a means to an end. So if you are a manager with a P2-dominant mind, while you will manage an organization to your principles you will also tend to have favorite staff who you will treat differently; in other words, you can play favorites. This is a major tendency you will have to watch. You will also tend to make major snap decisions on issues, and stand on the principle of the matter and have heated arguments with those who don't agree. You'll get all fired up about one thing and go to great lengths to prove that you're right. If people agree with your stated position, they're in; if they disagree, they're out. You must remember that not always does the end justify the means.

For a person very high in P2, one of their great challenges is to avoid falling short of their own performance criteria, because they expect to be good at everything, instantly. For the P2 function the learning curve doesn't exist. Instead, it is a vertical line! If the P2 function decides to focus, it expects to master anything in a fraction of the time it usually takes.

HOW DOES P2 AFFECT COMMUNICATION?

If your mind is P2-dominant, you can sometimes preach to others on a pet subject. Often you can push the conversation in one direction, that is onto one of your soapboxes. You can be totally insensitive to others who are not in line with your ideas. You can be very passionate about a cause or a topic, and will talk over the top of others and will not keep conversations to set timeframes if you believe you don't need to. P2 can be, at its strongest, bombastic or rude.

I should underline that the P2 function is incredibly strong. It has high fight power and high impact power, but this blast is not necessarily sustained.

P2 enables the mind to work faster. P2 minds are effective rather than efficient. The P2 mind is a walking argument. If you are dealing with people who have high P2, they will have high energy and they will be good at debating, arguing the point fluently, and on occasion will get exceedingly angry. They will tend to be very enthusiastic, and they have high expectations of themselves and others.

In a nutshell

If you are high in the P2 function, you will tend to feel passionate about ethical issues. You will tend to see things as being right or wrong, good or bad, black or white. While it is a very polarized part of the mind, it is also the mother of action.

So when you have to achieve, you can use your P2 function to totally focus and say to yourself, 'This is how I'm going to do it' and blast through every obstacle with sheer passion and energy.

STRENGTH	WEAKNESS
Committed, focused and attached to doing whatever it takes to achieve the outcome.	Committed, focused and attached to doing whatever it takes to achieve the outcome.
OPPORTUNITY	**THREAT**
To detach and rejuvenate.	Can burn out.

P2 and Management

- Will be a high energy, passionate leader.
- Manages an organization to a set of principles.
- Will tend to have favorite staff/people and treat them differently.
- Will make snap decisions on things.
- Will stand on the principle of the matter.
- Will often have heated arguments with those who don't agree.
- Will get all fired up about one thing and work to prove they are right.
- Will have an obvious set of beliefs. If people agree, they are in; if they disagree, they are out.
- The end can often justify the means.

P2 and Communication

- Can sometimes preach to others if their 'pet subject' is brought up.
- Can often push the conversation in one direction, that is one of their soapboxes.
- Can be totally insensitive to others not in line with their ideas.
- Can be very passionate about a cause or topic.
- Will talk over others and will not keep to set timeframes unless they believe they should.
- Can be bombastic or rude.

Chapter 8

The Human Spirit's Search for Information, The Mind's Search for Wisdom

Albert Einstein said, "The important thing is not to stop questioning. Curiosity has its own reason for existing. One cannot help but be in awe when he contemplates the mysteries of eternity, of life, of the marvellous structure of reality.

It is enough if one tries to comprehend a little of this mystery every day. Never lose a holy curiosity." That was Einstein's spirit talking about his great thirst for wisdom and knowledge.

The mind is a voracious sponge, constantly scanning, reading, sensing and recording information. The 'I' score refers to this function. The spirit's thirst for all information is phenomenal.

In fact, there are two kinds of information: quantitative (information collected by the I1 function) and qualitative (information which is collected by the I2 function).

Chapter 9

Factual Data and Wisdom - I1

The I1 function collects facts and figures on everything. When making a decision, I1-dominant minds will always want to know the details. I1-most-dominant minds tend to study a specific topic in close detail. They may know every conceivable fact about a chosen subject, and are adept at cataloguing and cross-referencing data. I1-dominant minds will often delay decision making in order to categorize more facts or data. They will categorize information and cross-reference it in their own minds with other information they have collected. I1 minds collect information, communicate and learn, visually.

They are usually very good at remembering phone numbers and people's names. I1-dominant minds tend to enjoy conversations where they can regurgitate facts or exchange information. When two I1 minds get together, they tend to exchange details about a specific topic. The education system is largely focused on training and evaluating a person's I1 function. I1-dominant minds would have enjoyed school and would have performed well at tertiary education.

I1 is the factual, quantitative function of your mind. I once worked with a consultant who is incredibly high in I1. I was astonished when I saw his incredibly high score on the profile test, and thought it would be fascinating to work with a person who has such a highly developed I1 function. The following description of one of his meetings, gives I believe, a rare insight into the I1 function in action.

John started, 'I refer to your notes from the previous four meetings. The first meeting on the 23rd of the third of this year, the second meeting on the 15th of the fourth.' He went through each meeting, and summarized each piece of information. Now this was totally appropriate because, on that project, he had around the table, a group of people who were also incredibly I1. He asked, 'Does everybody have the minutes of the meeting from the 9th?' One of the other meeting participants responded, 'John, I don't have that. Could you go and make a copy of that for me?'

We spent the first forty-five minutes of the meeting collecting largely irrelevant information about previous meetings. We didn't decide a thing; all we did was catalogue data. I'm very high in the Ps, so for me this just seemed to be taking an eternity, but for all the I1s in the room, this was systematic information collection, and was absolutely essential before the next step could be taken.

THE I1 FUNCTION'S GREATEST STRENGTH IS ITS GREATEST WEAKNESS

The I1 function's strength is to focus on the detail and work with quantitative information. Its weakness is that it can only focus on detail and work with quantitative specific information. Its greatest opportunity for personal development is to get comfortable with processing qualitative vague information. And its threat to happiness and success is its inability to deal effectively with ambiguity, which will render it useless.

The I1 function says, 'Give it to me in detail.' But what happens if you do not have the detail? 'Well,' it will say, 'we can only proceed when we have the detail.' The problem is that life requires us to make hundreds of decisions with only vague information.

SO HOW DOES THIS APPLY TO RELATIONSHIPS AND WORK?

First of all, the I1 function is detail-focused, so that means people appreciate its eye for detail. If you naturally access your I1 function you will have an excellent eye for spelling, punctuation and grammar; you are excellent at information retrieval and you will always want to have the facts at your fingertips. Colleagues will value your ability to provide detailed background information on issues, proposals, dates, names and addresses.

WHAT ARE YOUR WEAKNESSES?

You tend to work badly when there are very few facts, and you can sometimes get bogged down in detail rather than seeing the big picture. Endlessly collecting information can slow you down because you can waste time finding irrelevant detail before you start. In short, your I1 function will tend to encourage you to spend too much time *researching* rather than *doing*.

SO HOW DOES THE I1 FUNCTION AFFECT MANAGEMENT?

If you naturally access your I1 function you will have an excellent, well-categorized mental library. You will be absolutely pedantic about files and information. You will assess employees' merits on both their understanding of a specific topic and their general knowledge. When discussing something, it is assumed that every fact must be correct and accurate, or the discussion is worthless. Every form, every memo, every note, everything must be kept and be able to be retrieved in hard copy or in your mind.

IF YOU NATURALLY ACCESS YOUR I1 FUNCTION, HOW WILL YOU COMMUNICATE?

You will probably have an excellent vocabulary. You will tend to listen for interesting or new facts. You will feel happy when exchanging facts. You will most likely love jargon or buzz words or buzz topics. However, you will often be oblivious to how people are feeling or to their hidden agendas. And you can fall into the trap of exchanging data but not resolving issues, simply because you feel energized by exchanging quantitative data.

HOW CAN YOU IDENTIFY SOMEONE WHO NATURALLY ACCESSES THEIR I1 FUNCTION?

There is an old proverb that says, 'He that cannot ask, cannot live.' According to this proverb it's the I1 function that earns us the right to live. It loves learning and experiencing life. How do you identify a person who naturally accesses their I1 function? Well, you will know them first of all because they will remember great quantities of information.

They will only want to know what can be seen or written down. 95 per cent of I1 factually driven people are visually oriented, so they will tend to take information through their eyes, rather than through their ears. They often have a photographic memory, or the ability to remember facts and figures easily. They will usually remember names, and be good at spelling, and punctuation.

Often highly rewarded, I1-dominant minds are usually considered to be our best academic achievers and students. If you are high in I1, it usually means that you collect specialist information in your given area of interest.

You will probably enjoy *Trivial Pursuit*! Another characteristic of I1 is its amazing ability to process vast amounts of information and life experiences quickly. The I1 function enables the mind to process a changing situation quickly and respond rapidly in a crisis situation.

In a nutshell

People who naturally access their I1 function tend to be good with measurable facts and details. When you need to see the reality of a situation and look at 'just the facts', you can access your I1 function.
To do this, put aside your own opinions, feelings and hunches and focus on what you can see and measure and describe objectively. This can give you a refreshing clarity from which to tackle a problem anew.

STRENGTH	WEAKNESS
Committed, focused and attached to doing whatever it takes to achieve the outcome.	Committed, focused and attached to doing whatever it takes to achieve the outcome.
OPPORTUNITY	**THREAT**
To detach and rejuvenate.	Can burn out.

I1 and Management

- Will have an excellent, well categorized library.
- Will be absolutely pedantic about files and information.
- Will assess employees' merits on their understanding of their specific topic and their general knowledge.
- Will be a perfectionist and will expect no less from the staff.
- When discussing something - it's assumed that every fact must be right or the discussion is worthless.
- Every form, every memo, every note - *everything* - must be kept and be able to be retrieved.

I1 and Communication

- Tends to have an excellent vocabulary.
- Tends to listen for interesting or new facts.
- Tends to feel happy when exchanging facts.
- Loves jargon or buzz words or buzz topics.
- Often oblivious to how people are feeling or to any hidden agendas.
- Can talk facts all day and not resolve issues.

Chapter 10

Qualitative Earthly Wisdom - I2

Bertrand Russell says, "We know too much and feel too little." Remember that in our search for information we use two functions: one collects I1 facts and the other collects I2 emotions and concepts.

Your I2 function enables you to empathize and gives you access to your ability to connect with others. It's qualitative rather than quantitative. To understand what is happening at a people level, we often sense the truth of the situation thanks to our I2 function.

I2-dominant minds are sensitive and emotionally aware. They can easily sense the feeling in a room from those present. They are empathizers. I2-dominant minds seem to know just how others are feeling in the most difficult situations. The I2-dominant mind's world is a complicated one that can sense the emotional fears and inadequacies of other people.

I2-most-dominant minds never feel totally confident or in control. People with high I2 scores may sometimes wonder why they do not seem to be able to be as balanced or consistent as their I1 friends. The primary reason for this is that I2 picks up pain, excitement and pleasure vicariously through others and is often a passenger on someone else's emotional journey.

I2-dominant minded people can sense how others are feeling. This makes them excellent at listening. They usually communicate incredibly well if they are not intimidated by the person with whom they are speaking.

THE I2 FUNCTION'S GREATEST STRENGTH IS ITS GREATEST WEAKNESS

If you naturally access your I2 function, you will be able to pick up how others are feeling. That is a great strength. What is your weakness? You can pick up how others are feeling and often you don't want to know (believe me!). Your greatest opportunity is to learn to block out unwanted emotions. And your greatest threat to happiness and success is that you can be swamped by powerful, external, irrelevant emotions. If someone is angry but they are not necessarily angry with you, your I2 function may make the wrong connection, and assume that you are the cause of the anger.

HOW DOES THAT RELATE TO RELATIONSHIPS AT WORK?

If you naturally access your I2 function you will be sensitive to the way others are feeling. You will think qualitatively and 'big picture' with broad themes or trends rather than quantitatively in detail. This enables you to deal very competently with vague situations with limited information. What are your weaknesses? You can be vague! You can let the emotion of the situation overwhelm you. You can miss details, and you can be inconsistent. This is one of the characteristics of the I2 function that is not really understood. You can feel one emotion in one environment and a different situation can produce a completely different set of emotions.

THE I2 FUNCTION: BROAD THEMES OR TRENDS AND MANAGEMENT

The I2-dominant manager will be the legitimate, socio-emotional leader. They will make decisions based on what will cause people the least pain. This is no easy task. For example, what happens if an Army General, sending a whole regiment into battle, naturally accesses the I2 function?

This will be a very painful time as he feels the loss of his men. The I2 function usually takes at least two days to make a decision about most things. And if it is brand new information, your I2 function may need a week or even two weeks to feel comfortable. If you are at a conference and you are listening to new information, the things that you learnt at lunch-time you may start putting into place by lunch-time tomorrow or the day after.

Often if you naturally access your I2 function and have attended a training program, all the pennies will drop a week later. You feel like going back and saying, 'Hey, look. I've got all these questions now.' (Conversely all the people high in I1 will have all their questions there and then on the spot because they will have processed the information immediately.)

While I1's in the audience are just as likely to ask the presenter their questions immediately, I2's will send an e-mail a week later saying, 'I didn't quite understand this section. It didn't quite make sense. Can you explain it to me again please?'

So I2's will tend to take a long time to make most decisions. They will base all their decisions such as employment of staff, what they do with their family, or an annual holiday - on what feels best.

An I2-dominant manager will spend much of the time counselling and listening to staff. Therefore, they will have great difficulty firing non-performers, and will often not appear strong or aggressive. Of course, this assumption is false. Being intuitive or empathetic is not a weakness. I2-dominant people will be excellent listeners. They will focus on how staff are feeling and respond to what is happening in the personal lives of others. They will often defend the underdog, and will want to keep the group happy. They are fantastic encouragers and great empathizers.

However, because they will respond slowly and need time to go away and think about the situation, conversations can take days to complete. If you ask the I2 function about a new idea, the response may be, 'Hmmm, it's good. Just something isn't sitting right. I'll need to get back to you on that.' The I2 function needs space. Rush the I2 function and it will 'close down', because it knows it cannot think at its best in a rushed environment.

"Men as well as women," said Lord Chesterfield, "are much oftener led by their hearts than by their understandings." Isn't that true? The empathetic part of the mind is very persuasive. It picks up the emotional tone of the room and will feel it. If the I2 mind is stressed or unhappy it will tend to show it.

Because the I2 function is both sensitive and quiet, it will often seek reassurance and encouragement because its biggest challenge in life is detecting *which emotions are from within* and *which belong to others*. If you naturally access your I2 function, you will be able to sense instantly when you walk into a room, what people are feeling. You'll know how to charm them, work with them and get them on side, and they will feel as though you are their greatest ally.

You will be able to get the best from them simply from an emotional point of view. So the ability to find a person's mood and zone into their feelings and emotions and thoughts is the gift of the I2 function. When solving a problem, an I2, the empathizer, will want to feel right about it before making a decision. So if you present a new idea, the I2 will not necessarily want to get straight into it but will say, 'Look, I've just got to get used to this for a few days.' As a society we need to learn to give more time to those who naturally access their I2 function.

THE CHALLENGES FOR THE I2 FUNCTION

A negative glare or a negative response will discourage the I2s. At work they are not usually as reliable or consistent as an I1 mind, because they tend to be picking up all the office emotions which affect performance. They are either high performers or low performers, and can be both in the same day! The I2 function won't study until it feels it wants to study, it won't learn until it is ready to learn. You can't push it; the empathizer does it at its own pace. We can all experience great frustration when we use this function. Sometimes the student will say, 'OK, time to study,' but the I2 function may be clogged with other issues and unresolved emotion and will simply close down.

So I2 is not an 'on demand' function; instead it runs at its own pace. When you look at compatibility, this issue of pace is critical. I2 is a slower pace. It is the softest, quietest, most contemplative pace of the functions, and it must be given space and time.

In a nutshell

When you need to understand the emotional climate of a situation, you can access your I2 to help you. Do this by putting aside your own thoughts, feelings, opinions and intentions and paying attention to the feelings of the other person(s).

Sit calmly and quietly and listen and try to be beside them on their journey. You don't have to do anything else - no action. Just understand.

STRENGTH	WEAKNESS
Can pick up how others are feeling.	Can pick up how others are feeling.

OPPORTUNITY	THREAT
To learn to 'block out' unwanted emotions.	Can be swamped by powerful external emotions.

I2 and Management

- Will be the legitimate and socio-emotional leaders.
- Will make decisions based on what will cause people the least pain.
- Will take a long time to make most decisions.
- Will base direction/employment of staff on what feels best.
- Will spend much of the time counselling and listening to staff.
- Will have difficulty firing non-performers.
- Will often not appear strong or aggressive.

I2 and Communication

- Will be excellent listeners.
- Will focus on how staff are feeling and responding to work and personal life.
- Will often defend the underdog.
- Will want to keep the group happy.
- Excellent counsellors/encouragers/affirmers.
- Will respond slowly and need time to go away and think about it.
- Conversations can take days to complete.

Your First Step in Your Life Quest

Chapter 11

Putting it Together to Form a Leadership Style

So now you have a good idea of each of your six thinking functions. Your first two define the soul. C1 is the first kind of creativity, which, if you remember, enables you to multi-task, jump from one topic to another, and pay attention to anything new. C2, imagination, is dreamy, future-centered and has the ability to envisage a situation, as it will be, in the future.

The next two functions define your willpower, which takes two forms. The first type of willpower is P1, which is systematic and logical, and takes one step at a time. Your second kind of willpower focuses on values and beliefs, decides what is right, what is good, what must be done, and achieves high performance. That is the P2 (blast through) function.

Finally, your mind is constantly collecting information about the world. It does that in one of two ways, either by increasing your I1 function which enables you to recall factual information, is quantitative and demands 'show me, don't tell me'; or by increasing your I2 function which is qualitative, empathetic and focuses on feeling.

These six critical elements are all parts of your mind. When you're making a decision, you may use only one of those, or you may use all six. ***Your task is to learn how to use the right functions for the right task.***

If you really understand the functions your mind naturally uses and those it ignores (your strengths and your weaknesses), you are ready to move on to the next stage. The next stage is very exciting because now you can start looking at your unique combination of thinking functions. When the three functions you use by nature are combined, a three-dimensional personality emerges. In effect you 'transform' energy into a higher level of consciousness. Only at this higher level of consciousness does the true 'self' emerge. (Your true self has a leadership style waiting to be developed and used.)

This three-dimensional personality takes one of eight different forms. These are illustrated and summarized as follows:

Diagram

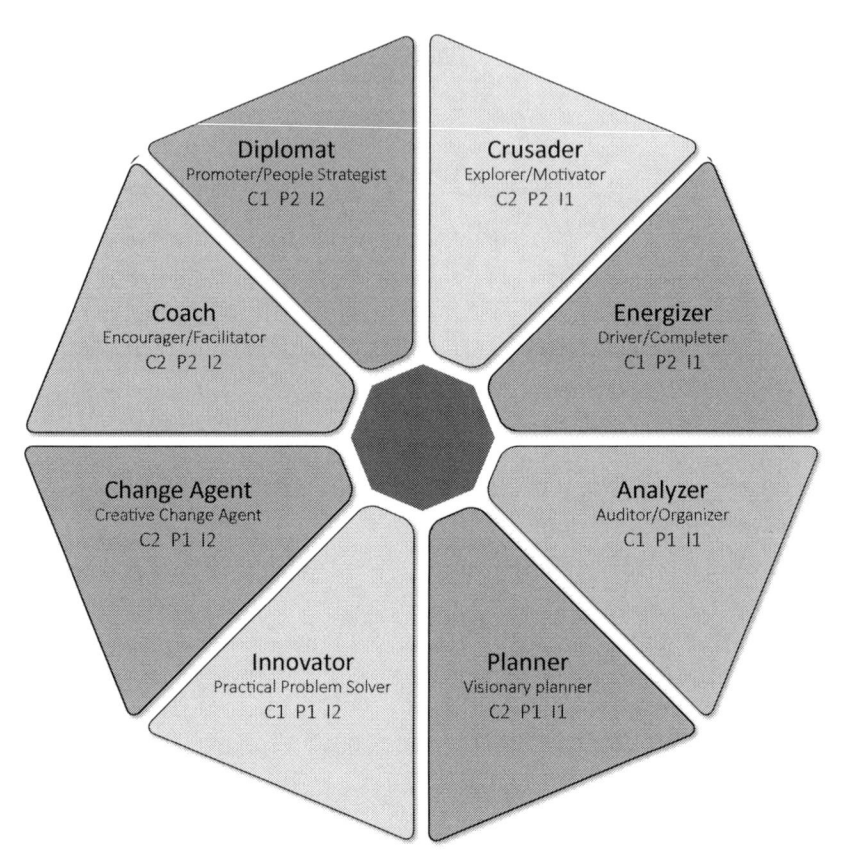

- **Diplomat** — Promoter/People Strategist — C1 P2 I2
- **Crusader** — Explorer/Motivator — C2 P2 I1
- **Coach** — Encourager/Facilitator — C2 P2 I2
- **Energizer** — Driver/Completer — C1 P2 I1
- **Change Agent** — Creative Change Agent — C2 P1 I2
- **Analyzer** — Auditor/Organizer — C1 P1 I1
- **Innovator** — Practical Problem Solver — C1 P1 I2
- **Planner** — Visionary planner — C2 P1 I1

1. Crusader (Explorer/Motivator)

The Crusader will do 'whatever it takes' to achieve their vision. They are very high energy and motivational by nature, often inspiring with the highest principles and a naturally optimistic style. The Crusader is a persuasive communicator, is excellent at securing resources for their vision and fills team members with the conviction to achieve their crusade. Crusaders focus on clarity of role and keeping team members accountable.

2. Innovator (Practical Problem Solver)

The Innovator is able to solve problems that are complex, undefined or constantly changing. They are excellent at managing groups of people in high stress, dangerous or crisis situations. The Innovator is practical and creative and can solve things 'on the hop'. The Innovator is the natural leader when the right emergency action is needed without preparation.

3. Diplomat (Promoter/People Strategist)

The Diplomat has the ability to promote the good work of the team both within the team itself and to important external stakeholders. This is essential if the team is to receive additional resources and for increasing the team's circle of influence. The Diplomat is particularly good at devising strategies for achieving objectives with the least exposure, cost or risk to personal reputation or credibility.

4. Coach (Encourager/Facilitator)

The Coach creates an environment where the unique strengths of each individual can be used for the best team outcome. This involves creating a sense of abundance, outlining the principles of team interaction, getting agreement for objectives and facilitating discussion that fosters the best contribution for each team member, while reminding all team members of the team vision and purpose. The Coach's role is to ensure the team is functioning as a team rather than as a group of individuals.

5. Analyzer (Auditor/Organizer)

The Analyzer ensures agreed processes are followed; documents are accurate and updated; quality is maintained; finances are documented, fair and accountable; and ensures legal issues are squared off. The Analyzer ensures there is a full audit trail and that records of meetings, agreements and resolutions are accurate and readily available.

6. Planner (Visionary Planner)

The Planner can see what is ahead for the team both internally and externally, and can create systems and processes that draw on relevant data and achieve the agreed vision. These systems are then documented in a user-friendly way. The Planner has an excellent sense of cause and effect and the ability to sequence activities appropriately.

7. Energizer (Driver/Completer)

The Energizer is interested in action and completing tasks. They focus on clarifying exactly what needs to be done, by whom, with what resources and in what timeframe. They have an innate sense of urgency and don't walk away from conflict if that is required to agree on tasks and responsibilities. The Energizer pushes the team to make decisions, to allocate resources and agree to timeframes. They energize the team, and roll their sleeves up and get on with the task at hand. They are practical and push teams to complete the task.

8. Change Agent (Creative Change Agent)

The Change Agent can see when systems are not going to produce the desired outcome or where processes are falling short. The Change Agent can create new paradigms, frameworks or models that better align the process with the vision and the people. The Change Agent enjoys prototypes or new projects, is analytical by nature, is gregarious yet fiercely independent, ensures the leadership 'walks the talk' and is credible.

To better identify which leadership style you are, complete the Leadership Style Inventory described in Appendix Four.

Section 2 further details each leadership style including aspects such as natural leadership styles, and helpful hints for managing yourself and others who may have this leadership style.

For each leadership style the Mirror is also investigated. For a full explanation of a Mirror see "Chapter 20" on page 183.

What is your natural leadership style? Do you have blind spots that perhaps others have seen but you haven't? Take the next step forward on your personal quest with us and find out.

SECTION 2

Leadership Styles

Leadership Styles

Leadership Styles

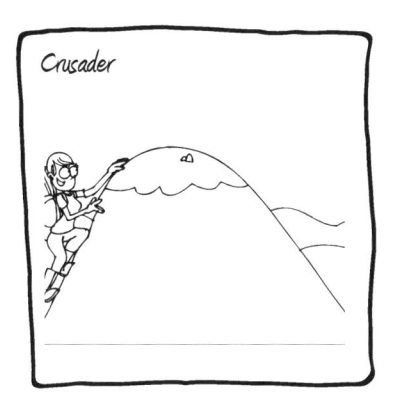

Chapter 12

The Crusader
An In-Depth Look at the Crusader

God grant me the serenity to accept the things I cannot change,
the courage to change the things I can and the wisdom to know the difference.
Anonymous

What we've got to thank Crusaders for:

- Clear rules
- Code of conduct
- High manufacturing standards
- On time, on budget
- High precision specialist medical equipment
- High performance cars
- Total Quality Management (TQM) movement
- Business excellence

THE CRUSADER PROFILE

Whoever thinks a faultless piece to see, thinks that ne'er there was, nor is, nor e'er shall be.

Alexander Pope

OVERVIEW

Crusaders are passionate, disciplined and dependable protectors of morality, justice and honesty. They are the defenders of what is true and correct. With a clear sense of what is 'right', Crusaders work long hours doing many of the tasks that the rest of us take for granted – cleaning, maintenance work, completing checks and audits, checking the quality is right, rechecking figures, finalising work schedules, fine-tuning project plans or lesson outlines or doing whatever it takes to get it right or as close to perfect as possible.

Crusaders respect rules, quality management and the accepted procedures. They respect authority and the established protocol. Serious, stern-looking and always ready to correct others, Crusaders are by nature frugal, independent, reliable, conservative and task-oriented. They teach us the true meaning of honor and, in a team, foster commitment from others.

> *I went to a hardware shop to buy some special cleaner – I was buying a number of things. When I got home and looked at the docket I realized I'd got six bottles of this cleaner but they'd only charged me for one. I felt really awkward about this, and very quickly decided that I would just have to go back and pay the girl for the other five bottles. Needless to say, the girl was quite surprised, which to be truthful quite amazed me, because I like to think everyone would do something similar. I think as I've got older I've realized too, in some way, disbelief that not everyone does this. And that some people may think you're a bit strange for doing it. But I couldn't live with myself if I hadn't.*

FOCUS OF ATTENTION

Crusaders (the White Knight leadership style) fight for what is true and right. This can mean fighting for the underprivileged, the disadvantaged, the marginalized or the underdog. Crusaders demonstrate to others what ethics, justice, integrity, excellence, magnanimity, benevolence and compassion really mean.

KEY CHARACTER DRIVERS

There are three key Intelligences that drive the Crusader:

C2 – Vision

P2 – Passion

I1 – Data

THE SUBTYPES

Each of the eight types is made up of three Intelligence Circuits (ICs). The Crusader has C2 Vision, P2 Passion and I1 Data. As we adapt to our life circumstances we tend to favor one of the three. This subtly changes the personality and gives rise to subtypes. All Crusaders will be able to relate to all three of the subtypes at some time in their life.

THE VISIONARY CRUSADER

The Visionary Crusader fights to keep ideas and ideologies pure. This subtype does this by firstly keeping themselves pure through daily exercises or rituals that require a high degree of self-discipline. Then through meditation, reading, study or training, the Visionary Crusader keeps their eye on the original and 'pure' doctrine, practice or procedure to ensure it is kept authentic.

The Visionary Crusader is very prone to attachment – which denies the constant fluid state of the universal system. While attachment is important for keeping promises, being true to your word and being a person of integrity, it also has some downsides.

In Eastern religions this attachment is considered the source of all suffering. Attachment focuses energy outside the individual and on another person, ideology or object. When the object of the attachment is removed the Visionary Crusader's focus tends to remain on the lost lover, the lost opportunity, the lost reward, the disappointment.

This subtype should also watch that they don't become over-intellectual and ungrounded, addicted to spirituality as a way of escaping day-to-day responsibilities; or they may become involved in psychotic episodes where the Visionary Crusader becomes totally unpredictable and manic or simply overwhelmed by life.

> *Ideals*
> *I think the world would be a good place if everyone was considerate of other people: honesty, justice, and respect for yourself as well as others. I live in an ideal world where people are nice to each other. I go out of my way to be friendly to people.*

THE POWERFUL CRUSADER

With P2 as their most dominant driver, the Powerful Crusader subtype fights for compliance, getting it right and completing the long list of 'shoulds' associated with any role or any task to be undertaken.

This subtype is particularly focused on compliance and ruling with an iron fist. When in full swing the Powerful Crusader leaves no room for others to express their creativity or individuality – there is a right way to complete the task, and everyone's role is to learn to do it the RIGHT WAY. This subtype is really where the Crusader gets its name from because it is the Powerful Crusader who goes on crusade. This subtype needs to be careful that they don't become what John Bradshaw calls a human doing rather than a human being – constantly pushing themselves to achieve and produce as a means of securing approval and feeling OK about themselves.

> *Being Disciplined*
>
> *I was very disciplined about my study in University. I got an OP2 at school through discipline and sheer determination. I was going to do well no matter what. I'm very disciplined about things I think are worthwhile, and other things I don't think are so important, I'm probably not so disciplined about, depending on my vision and the vision changes. I suppose the vision is that I'm good at everything I do.*

Powerful Crusaders tend to push themselves so hard that they suffer from chronic fatigue or burnout because their bodies simply can't keep up. They also need to watch that they don't become dominating and controlling bullies wanting to know everything that everyone is doing and constantly trying to micro-manage and control everyone's lives for their own personally desired outcome. At all times this subtype needs to check that it is using, rather than abusing, power.

> *I have learned through bitter experience the one supreme lesson: to conserve my anger, and as heat conserved is transmuted into energy, even so our anger controlled can be transmuted into a power which can move the world.*
>
> *Mahatma Gandhi*
> *Former Indian Spiritual/Political Leader*

Leadership Styles

If you are going to achieve excellence in big things, you develop the habit in little matters. Excellence is not an exception, it is a prevailing attitude.

Colin Powell

Former United States Secretary of State

Being 'Forceful'

I work in a hospital and at times I can be very forceful. If someone else is at risk, and you're seeing the consequences of your behavior, you get very protective of your patients. I want to make sure other people are following the standards as what they do impacts other people. When I see that happen, I take these responsibilities seriously. I do fear that other people perceive that I am too dominating, when I actually feel like I come across meek and mild.

THE WISE CRUSADER

With I1 as their most dominant driver the Wise Crusader focuses on completing tasks so that the things they create look like the 'idealized' version of their creation. Christmas dinner, for example, must have the entire color, decoration and food one would expect the ideal Christmas dinner to have. Home must be spotless; cars should be clean and serviced. Educationally, Wise Crusaders value education and resist being promoted past their perceived level of training.

This subtype is often called the perfectionist. As I1 rises to very high levels, Wise Crusaders can become fascinated with clairvoyance, the third eye, mysticism and psychic intuition. While this is an expansive area of study, the Wise Crusader needs to watch that they keep grounded and carefully analyze the dreams, visions and insights that they find so fascinating and don't escape into the mystical world completely.

Being passionate

I am passionate about cooking. When people come over for dinner I want to cook the best possible meal, and I want it to look just right. I want it to present well. It has to coordinate and most importantly it has to BE good. I take great delight watching other people enjoy it.

Brand

I love buying good quality clothes. The brand of the clothes is probably very important to me – but really as notification of quality rather than a label shown so you can see it.

LEADERSHIP STYLES RELATED TO THE CRUSADER

When people discuss leadership styles, many of the characters they use will fall into the same category as the Crusader, much the same way that there may be fifty-seven species of fern but regardless of the species, it still belongs to the fern family.

By way of example, some of these are:

- The Perfectionist
- The Olympian
- The Soldier
- The Rescuer
- The Reformer
- The Advocate
- The Warrior
- Theseus – Athenian Bull Slayer
- The School Ma'am
- The Attorney
- The Mentor, Tutor
- Arjuna (in the Bhagavad-Gita)
- The Queen
- The Defender
- The Amazon
- The Crime Fighter
- The Revolutionary
- The Pioneer
- The Celibate Nun/Monk
- The Sheriff
- The Hero/Heroine
- The Explorer
- The Environmentalist
- The Magistrate
- Ulysses
- The Settler
- The Soldier of Fortune
- The Legislator
- The Mercenary
- The Pilgrim
- Hidesata (in Japanese legend)
- The Lobbyist
- The Gunslinger
- The Entrepreneur
- Bernado del Caprio (19th Century Spanish hero)

CHILDREN'S STORIES/NURSERY RHYMES

- The Princess and the Pea
- Sir Lancelot, the White Knight

THE MIRROR

While the Crusader is moral, principled and idealistic, the Crusader's Mirror, the Innovator, is sexy, impulsive and laid back with a youthful sexual charm, an easy humor and a love of parties. When the Mirror is in control the Crusader loves having fun, breaking the rules, being disorderly, talking loudly, behaving badly and generally doing all the things the Crusader abhors. The Mirror is particularly likely to get the

Crusader into trouble when a little alcohol is applied.

When a young Mirror Innovator appears on the scene they will charm people through overt seduction and physical contact. This matures to empathetic listening, warmth, an acceptance of all people and an incredibly generous spirit that is always available to help in a crisis at any time, day or night.

When integrated into the personality, the Innovator gives the Crusader patience, acceptance, warmth, generosity and the ability to solve problems patiently. It even gives them the ability to enjoy life and amuse themselves.

UNDERSTANDING CRUSADERS

Crusaders best manage themselves by:
- Not letting themselves get locked into one vision and becoming inflexible
- Not misinterpreting team members' rejection of the vision as being a rejection of them and their leadership
- Not pushing people so hard they burn out
- Not pushing everyone to work at the Crusader's fast pace and instead giving them time to think things through

As team members, Crusaders make the best contribution when:
- They are given a vision that is big enough to be worthy of their energy, commitment and enthusiasm
- They have a role that requires re-energizing or motivating teams of people
- They have new and interesting challenges that require decisive decision-making and quick action

When managing Crusaders:
- Provide regular written feedback about what they are doing well and what you would like them to do differently and explain why
- Give them at least one project that stretches them into unfamiliar territory
- Give them projects with an element of competition, so that their effort can be acknowledged

Leadership Styles

How Crusaders will behave during meetings:
- Will need clarity around why the meeting is required, why all the participants are required and how the team's effectiveness will be measured
- Will want there to be tangible action as a result of discussion – even if the decision is not to make a decision, the outcome must be said and noted
- Will tend to run roughshod over sensitive members of the meeting

Personality strengths that help the Crusader to further their development:
- Able to break through virtually any barrier to achieve results
- Passionate and inspirational
- Fantastic at debating that the extra effort to make it better is worthwhile

Personality weaknesses that can stand in the way of the Crusaders development:
- Insensitive
- Totally task-oriented
- Can suffer from burnout
- Can link ego with vision and become inflexible

Opportunities for Crusaders to develop:
- Need to learn how not to offend
- Need to learn how to change direction quickly
- Need to learn how to connect with people
- Need to learn how to value themselves in ways other than just outcomes

Threats to a Crusader's development:
- Can create many enemies who retaliate
- Can get bored when there are no new conquests and will go looking for trouble
- Can lose 'connection' with people and become lonely
- Can become too outcome-focused, Energizer themselves as not adding value, suffer from self-imposed disappointment and get frustrated and depressed

WHEN NEGOTIATING WITH CRUSADERS

When negotiating with Crusaders the way you position information is very important. While Crusaders are attracted to messages centered around due process and quality, the two other themes which are most convincing to them are, *'Show me that you are willing*

Leadership Styles

to do what it takes to make this vision happen' and *'Show me this idea is the best way forward.'*

These are discussed in more detail below:

'Show me that you are willing to do what it takes to make the vision happen'

There are two groups who access their P2 and C2 by nature, the Coaches and the Crusaders. This group:

- Looks for passion and commitment for a clear and exciting vision
- Sees the leader's role as the motivator and inspirer of their people
- Will assess the leadership's ability based on their ability to inspire and motivate their team or stakeholders
- Must be convinced that the vision is right and that the endpoint will justify all the hard work to achieve it
- Likes to see how the organization is performing relative to the rest of the market
- Likes benchmarking comparisons
- Puts enormous store in reputation and community standing. The 'person' is as influential as their message
- Respects institutions, laws and precedents, and wants to see that the organization is 'doing the right thing'
- Looks for tangible evidence that the leader and their team are absolutely committed to achieving the vision and the leader supports bonus payments or incentives on this basis
- Is focused on teamwork, synergy and big picture strategies rather than implementation of plans and processes

'Show me this idea is the best way forward'

There are two types that access the P2 and I1 functions by nature, the Energizer and the Crusader. This segment makes up approximately 37 per cent of the general population. This group:

- Cannot tolerate indifference, lack of passion, coldness or apathy
- Wants to be sold the benefits of new ideas particularly if these benefits can be quantified Wants to keep the discussion tangible and concrete with specifics
- Doesn't like concepts, models, abstract ideas, hunches, intuitions or possibilities
- Believes there is a valid code of conduct and that there is a right and wrong way of

doing things. They will want to see that leaders are approaching tasks the RIGHT way
- Believes in following the rules, respecting the status quo, paying taxes, doing jury duty and being fair
- Wants communication to be precise, passionate, action-oriented and respectful of institutions and roles/positions. They also want their leaders to be strong yet approachable and to protect those within their responsibility
- Likes to see that goals are articulated, milestones are set, and that these goals are achieved. Also wants to see the leadership is passionate and will do whatever it takes to keep the energy and focus maintained

FAMOUS CRUSADERS

- Angelina Jolie (Actor, UN Goodwill Ambassador)
- Aung San Suu Kyi (Burmese Politician, Nobel Peace Prize winner)
- Carl Benz (Founder, Mercedes-Benz)
- Celine Dion (Singer)
- Charles Dickens (Author)
- Coco Chanel (Founder, Chanel)
- Edward Deming (Engineer)
- Emily Post (Author)
- Estee Lauder (Founder, Estee Lauder cosmetics)
- Henry David Thoreau (Author)
- Hillary Clinton (US Secretary of State)
- John Paul II (former Catholic Pope)
- Katherine Hepburn (Actress)
- Mahatma Gandhi (Leader, pacifist)
- Margaret Thatcher (Former British Prime Minister)
- Martin Luther King, Jr. (Activist, Nobel Peace Prize winner)
- Mary Poppins (Character)
- Plato (Philosopher)
- Vanessa Redgrave (Actor)
- William Wallace (Scottish Revolutionary)

> *I have a dream that my four little children will one day live in a nation where they will not be judged by the color of their skin, but by the content of their character.*
>
> Martin Luther King, Jr
> American pastor, activist, humanitarian, and leader in the African-American Civil Rights Movement

CRUSADERS AT WORK

Crusaders enjoy the big picture They are brilliant at painting very clear pictures of how things could be in the ideal world. Being vision-centered they cope with change easily as long as it aligns with their vision. Their energy and enthusiasm are heightened when focused on a project they are committed to and believe in.

Dependable

On a report card, or anything I've ever done where there's some form of assessment, they've always said I'm a very responsible person – being answerable to whatever you're called to do or told to do. People would never check up on me. If I said I was going to do it, I'd do it.

For the Crusaders, no vision means no energy. They are keen to cooperate if their vision and ideas are valued; if not, their willingness to contribute diminishes quickly. These wunderkind human beings can achieve the impossible, bringing to life dreams that others would consider unachievable. If a Crusader decides a project should go ahead, it will usually happen. The Crusader is excellent at getting projects off the ground and insisting on quality.

They are highly motivated to achieve their vision in what they believe is right. Efficiency fades when Crusaders are required to change tack halfway through a project. They will not willingly adhere to processes or procedures implemented by others. Their opinions are based on values rather than analysis or logic. They would rather beat their own path. When assigned a project, they will be very determined to see their vision take shape. Often they will seek to hand over a project if it is too small They will either work on a project to meet a deadline or, if it does not fit the vision, will tend to be attracted to a newer project or idea that does. They suffer boredom when there is nothing to strive for.

Colleagues may bore them easily if they do not share their vision. They like people who value their ideas and also tolerate their highs and lows. They don't respect people who allow logic to stifle creativity. Crusaders are most comfortable with like-minded people. A Crusader's confidence rises and falls. When they have a vision and an outlet for its expression they ooze confidence.

We shall never have friends if we expect to find them without fault.

Thomas Fuller
English Preacher, Historian and Scholar

A Crusader must be able to express their vision and creativity. They are natural energizers, motivated and enthusiastic, but can become depressed and frustrated when their vision is repressed. They are excellent at delegating, and will make clear the implications of achieving or not achieving the objective.

> *If I asked someone to go and get something for me I'd always make a concerted effort to always tell them how much I'd appreciated it.*

They tend not to naturally empathize with others. They are more interested in winning the battle than being loyal to those who don't share their vision. They cope with aggression either by arguing the point or by escaping to the creative vision part of their mind. They often respond with aggression.

Their ability to analyze is often clouded by their ability to Energizer. They will make quick decisions generally based on preconceptions and attitudes, and when asked to make a decision regarding a new topic, they will spend a lot of time looking for facts to substantiate their decision.

Crusaders cope with stress by daydreaming or focusing on how things could be, rather than how they are. They will place themselves under a lot of stress to achieve their vision. Crusaders enjoy competition and generally win. Their assets are their convincing speech, excellent arguments and factual recall to back them up. They are fluent communicators and accomplished negotiators with excellent memories. They like power and are sometimes ruthless with it.

A Crusader's humor is often weird or bizarre, and anything taboo or offensive amuses them. They will always want things done properly. They will unconsciously exaggerate at times to win a point.

Crusaders are zany and in their passion to express possibilities, they will paint pictures, sometimes ignoring reality and the current truth. Crusaders are at their most formidable when turning an organization or situation around, swaying large numbers of people and working as up-front, blast-through change agents or conquerors of new territory.

LEADERSHIP STYLE OF THE CRUSADER

Each Neuro-Rational Type, due to its combination of thinking functions, has a different leadership style. These leadership styles tend to be expressions of the underlying world view of each personality. The most effective leaders use a variety of styles, choosing the appropriate style, timing and intensity to manage each situation.

A groundbreaking survey of 3871 executives selected from a database of more

The Mentoring Style

Fred Hollows, the famous eye surgeon, was a Crusader (Powerful Crusader subtype). Head of the Eye Department at a Sydney hospital in 1966, he learned of the great incidence of eye disease among Australian Aborigines. Because he always believed strongly in equality, he set about establishing the first Aboriginal Medical Center, later launching a nationwide program in Australia, then he moved his crusade to Africa. Hundreds of thousands of people benefited as he worked for excellence and affordability among the needy.

Dr Hollows was able to inspire people to follow his moral crusade – doctors and other staff volunteered and people donated millions of dollars. He was indomitable. He said, 'I believe in helping people help themselves ... When I've seen an opportunity I haven't sat down and called a committee meeting. We've gone and done it'. He was known as the 'wild colonial boy' partly because of his wild temper. One biographer politely said that he could be 'very gruff when things weren't going as he thought they should and this made him some enemies. But his family and friends loved him deeply' (Leary online, 2002 ABC, Privacy Policy).

True to the Mentoring style, Fred Hollows was dynamic and totally focused on the detail and excellence of the work they did – driven by the moral crusade. And in the process he trampled on some toes.

In their compelling book Memories of Fred, Pat Fiske and Michael Johnson offer the following recollections which demonstrate Dr Hollows' leadership style. Pat Fiske, cycling, running and climbing mate and director of the film about Fred's life and work, For all the World to See, said, 'He often gave me hell, as he did others. I had a love-hate relationship with him. There were times when I was so angry and frustrated during arguments when he would just cut me off with his shouting and self-certainty, stifling any chance of debate ... But I got heaps out of the friendship – he was dynamic, exciting to be with and always had you on wood. He had a powerful sense of self, a self-confidence that swept you along with him ... He made you feel an important member of the team. I treasure many happy memories.'

Paul Torzillo, medical student and Volunteer Driver Aboriginal Medical Service 1970s, said, 'Fred loved being a doctor and was proud of the profession. He was concerned with competence and professionalism and imprinted their importance on me for the rest of my career. I was always amazed at Fred's ability to interact with all comers. Even more amazing is how highly regarded he was, very often by people who didn't particularly share his political views! He was often challenging and provoking and frequently insulting – I think it was this ability to engage people which helped him recruit so many people to work with him ... Fred was absolutely serious and committed to the indigenous cause. Fred enjoyed being around blackfellas, he liked their company, found them interesting and enjoyed the time.'

Adapted from the Fred Hollows Foundation online www.hollows.org

The Leadership Style of the Crusader

Situation	Explanation
1. The leader's modus operandi	One-to-one mentoring to help set high standards
2. The style in a phrase	'Do it again until you get it right'
3. Underlying emotional intelligence competencies	Self-discipline, a sense of justice, fairness
4. When the style works best	When change is being driven by moral crusade
5. Overall impact on climate	Medium positive

than 20,000 executives[1] found distinct leadership styles which consistently appear in organizations. Daniel Goleman (2000) attributes these different leadership styles to different emotional intelligences. These intelligences equate to the Intelligences.

The leadership style most closely aligned to the profile of the Crusader is a *Mentoring* style. The author's experience shows that the Mentoring style has a medium-positive effect on the overall climate of the organization. The primary focus of the Mentoring style is the vision of the moral crusade which is to be achieved through personal performance.

Some of the attributes of the Mentoring leadership style are as follows:

- **Clarity.** The visionary (strong C2 element) nature of the Mentoring leader generates motivation because people come to see clearly how their work fits into the larger vision of the organization. For the Crusader leader clarity is how the individuals are performing in relation to their personal best.
- **Inspire commitment.** Their visionary focus allows them to frame the individual tasks in the context of the overall vision (I1 articulated vision). Therefore, people can see how their work matters and why it is important. It brings significance to the employees' daily activities and so increases their sense of commitment.
- **Very high standards.** With a strong sense of vision, the leader defines standards that underpin the overall objectives. The Crusader is focused on detail and excellence of output. The emphasis is on results on – creating things of a very high standard. Key words are 'excellence', 'best in class' and 'best of breed'.

---

1 Survey was originally analyzed by Kelner, S., et al. (1996).

Disciplining yourself to do what you know is right and important, although difficult, is the highroad to pride, self-esteem, and personal satisfaction.

Margaret Thatcher
Former British Prime Minister

- **Feedback.** In providing feedback (assisted by I1), the single objective is whether the performance has furthered the vision. Therefore, determinates of positive or negative feedback are fixed and not subject to whims. The Mentoring style is one-to-one and always fair.
- **Objectives.** These are clear and stated up front, as are the rewards for performance.

It's important that everyone in the team contributes equally and performs their role to the best of their ability. When I was a team leader, I wanted the people I was in charge of to learn from me so that they could be proud of themselves and I could be proud of them. I tried to treat them as equals. I tried to make every experience a learning experience. I would never try to withhold information from them and I would try to encourage them in their career. I always tried to compliment them on a job well done. When managing difficult staff that didn't play by these rules of mutual respect, I had to have very strong self-control and not behave in a way that was reactionary to whatever they were doing. At great expense to myself, I still tried to treat them fairly and equally. In doing so, I think I became quite discouraged that some people had no interest in making an effort in getting along with other people, or being respectful, when personal differences were evident.

I struggled with doing the right thing by these people. I might not have liked them, or really honestly wanted to respect them, but I believed it was important that everyone had a right to be respected and treated well. Internally, I struggled greatly with the fact that they weren't treating me well. I suppose in one way I was hurt, in that no matter how hard I tried, they treated me with great disrespect, with absolutely no concern for my feelings even though I was constantly thinking of ways of working in with their requests.

SCHOOL OF STRATEGIC THOUGHT[2]

The natural differences are not limited to leadership styles alone; they also extend to a natural inclination towards different strategic thought. These differences have been researched by Mintzberg, Ahlstrad and Lampel (1998). For the Crusader, their approach to strategy belongs in the positional school. This suggests that only a few key strategies (or positions in the economic marketplace) are desirable.

THE GENIUS OF THE CRUSADER – PATHFINDING

The Genius of the Crusader is in pathfinding, an ability to conquer new territory. This means they thrive on danger or unknown territory, or creating new frontiers. As long as the crusade aligns with the stated vision, Crusaders will undergo enormous short-term pain for long-term gain. They will be the ones who blast through to achieve the results. This makes Crusaders excellent for starting up businesses or projects, for rejuvenating dead concepts or creating new visions. Buckingham and Clifton (2001) describe this strength as follows:

- Excellence in standards, as opposed to mediocrity.
- The stance is that it takes just as much effort to transform something strong into something superb as it does to take something mediocre to something above average, so why waste time on the latter.
- The person focuses on strengths, be that their own or another's. They can discern where strengths are being met (or underused) and focus on encouraging, challenging and developing them to reach excellence.
- Because of this focus on sorting, they are seen as discriminating. This person prefers the company of people who appreciate their strengths and who have developed their own strengths.
- They avoid people who see them as deficient and try to round out their own or other people's talents. Instead, they prefer to focus on what they can do well and take that to excellence. They consider their positive attitude as more fun, more productive, even though demanding.

---

2 The natural differences are not limited to leadership styles alone; they also extend to a natural inclination towards different strategic thought. These differences have been researched by Minzberg, Ahlstrad, and Lampel (1998).

Leadership Styles

Chapter 13

The Coach
An In-Depth Look at the Coach

Merlin: Love is a force.
Young King Arthur: Is it very powerful?
Merlin: Yes. Some would say the greatest power in the Universe.

Merlin
MAGICIAN

What we've got to thank Coaches for:

- Creating a sense of magic
- Healing and inspiration
- Creating a sense of purpose out of pain
- Empowering people to use their gift
- Coaching people to achieve their best
- Making the impossible come true
- Creating spaces with an 'other-worldly' feel such as theme parks and restaurants

THE COACH PROFILE

One's own self is well hidden from one's own self: of all mines of treasure, one's own is the last to be dug up.

Nietzsche

German Philosopher

OVERVIEW

Coaches have the unique ability to see the potential in others and create environments that empower them or enable them to reach their full potential. They have a natural fascination with their own quest for meaning, the purpose of life and the deeper and more mystical parts of life.

> *I've sung for thousands and held every one of them in my hand, even the Policemen. I've preached to stone faces and watched the tears start. I've had at least one person from each of my former Churches go into Ministry and one other tell me he had 'joined up' because he'd heard me being crazy once on a Christian Radio Show.*
>
> *When I was about nine years of age, my best friend and I put on a concert. We created instruments from cardboard, made a stage of sorts, created costumes and sold tickets to the neighbors. I was in another world ... wished I could have stayed there.*

Coaches can inspire with their amazing ideas and big dreams, their zest for life and their optimism, energy, passion and warmth. For the Coaches everything is interdependent, so their home and work lives will merge as will their various business ventures, their ideas and their philosophies. This can sometimes mean that relatively small issues are combined to create large, complex and difficult situations. When this happens the Coaches can see that any movement will impact on so many areas that they can become paralyzed for fear of 'upsetting the apple cart'.

Regardless of their training or level of professional development, Coaches have the ability to create teams of people all working to the same objective, all for their own personal reasons. The Coaches will take the role of listener, friend, supporter and adviser for each team member.

Coaches are very sensitive and can intuitively 'pick up' the feelings of others. This can mean that the internal emotions of Coaches are greatly affected by the people around them. By nature Coaches will avoid long-term exposure to trauma, stress, crisis and conflict because of the enormous emotional stress it causes them.

> *Healing*
>
> *Just to prove you don't have to be an angel to do miraculous things, I have been the instrument of the spontaneous healing of illnesses, chronic conditions, psychological trauma, dementia, but so far not Athlete's foot.*
>
> *When I focus on the problem and not get emotionally involved I can prescribe the correct homeopathic remedy. I feel involved but objective and it's great to see people relaxed and comfortable about what's happening.*

FOCUS OF ATTENTION

Coaches focus on creating a safe environment where everyone can reach their full potential. At their best, Coaches are modest, confronting, inspirational, visionary, liberating, empowering and healing.

> *Creating a safe environment*
>
> *When I was a boy we used to go on holiday to a seaside place with lots of sand dunes. I would spend all day running across the dunes with my plastic raincoat tied around my neck as a cape. I was Aqua Boy and it was my job to keep all the people in the caravans safe from the... I don't know... things they needed to be safe from. Nothing's changed.*
>
> *My home is my castle. I love to create an environment where when we come back to it, even if we've been away just a short time, it's restful and refreshing. It's a haven. That's so important to me.*

KEY CHARACTER DRIVERS

There are three key Intelligences that drive the Coach:

C2 – Vision

P2 – Passion

I2 – Heart

Once you have mastered time, you will understand how true it is that most people overestimate what they can accomplish in a year - and underestimate what they can achieve in a decade.

Anthony Robbins,
Motivational Speaker

THE SUBTYPES

Each of the eight types is made up of three Intelligences. The Coach has C2 Vision, P2 Passion and I2 Heart.

As we adapt to our life circumstances we tend to favor one of the three. This subtly changes the personality and gives rise to subtypes. All Coaches will be able to relate to all three of the subtypes at some time in their life.

THE VISIONARY COACH

Visionary Coaches are future centered, often with visions that are not logically connected to their current line of thinking.

The Visionary Coach will tend to have close friends with whom they are open and honest, and they will generally keep their personal thoughts and ideas from others.

They tend to daydream or focus on what could be, rather than what is. They are sensitive to stress and prefer low-stress situations where they can relax and express their imagination without fear of ridicule or misunderstanding.

Their spiritual world will not work to a pattern and will not be disciplined. A Visionary Coach often has bizarre or taboo thoughts and ideas which may even offend themselves. They have a brilliant imagination and can visualize well and tap into the wisdom of heaven.

THE POWERFUL COACHES

Powerful Coaches have strong opinions about most things and will want issues resolved. They filter thoughts through their opinions and beliefs. Powerful Coaches will tend to make decisions quickly, often based on the principle of the matter, will argue well, and are motivated by a belief in the value of what they are doing. The Powerful Coach's motivation comes from believing that what they are doing is important and in line with their philosophy of life.

One of the greatest challenges for Powerful Coaches is to control their anger and to understand that others can have their own ideas that may not agree with theirs. They like to be acknowledged for a job well done, and it is important to them to live up to their own very high self-expectations. The Powerful Coach is highly competitive and a high achiever.

THE SENSITIVE COACHES

Sensitive Coaches are very attuned to how others are feeling – they are true empathizers, putting people first at all costs. They have an intuitive ability to sense what is happening around them.

The Sensitive Coaches are naturally shy although they may hide it well. They will be extremely sensitive to the needs of others, often to their own detriment. They do not want to offend or upset others, and will tend to say nothing when they are upset or angry unless they are compelled to. Sensitive Coaches need to be careful that their unexpressed anger does not turn to resentment. Resentful Coaches will go to great lengths to get even. When doing this, they will use great subtlety so that no one can read their behavior.

Sensitive Coaches will think in terms of people, not facts, and intuitively sense how others are feeling. They will place relationships at the very top of their priority list and they make very sensitive partners. They will be caring and loving parents and the glue that binds a family.

> *Unconditional Love*
>
> *My friend and I worked for eleven years to keep an elderly lady we came to love, out of a nursing home. She lived in nauseating squalor; we fixed it time and again. She would get terribly depressed and not get out of bed (for anything) for days. She had a heart of gold and severe bi-polar disorder. The illness would make her turn on us time and time again. The last time it happened, it destroyed the life I had then. I rang her a while back, just to say, 'I love you.' What else?*
>
> *We lived for a time in the rainforest and during this period had a friend live with us. He was often unreliable, dirty, messy and uncommunicative, but generous to a fault. He lived with us for five years, drove me batty at times but if he needed a place to live I'd welcome him back anytime.*

LEADERSHIP STYLES RELATED TO THE COACH

When people discuss leadership styles, many of the characters they use will fall into the same category as the Coach, much the same way that there may be 57 species of fern but regardless of the species, it still belongs to the fern family.

By way of example, some of these are:

- The Guru
- The Spiritual Adviser
- The Caregiver
- The Evangelist
- The Preacher
- The Healer
- The Property Developer
- The Therapist

- The Counsellor
- The Kindergarten Teacher
- The Prophet
- The Monk
- The Motivational Speaker
- The Minister
- The Hypnotist
- The Soothsayer

- The Entrepreneur
- The Shaman
- The Fortune Teller
- The Magician
- The Actor
- The Entertainer

CHILDREN'S STORIES/NURSERY RHYMES

- Merlin the Magician
- Santa Claus
- Wendy from Peter Pan
- The Fairy Godmother

THE MIRROR

While the Coaches see themselves as gentle, visionary, passionate people with an ability to heal the past and create a better world, their Mirror, the Analyzer, is obsessed with order, details, stability and security. Coaches can be confusing because while their language is passionate, optimistic and nurturing, their behavior, which is influenced by the Mirror Analyzer, suggests they are penny-pinching, controlling and almost obsessive-compulsive.

At home, the Mirror may express itself through constantly monitoring the household's financial position on a spreadsheet, isolating investments into a number of different funds, each having different risks, keeping friendships separated, feeling comfortable only when things are totally clean and ordered, and insisting on folded

Leadership Styles

> *If you can dream it, you can do it. It's kind of fun to do the impossible.*
>
> Walt Disney
>
> Walt Disney was the man behind Mickey Mouse, Donald Duck and other cartoon favorites. He created one of the largest amusement parks in the world and brought many of our favorite fairy tales to life.

clothes, clean cars, ironed shirts, neatly stacked books and spotless tables and desk tops.

At work, the Mirror unobtrusively shadows the noisy, energetic and inspirational Coach, ensuring meetings are minuted, costs are managed and itemized, information is filed and budgets are micro-managed.

Young Mirror Analyzers are quiet and gently question the Coach's qualifications, level of knowledge and professional credibility. This often encourages the Coach to undertake study to achieve formal qualifications for the work they are doing.

As the Mirror matures, the strength and volume of the Mirror Analyzer's concerns become harder for the Master Coach to ignore, and the Coach's authenticity and practical abilities are constantly questioned. This usually leads to the Coach beginning the process of learning the 'nitty gritty' detail of the work they have been getting others to do for them.

When the Mirror is fully integrated into the personality, the Mirror Analyzer gives humor, flexibility, structure, intellectual rigor, depth and grounding to the already visionary, passionate and intuitive Coach.

UNDERSTANDING COACHES

Coaches best manage themselves by:

- Disciplining themselves to attend to detail
- Not letting themselves get locked into one vision and instead remaining flexible and open to new ideas
- Disciplining themselves to make the hard decisions when dealing with staff and giving negative feedback
- Ruthlessly staying in touch with reality

As team members, Coaches make the best contribution when:

- They are required to integrate or bring together different systems, paradigms or ideas
- They are given freedom to define their task, timeframe and deliverables
- They can encourage, motivate and nurture team members as socio-emotional leaders
- The system for measuring their effort is clear and stakeholder feedback is sought

When managing Coaches:

- Provide them with clear timeframes, deliverables and available resources
- Have them break the project into phases and insist they report back to you in writing at each phase end, with an analysis and next action
- Ensure they don't start integrating elements that are not part of the project
- Help them work through detailed issues around legal implications, financial details and process specifics
- Firm up their recommendations with detail you may have to insist they – research some more and come back with specifics

How Coaches will behave during meetings:

- Will want to see everyone participating and making a contribution
- Will reassure the offended, disgruntled or angry
- Will want to talk about frameworks, paradigms and visions
- Will want the meeting to run to time

Personality strengths that help the Coaches to further their development:

- Is able to create reality
- Can see the big picture
- Is inspirational and motivational

Personality weaknesses that can stand in the way of the Coach's development:

- Are not happy with anything that's not perfect
- Don't focus on detail, which often trips them up
- Find it difficult to motivate practical, hands-on people

Opportunities for Coaches to develop:
- Need to ground themselves and get in touch with reality
- Need to be 'present' in the here and now
- Need, in difficult times, to learn how to take life one step at a time

Threats to the Coach's development:
- Can become so out of touch their skills and thoughts are irrelevant
- Can have major trip-ups because they are focused on past and future rather than the here and now
- Can be overwhelmed and 'break down' in times of crisis if there is no obvious way out

WHEN NEGOTIATING WITH COACHES

When negotiating with Coaches the way you position information is very important. Coaches are attracted to messages centered around two main themes which are most convincing to them: *'Show me that you are willing to do what it takes to make this vision happen'* and *'Show me this solution will empower the team to achieve the objectives.'*

'Show me that you are willing to do what it takes to make the vision happen'

There are two groups who access their P2 and C2 by nature, the Coaches and the Crusaders. This group:
- Looks for passion and commitment for a clear and exciting vision
- Sees the leader's role as the motivator and inspirer of their people
- Will assess the leadership's ability based on their ability to inspire and motivate their team or stakeholders
- Must be convinced that the vision is right and that the endpoint will justify all the hard work to achieve it
- Likes to see how the organization is performing relative to the rest of the market
- Likes benchmarking comparisons
- Puts enormous store in reputation and community standing. The 'person' is as influential as their message
- Respects institutions, laws and precedents, and wants to see that the organization is 'doing the right thing'

- Looks for tangible evidence that the leader and their team are absolutely committed to achieving the vision and support bonus payments or incentives on this basis
- Is focused on teamwork and synergy and big picture strategies rather than implementation plans and processes

'Show me this solution will empower the team to achieve the objectives'

There are two groups who access their P2 and I2 by nature, the Diplomats and the Coaches. This segment makes up approximately 12 per cent of the general population. This group:

- Is very sensitive to non-verbal communication, reading between the lines, gestures and facial expressions
- Has a huge influence on the population because they are the novelists, dramatists, television interviewers, playwrights, poets, biographers and popular journalists
- Asks questions about the meaning of actions, the purpose of the organization, the role of leaders and the impact this all has on the organization's stakeholders
- Sees good in everyone and assumes everyone is doing their best with the best intentions
- Has very little interest in buying and selling, or commercial occupations; and is much more interested in bringing out the best in people and enabling people to reach their full potential
- Will be, by nature, naive about the 'complexities' of law and business

---

Imagine that men are from Mars and women are from Venus.

One day long ago the Martians, looking through their telescopes, discovered the Venusians.

Just glimpsing the Venusians awakened feelings they had never known. They fell in love and quickly invented space travel and flew to Venus.

John Gray
Author - 'Men Are From Mars, Women Are From Venus'

Leadership Styles

FAMOUS COACHES

- Al Gore (Former US Vice President)
- Anthony Robbins (Motivational Speaker)
- David Fritz (Author)
- David Hawkins (Author)
- Dr John Gray (Author, Men are from Mars, Women are from Venus)
- Eva Perón (Spiritual Leader of Argentina)
- George Lucas (Film maker, Star Wars)
- Howard Hughes (Entrepreneur, inventor)
- Jim Yong Kim (World Bank President)
- Louis Armstrong (Musician, Singer)
- Luciano Pavarotti (Singer)
- Merlin the Wizard (Character)
- Muhammad Yunus (Microfinance Founder, Nobel Peace Prize winner)
- Napoleon Hill (Author)
- Oprah Winfrey (TV Personality)
- Ronald Reagan (Former US President)
- Sir Michael Parkinson (TV journalist)
- Steve Jobs (Founder, Apple)
- Walt Disney (Founder, The Walt Disney Company)
- William Shakespeare (Writer)

COACHES AT WORK

Coaches are extremely loyal to close friends, family and selected acquaintances. They tend to be largely misunderstood by others. Coaches are highly sensitive, very empathetic and understanding of others. They will be supportive of others as long as they demonstrate an interest and willingness to pursue the Coach's vision.

At first tier, Coaches have a changing temperament. They can be endearing one minute and moody the next. They can become quite depressed once a project has been completed and they have no vision for the future. Similarly, if things are moving too slowly they can easily become bored. They are very spontaneous and creative and more than willing to experiment.

Coaches respond well to people who are balanced, predictable and disciplined and at first tier they will generally put people into two boxes – those to be trusted and those not to be trusted. They are very likely to exaggerate. They are highly competitive and enjoy being recognized for their achievements. Coaches thoroughly enjoy creating magic and, as storytellers, they are dedicated to communicating the essence rather than the detail.

Creating Magic

I can't imagine life without magic. How dull! Every kid, and adult, should watch the movie 'Never Ending Story'. Reality is too hard and boring. I like to create magic and fantasy even if it's only in my head. At least it makes the day more interesting.

Starts when I wake up, sometimes before. Couldn't be without it, wouldn't want to.

The Coach is neither analytical nor objective. Responses are based on their values and beliefs, gut reaction and vision.

At first tier, Coaches will feel stress which drives them to either work harder, become more intense, talk faster or become abrupt. If confronted with aggression they will either argue, be lost for words or take it as a personal attack. They have long memories. A Coach is most formidable when leading groups to over-achieve, resolving complex personal problems and giving life meaning.

Hard work

If it's what I want to do, I'll work round the clock until I fall over. If it's not what I want to do, I'll hide behind the clock till some other bugger does it.

If I can see the reason or point to what I'm doing I'll work endlessly. If I can't engage with it or it doesn't capture my interest, I'm without energy and the whole thing is a pain in the neck.

THE LEADERSHIP STYLE OF THE COACH

Each Neuro-Rational Type, due to its combination of thinking functions, has a different leadership style. These leadership styles are a function of the center of focus of the Neuro-Rational Types, and tend to be expressions of the underlying world view of the personality.

In motivating people, you've got to engage their minds and their hearts. I motivate people, I hope, by example – and perhaps by excitement – by having productive ideas to make others feel involved.

Rupert Murdoch
Media Mogul

The Leadership Style of the Coach

Situation	Explanation
1. The leader's modus operandi	Develops people for the future
2. The style in a phrase	'Try this'
3. Underlying emotional intelligence competencies	Developing others, empathy, self-awareness
4. When the style works best	To help an employee improve performance or develop long-term strengths
5. Overall impact on climate	Positive

A groundbreaking survey of 3871 executives selected from a database of more than 20,000 executives[1] found distinct leadership styles which consistently appear in organizations. Daniel Goleman (2000) attributes these different leadership styles to different emotional intelligences. These intelligences equate to the Intelligences.

Each leadership style has a different impact on the work environment and on organizational performance. The most effective leaders use a variety of styles, choosing the appropriate style, timing and intensity to manage each situation.

The leadership style identified by Goleman's research that is most closely aligned to the profile of the Coach is the *Coaching* style.

The author's experience supports the insightful research reported by Goleman. In most situations, the Coaching style is one of the most effective leadership styles as it drives up many aspects of corporate climate. The primary focus of the Coaching style of leadership is developing the unique capacities and abilities of the co-workers.

Some of the attributes of this leadership style are:

- By identifying the unique strengths of an individual and tying them to their personal and career aspirations, the Coaching style **increases loyalty and engagement**.

- **Empowering.** By identifying the unique strengths of an individual (a combination of C2 and I2) the Coaching leader draws commitment from employees.

---

[1] Survey was originally analyzed by Kelner, S., et al. (1996).

The Coaching Style

Daniel Goleman (2000) tells the story of Lawrence, production manager of the manufacturing division of a large company. When sales dropped, he decided in collaboration with the CEO, to close the unit and reassign the staff. When the team leader of the unit, James, heard about this, he bypassed his boss and requested a meeting with the CEO.

When Lawrence learned of this, he met with James. But instead of berating him, Lawrence coached him: first he talked over the reasons for closing the unit and James' career path. Then he coached him on how to make a good impression in his meeting with the CEO.

A Coach leader can see the potential in each of their team members and will want to see them grow and flourish.

They will not dismiss a worker if they feel their intentions are good, so they will give them a second (and third) chance to succeed.

- **Feedback.** Coaching leaders provide plenty of feedback and instruction. It requires constant dialogue, so employees know their boss is watching them and cares about what they do. This helps to increase flexibility and creates an environment where risk-taking can occur.
- **Conceptualisation.** The constant dialogue ensures people know what is expected of them and how their work fits into the larger vision or strategy of the organization.
- **Delegating.** This leadership style is the best at delegating. They give challenging assignments, even if this results in short-term failure for long-term learning. The message that is implicit is, 'I believe in you, I am investing in you, and I expect your best efforts.' Often employees will rise to the challenge with their heart, mind and soul.

The Coaching style works well in almost any business environment. It is most effective when the employee desires to be coached and is already aware of their weaknesses. If employees are resistant to change then it is ineffective. It is also ineffective as a method of leadership if the individual using it is inept at providing feedback that motivates, and instead creates fear and apathy.

Giving people a second chance

It wouldn't occur to me not to – I've been forgiven so many times. We all make mistakes, how can I expect to be forgiven if I don't forgive. Life is short. Relationships are everything. Forgive, forget and move on.

SCHOOL OF STRATEGIC THOUGHT

The natural differences are not limited to leadership styles alone; they also extend to a natural inclination towards different strategic thought. These differences have been researched by Mintzberg, Ahlstrad and Lampel (1998). For the Coach, their approach to strategy belongs in the Entrepreneurial school. This suggests that strategy formation results from the insights of a single leader and stresses intuition, judgement, wisdom, experience and insight. The 'vision' of the leader supplies the guiding principles of the strategy.

THE GENIUS OF THE COACH – ASSIGNING MEANING

The Coach's Genius lies in their ability to develop meaning for situations or events, to integrate information and to heal. This means creating a passion for the future, giving life meaning, healing old psychological wounds and integrating knowledge in a powerful way.

The *Genius* which most aligns with the Coach is what Buckingham and Clifton term *developing*.

Buckingham and Clifton (2001, p. 95) describe the Coach as the *developer* as a person who, when they see others, see only their potential.

That means:

- They do not see others as they are, but rather as they can be. In fact, everyone is seen as 'a work in progress, alive with possibilities'.

- It is the possibility of each person's potential growth which they find attractive.

- Their interactions with each individual are focused on seeing them reach success.

- They look for ways to challenge people to help them grow, and they watch carefully for signs of growth.

- People seek this person out for help and encouragement because they know that the Coach genuinely wants to see them reach their potential and will be as fulfilled as the person they help.

Leadership Styles

Chapter 14

The Diplomat
An In-Depth Look at the Diplomat

You will get all you want in life if you help enough other people get what they want.

Zig Ziglar
Motivational Speaker

What we've got to thank Diplomats for:

- Diverse teams
- Diplomacy
- Agreements/Contracts/Treaties
- Effective negotiation
- Empathetic counselling
- Effective conflict resolution
- Fair HR practices
- Customer relationship/management/service
- Balanced lifestyle
- Democracy

THE DIPLOMAT PROFILE

> *People are always blaming their circumstances for what they are. I don't believe in circumstances. The people who get on in this world are the people who get up and look for the circumstances they want, and if they can't find them, make them.*
>
> George Bernard Shaw
Irish Playwright

OVERVIEW

Diplomats are charming, enthusiastic, energetic and ambitious. They have an unmatched ability to sell ice to the Eskimos and have the Eskimos thank them, pay for their airfare and invite them back.

Regardless of their training or level of professional development, Diplomats like competition, negotiation, promoting ideas and people, and rising to the top.

> *It was never hard to get promoted or get selected for a job – as I had the track record of producing results and had built relationships along the way.*

Diplomats are some of the most senior administrators and leaders in Australia. They live to work and rise to challenges, particularly complex people issues that others cannot nut out. Diplomats are passionate about projects with which they are involved, and manage to get everyone in the team working to achieve their objectives for their own reasons.

Diplomats can be high-profile if it is required, but prefer to work behind the scenes, enhancing their own career and credibility with each initiative.

Diplomats are excellent at creating a successful image. They rarely look concerned and appear to have the perfect lifestyle, living in the right suburbs, driving the right cars and holidaying in the right places.

> *I genuinely believe that we are great at building teams but often our quest to win and succeed can alienate the team. We can be very driven – I look back on my career and can reflect that whilst others may have been studying hard to get to the top, I would 'just do it' and try and outperform by delivering more or better results.*

> *We should seek by all means in our power to avoid war, by analyzing possible causes, by trying to remove them, by discussion in a spirit of collaboration and good will. I cannot believe that such a program would be rejected by the people of this country, even if it does mean the establishment of personal contact with the dictators.*
>
> Neville Chamberlain
> Former British Prime Minister

Diplomats are the ultimate mediators. They are altruistic at heart and dedicated to authenticity and bringing out the best in others.

> *It is an exceptional feeling to know we can move people to greatness, alerting them to their true capabilities, and awakening them in preparation for their wonderful journey ahead.*

FOCUS OF ATTENTION

Diplomats are brilliant at working in any field that requires people-to-people skills. They are particularly good at finding ingenious ways of achieving results when all else has failed. At their best, Diplomats are charming, good at negotiating and diplomatic. They strive for esprit de corps, and are kind, genuine and venerable.

> *If the eyes are the windows to the soul, then a smile has opened the windows. Confident body language speaks volumes in a first meeting or presentation. Much is analyzed in the initial introduction. Other statements where there is continuance to build relationships would involve: 'You catch more flies with honey', and also, 'It's all in the delivery.'*

KEY CHARACTER DRIVERS

There are three key Intelligences that drive the Diplomat:

C1 – Spontaneity

P2 – Passion

I2 – Heart

THE SUBTYPES

Each of the eight types is made up of three Intelligences. The Diplomat has C1 Spontaneity, P2 Passion and I2 Heart. As we adapt to our life circumstances we tend to favor one of the three. This subtly changes the personality and gives rise to subtypes. All Diplomats will be able to relate to all three of the subtypes at some time in their life.

THE CREATIVE DIPLOMAT

The Creative Diplomat will enjoy new ideas, thoughts and solutions and will be able to adapt other people's concepts, designs and processes to support their objectives. They will lose interest in old projects and people quickly, wanting instead to constantly meet new challenges. Creative Diplomats are quick-minded, sexy, funny, innovative, witty and enthusiastic.

THE POWERFUL DIPLOMAT

The Powerful Diplomat will have strong opinions about most things and will want issues resolved. They are keen to succeed and want to outperform people's expectations. They will be motivated at times and generally enthusiastic.

The Powerful Diplomat is the master strategist who is able to achieve virtually anything behind the scenes. Kings may come and go, but the Powerful Diplomat is always there behind the scenes pulling the strings.

THE SENSITIVE DIPLOMAT

The Sensitive Diplomat will be very aware of how others are feeling – a true empathizer, putting people first at all cost. They do not want their opinions to offend and so often suppress their thoughts. The Sensitive Diplomat will not necessarily need to tie up all the loose ends, but rather will constantly stay on the emotional pulse of the person or people they are with.

> *Meeting new people*
>
> *Meeting new people is like a movie preview. You may have read the title. You may have read the reviews, but it is only when you immerse yourself, do you find truth, understanding and appreciation.*

LEADERSHIP STYLES RELATED TO THE DIPLOMAT

When people discuss leadership styles, many of the characters they use will fall into the same category as the Diplomat, much the same way that there may be fifty-seven species of fern but regardless of the species, it still belongs to the fern family.

By way of example, some of these are:

- The Messenger
- The Herald
- The Courier
- The Communicator
- The TV Journalist

- The Trickster
- The Goddess
- The Gossip
- The Networker
- The Black Widow

- The Negotiator
- The Flirt
- The Siren
- The Seductress
- The Enchantress

CHILDREN'S STORIES

- The story of Joseph and the Coat of Many Colors

THE MIRROR

While the Diplomat is flexible, charming, subtle, creative and intuitive, the Diplomat's Mirror is inflexible, blunt, direct, obvious and focused on reality. The Diplomat's Mirror, the Planner, is constantly demanding perfection, structure, details and proof of accomplishment. From the Feng Shui perspective, the Diplomat is described as pure female energy and the Diplomat's Mirror, the Planner, is described as pure male energy. Male energy in this context is characterized as being unyielding, confronting and bullish and looks for opportunities to express these strengths.

Mirror Planners have a very clear idea where they should be living, to whom they should be married and their income and lifestyle. The challenge is that these expectations are all below the awareness of the Diplomat, so even though they work hard and achieve all their objectives, if these don't line up with the unconscious requirements of the Mirror, the Diplomat will not find the satisfaction for which they are searching. The answer lies in discovering this unconscious vision and informing the Master so that it can be updated or replaced.

I've stayed good friends with most of my girlfriends.

Richard Gere
Actor

UNDERSTANDING DIPLOMATS

Diplomats best manage themselves by:
- Disciplining themselves to stick to a plan until it is absolutely clear the plan needs to be aborted and a new plan is in place
- Not constantly agreeing with everyone but instead sometimes put a stake in the ground
- Focusing on principles that will guide their lives
- Rationally considering options and consciously running through the pros and cons of options on an operational rather than political basis
- Not letting themselves get so tangled up in politics that they can't get the job done (alliances have strings)

As team members, Diplomats make the best contribution when:
- They need to bring together the interests of diverse and different groups
- They need to resolve conflict
- They are required to find resources for the team or promote the good work of the team within the team or even outside the team
- They have to deal with complex emotional issues around people

Solving problems

Diplomats have large networks of contacts/acquaintances and always know someone that can help with a problem.

Mark, Sensitive Diplomat

When managing Diplomats:
- Don't let your relationship with them become political
- Encourage them to rationally consider their position in a non-political way to give them a 'true north'
- Encourage them to keep reminding themselves of the team's wider vision
- Encourage them to structure their activity into phases, and document and review their achievements in writing in a structured way

A person should only be judged in the press by how effective they are in their chosen field.

John Travolta
Actor

How Diplomats will act during meetings:
- Will be fascinated with the group dynamics and power plays
- Will be enthusiastic and encouraging to those with power
- Will be reluctant to state their position
- Will easily get sidetracked or sidetrack discussion

Personality strengths that help the Diplomat to further their development:
- Natural strategists
- Flexible, passionate
- Understand people and how to motivate them
- Can understand how others are feeling

Personality weaknesses that can stand in the way of the Diplomat's development:
- Focus on self-gain rather than the bigger picture
- Can change their own mind so much, nothing gets done
- Can create games and politics just for their own amusement
- Can let emotions cloud their thinking

Opportunities for Diplomats to develop:
- Need to discipline themselves to keep things simple
- Need to become attached to a corporate vision – not just a personal gain
- Need to be authentic and state their position – even when it's not political

Threats to Diplomat's development:
- Can fall foul of the system if not careful
- Can get totally wound up in 'winning' rather than achieving, and waste their talents
- Can be seen by others as manipulative and therefore not trustworthy

WHEN NEGOTIATING WITH DIPLOMATS

The effective communicator is able to align their narrative and the point they are wanting to make with the leadership style of the audience. That is, they use the same language, approach and behavior with the leadership style of the person they are presenting to.

When negotiating with Diplomats the way you position information is very important. Diplomats are attracted to messages centered on two main themes which are most convincing to them: 'Show me how this can help us get some quick wins' and 'Show me this solution will empower the team to achieve the objectives.'

'Show me how this can help us get some quick wins'

There are two types who naturally access their P2 and C1 functions – the Diplomat and the Energizer. This segment makes up 36 per cent of the general population. When negotiating with this group:

- Present constant initiatives that will give the organization the edge
- Demonstrate new ideas, business ventures and people as an indication that the leadership is doing a good job
- Exhibit how the organization has taken advantage of the opportunities created by shifts in the market (for example, competitors failing)
- Show evidence that the organization is responsive to market trends
- Show fast activity that secures 'quick wins'
- Use strategies that are grounded and that last no longer than a few years
- Show clear milestones, responsibilities and target dates for achievement
- Be prepared to convince them on every point
- Be aware that they consider the credibility of the presenter as important as the message itself
- Demonstrate passion, success and drive

'Show me this solution will empower the team to achieve the objectives'

There are two groups who access their P2 and I2 by nature – the Diplomats and the Coaches. This segment makes up approximately 12 per cent of the general population. When negotiating with this group:

- Is very sensitive to non-verbal communication, reading between the lines, gestures and facial expressions
- Has a huge influence on the population because they are the novelists, dramatists, television interviewers, playwrights, poets, biographers and popular journalists

Leadership Styles

- Asks questions about the meaning of actions, the purpose of the organization, the role of leaders and the impact this all has on the organization's stakeholders
- Sees good in everyone and assumes everyone is doing their best with the best intentions
- Has very little interest in buying and selling, or commercial occupations; and is much more interested in bringing out the best in people and enabling people to reach their full potential
- Will be, by nature, naive about the 'complexities' of law and business

FAMOUS DIPLOMATS

- Ban Ki-moon (UN Secretary-General)
- Barack Obama (US President)
- Bill Clinton (Former US President)
- Bob Dylan (Singer, Songwriter)
- Dale Carnegie (Motivational speaker)
- George Clooney (Actor)
- Gregory Peck (Actor)
- Henry Kissinger (Former US Secretary of State)
- Jennifer Aniston (Actor)
- Jeurgen Schrempp (Author)
- Jimmy Carter (Former US President)
- John F. Kennedy (Former US President)
- John Travolta (Actor)
- Justin Timberlake (Singer)
- Luke Skywalker (Character, Star Wars)
- Marilyn Monroe (Actor)
- Neville Chamberlain (Former British Prime Minister)
- Prince William of Wales (Duke of Cambridge)
- Richard Gere (Actor)
- Tony Blair (Former British Prime Minister)
- Whitney Houston (Singer)

DIPLOMATS AT WORK

Diplomats are often very high achievers and their greatest strength is their ability to understand the motivation of everyone they meet. They are themselves highly motivated and enjoy praise. They are most productive when they are motivated and valued for their contribution. They are capable of achieving more in less time than many others. A Diplomat is naturally enthusiastic, optimistic and committed. They thrive on new ideas, causes or directions, and can achieve virtually anything they set their mind to.

Leadership Styles

> *I didn't come into politics to change the Labor Party. I came into politics to change the country.*
>
> Tony Blair
Former British Prime Minister

A Diplomat is willing to cooperate as long as they agree with the project or the person at the helm. They naturally have little long-term vision and will adopt the vision of others. They will then motivate others to take up the cause. They are more willing to contribute if they can run the show. If things are not going the way they would like, they either say nothing or ambush the idea. They will happily follow rules and regulations set down by others as long as they believe in them. If not, they will try to adapt or alter the plans.

They have a charismatic leadership style and seek the best in people. They are always sensitive to the needs of their fellow workers and can see their fears, strengths and weaknesses. People are attracted to their energy and passion. New processes are willingly adopted as long as they are in harmony with their beliefs and attitudes, and they cope well with change.

They are intolerant of people who disagree with them, but are more tolerant of close friends or loved ones. They resolve conflict by trying to win the argument, either overtly or covertly. They will be aggressive to anyone who is aggressive with them. They take criticism personally and will fight the person, not the issue or activity. The personalities involved, together with issues of loyalty, beliefs and their relationship to the conflict, stand central to their arguments. They are happy to take responsibility, but may worry or rely on intuition to solve problems and sometimes wait until the last minute to complete a task. A Diplomat doesn't make snap decisions. They will take the problem home, sleep on it and do what feels right.

Diplomats will be extremely supportive when a new project starts if they believe in the project and the people involved. They will use lateral thoughts and solutions to cope with stress, and will work faster and more efficiently when they are working to deadlines. Often, Diplomats rely on stress for improved productivity and subsequently have periods of high then low performance. Similarly, they will have periods of stability and instability.

A Diplomat's confidence will always appear high. However they are sensitive to criticism, although they do not always appear so. They are extremely loyal until double-crossed or betrayed. They are flexible as long as they are not asked to behave in conflict with their beliefs.

A Diplomat will always let their attitudes and beliefs color decisions. When analyzing a situation, a Diplomat will look at the people and their feelings rather than the facts. They will use humor that is often 'close to the bone'. Sometimes they get themselves into trouble for using intuitive humor. They can also play games at another's expense. Diplomats are highly competitive and will work hard for approval. They need constant recognition and strive to be the best. They can appear both optimistic and pessimistic. Their enthusiasm is cyclical.

Diplomats are at their best when starting and driving a new project and achieving the impossible – because they believe in it.

THE DIPLOMAT'S MIRROR IN THE WORKPLACE

At work, when a young Mirror Planner is unleashed, there will be episodes of shouting, abuse, ultimatums and even physical threats. These intensely emotional and angry outbursts can stay with those they interact with forever. Because the Master has no comprehension of this behavior, however, the Diplomat will not understand why friends, family and colleagues clear the decks when things start looking stressed or the Diplomat starts getting angry.

As the Mirror Planner matures, the intense aggression gives way to strong words or steely ultimatums, detailed planning and a focus on controlling others through procedures and due process.

When the Mirror is integrated into this personality, the Planner brings vision, endurance and principles, and grounds the otherwise charming, funny, flexible and politically brilliant Diplomat.

At home, the Mirror Planner manifests when the Diplomat is stressed and the strategy to create a desired outcome is failing. Once 'out' the Planner will state the obvious, focus on the detail, demand obedience and yell and shout. The Mirror Planner has no subtlety, grace or sophistication. Instead, the Mirror Planner insists on total clarity, loyalty and proof and will bully it out of their target. No enemy is too big for the Mirror Planner who knows no fear and sees nothing but clear evidence and fault.

THE LEADERSHIP STYLE OF THE DIPLOMAT

Each Neuro-Rational Type, due to its combination of thinking functions, has a different leadership style. These leadership styles are a function of the center of focus of the Neuro-Rational Types, and tend to be expressions of the underlying world view of the personality.

The Leadership Style of the Diplomat

Situation	Explanation
1. The leader's modus operandi	Creates harmony and builds emotional bonds
2. The style in a phrase	'People come first'
3. Underlying emotional intelligence competencies	Empathy, building relationships, communication
4. When the style works best	To heal rifts in a team or to motivate people during stressful circumstances
5. Overall impact on climate	Positive

A survey of 3871 executives selected from a database of more than 20,000 executives[1] found distinct leadership styles. Daniel Goleman (2000) attributes these different leadership styles to different emotional intelligences. Each leadership style has a different impact on the work environment and on organizational performance. The most effective leaders use a variety of styles, choosing the appropriate style, timing and intensity to manage each situation.

The leadership style identified by Goleman's research (2000) that is most closely aligned to the profile of the Diplomat is the *Affiliative* style.

The author's experience supports the insightful research reported by Goleman. In most situations, the Affiliative style is one of the most effective leadership styles as it drives up many aspects of corporate climate. The primary focus of the Affiliative style of leadership is in developing social capital with co-workers (a P2- and I2-based approach).

Some of the attributes of this leadership style are:

- **Social capital.** The Affiliative style values individuals and their emotions more than tasks and objectives. People using this style also create a sense of belonging by taking co-workers out for a meal or spending other one-to-one time with them to see how they are feeling.
- **Loyalty.** The focus on building strong emotional bonds generates strong ties of loyalty.
- **Communication.** People who like each other talk a lot. They share ideas and they share their inspiration.

---

1 Survey was originally analyzed by Kelner, S., et al. (1996).

The Affiliative Style

Daniel Goleman (2000) describes the archetypal Affiliative leader, Joe Torre, 'the heart and soul of the New York Yankees'. We are given specific examples of the ways in which Torre carefully nurtured individual team members during the stressful 1999 World Series.

A Diplomat leader will always be in touch with the personal situation of each team member and this is true of Torre. He was careful to praise and acknowledge the pain of two young men who continued to play despite their fathers' death.

Torre also praised two players whose continuance with the team was threatened by disputes with management. The Diplomat's noble quality of bridge-building was evident here: his message was for the management as much as for the two players.

Not only was this Diplomat open to others' emotions, but he also respected his own and was ready to share with his team his own deep family concern. Here we see the emotional intelligence competencies of the Affiliative style: empathy, building relationships and communication.

- **Flexibility.** Trust is engendered by the focus on creating a harmonious environment. This trust means the Affiliative leader does not need to impose unnecessary strictures on how employees perform their work (C1 and I2 working together).
- **Feedback.** The Affiliative leader provides plenty of positive feedback. Under some other leadership styles, individuals receive no feedback at all, or only negative feedback. Therefore, the positive words from the Affiliative leader are very motivating.

Competition

As the years go by, we often will learn that there are easier ways to getting results than just working hard. We don't like working in isolation and really need the emotional connection of other people. So work can be just like part of the extended family.

> *Go ahead, fall in love, be for somebody. But when the primary's over, let's fall in line and bring the White House back to our party.*
>
> Bill Clinton
> Former US President

> *Competition creates a healthy respect between individuals, encouraging heroes of those who have achieved their best, and at times making reluctant heroes of those gracious in defeat.*

The Affiliative style works well, but by focusing only on praise it can allow poor performance to go uncorrected. People perceive that mediocrity is tolerated. Furthermore, since constructive criticism is not provided, employees must find out how to improve on their own. When clear directives are required, the Affiliative style does not work.

The Affiliative style should be used to build team harmony, increase morale, improve communications or repair broken trust.

> *Relationships with people are important and I really don't like conflict and will do a lot to avoid it because it usually causes me emotional pain. I think that most matters can be resolved with a little goodwill and some discussion. Unless I consciously decide to deal with the hard emotional stuff, I will do anything to avoid it – for example, disciplining a staff member.*
>
> *If you really want to know someone, put yourself in their shoes. Understanding a person's thinking and desires aids in building relationships with them and provides a wonderful opportunity to interact and impart our most endeared experiences.*

SCHOOL OF STRATEGIC THOUGHT

The natural differences are not limited to leadership styles alone; they also extend to a natural inclination towards different strategic thought. These differences have been researched by Mintzberg, Ahlstrad and Lampel (1998). The Diplomat approaches strategy formation by seeing it as an overt process of influence, emphasising the use of power and politics to negotiate strategies favorable to particular interests. This lies in the power school of strategy.

If we see the chance for further growth in Asia, we will seize it, and I assume that will happen soon.

Juergen Schrempp
Daimler CEO

THE GENIUS OF THE DIPLOMAT – BUILDING BRIDGES

The Diplomat's Genius comes from their ability to build bridges between people. As a consequence they develop powerful interpersonal strategies and so can achieve their objectives with very little disruption. The Diplomat has the ability to influence entire organizations without anybody triggering resistance.

Buckingham & Clifton (2001, p. 110) describe the Diplomat's behavior as follows:

- The Diplomat is comfortable with intimacy. Spending time with their close friends gives them great pleasure and strength – and if they do not know you, they will naturally want to get to know you.
- They are interested in the minutiae of everyone's life, and will willingly tell you theirs.
- The Diplomat knows that this is risky, but is willing to take risks because this is the cost of genuine friendship.
- They see that two people risking together is necessary for sharing together, which is necessary for genuine caring.

Leadership Styles

Leadership Styles

Chapter 15

The Innovator
An In-Depth Look at the Innovator

Results? Why, man, I have gotten lots of results! If I find 10,000 ways something won't work, I haven't failed. I am not discouraged, because every wrong attempt discarded is often a step forward ... Of all my inventions, I liked the phonograph best ...

Thomas Edison

What we've got to thank Innovators for:

- Action heroes
- Innovation
- Courageous acts
- Breaking down unnecessary bureaucracy
- Spontaneity
- Action sports
- New gadgets
- New technology

THE INNOVATOR PROFILE

The simple act of paying attention can take you a long way.

Keanu Reeves, Actor

OVERVIEW

Innovators are inventors by nature and have an unquenchable thirst for knowing how things work. They love challenge, variety and new and interesting problems to solve. They get frustrated and demotivated with routine. Regardless of their training or level of professional development, Innovators like to work to a system that is efficient and practical. If 'the way it has always been done' does not achieve this, the Innovator will not hesitate to redesign the system or rewrite the handbook.

Innovators are usually easygoing with a childlike curiosity and a fascinating general knowledge about just about everything. They are gregarious, party animals that enjoy having fun and forgetting the time. They are rational and systematic and can take over command in any kind of real crisis. When the pressure is on, Innovators have the ability to mobilize large teams in an efficient, sequential and effective way. When Innovators take control, all the other types stand back and let them lead.

Innovators are very fluent speakers by nature and able to think very quickly on their feet. In discussions they will be 100 percent present and enjoy pitting themselves against others in a discussion just for the sport of it.

Because they are excellent problem-solvers, Innovators will often create problems for themselves to solve when things are becoming too routine and they are bored. This cycle of creating and then solving problems seriously limits their ability to accumulate wealth.

A warrior of light is never cowardly. Flight might be an excellent form of defence, but it cannot be used when one is very afraid. When in doubt, the warrior prefers to face defeat and then lick his wounds, because he knows that if he flees he is giving to the aggressor greater power than he deserves. In difficult and painful times, the warrior faces overwhelming odds with heroism, resignation and courage.

Paulo Coelho
Author of 'Warrior of Light'

FOCUS OF ATTENTION

Innovators are brilliant at solving problems. In a practical sense this can mean inventing a new gadget, approach or system or doing what it takes to get the show on the road. They walk beside colleagues and friends as they go through life, attending to the little things that get everyone through the day (The Good Samaritan). At their best, Innovators are reverent, disciplined, courageous, ingenious, enabling, harmonious and peaceful.

KEY CHARACTER DRIVERS

There are three key Intelligences that drive the Innovator:

C1 – Spontaneity

P1 – Logic

I2 – Heart

> *Having fun*
>
> *My 'Bucks Party' is a good example of how I like to have fun. It was held on a Saturday during the day. A group of friends and I went up to Binna Burra in the Springbrook Forest and we did a day of high ropes, low ropes, flying fox and abseiling. It was fantastic. We all had a great time. We went out for a quiet drink that evening but it was such an anti-climax after a day of testing and pushing our limits. I would much prefer to do this sort of activity than to go out drinking.*

THE SUBTYPES

Each of the eight types is made up of three thinking functions. The Innovator has C1 Spontaneity, P1 Logic and I2 Heart. As we adapt to our life circumstances we tend to favor one of the three. This subtly changes the personality and gives rise to subtypes. All Innovators will be able to relate to all three of the subtypes at some time in their life.

THE CREATIVE INNOVATOR

The Creative Innovator will enjoy new ideas, thoughts and solutions and will be able to adapt other people's concepts, designs and processes to support their objectives. They will lose interest in old projects and people quickly, wanting instead to constantly meet new challenges. They will be quick-minded, witty and enthusiastic for the latest thought or idea.

THE CONTROLLING INNOVATOR

The Controlling Innovator is totally committed to creating order, systems and discipline. They will want to see projects from beginning to end, have a healthy sense of humor, and be analytical and even-handed. They will be self-disciplined and stable. The Controlling Innovator will want loose ends tied up. Their structure will suppress their spontaneity unless they are relaxed. They are steadfast, resolute and immovable once they have decided on a game plan.

THE SENSITIVE INNOVATOR

The Sensitive Innovator will be very sensitive to how others are feeling a true empathizer, putting people first at all cost. They do not want their opinions to offend and so will often suppress their thoughts. They will not necessarily need to tie up all the loose ends, but rather stay constantly focused on the emotional pulse of the person or people they are with.

The Sensitive Innovator will tend to be totally different when they are with people than when they are by themselves. By themselves they will be organized, task oriented and structured; with others they will tend to be the social glue, heading off conflict and doing whatever it takes to keep everything on an emotionally even keel.

> *Being with people without forcing your own point of view*
> *I have been told I am a good listener and like to hear people's stories. I find there are very valuable lessons for me from everyone I talk to and*

The Phantom, one of the first and still one of the most popular costumed heroes of the comics, is the descendant of an English seafarer who, over 463 years ago, washed ashore in Bangalla after a pirate raid and swore an oath over the skull of his father's murderer, that he and his descendants would devote their lives to '... the destruction of piracy, greed, cruelty and injustice ...'

(The oath of the skull)

therefore give my full attention to them. Sometimes I feel that I am a bit boring after listening to other people's very interesting stories, but I have been told that I am far from it. Who knows?

LEADERSHIP STYLES RELATED TO THE INNOVATOR

When people discuss leadership styles, many of the characters they use will fall into the same category as the Innovator, much the same way that there may be fifty-seven species of fern but regardless of the species, it still belongs to the fern family.

By way of example, some of these are:

- The Provocateur
- The Workaholic
- The Gambler
- The Follower
- The Indigent
- The Friend
- The Sidekick
- The Right Hand Man
- The Consort

- The Casanova
- The Gigolo
- The Seducer
- The Sex Addict
- The Lover
- The Good Samaritan
- The Wanderer
- The Vagabond
- The Nomad

- The Disciple
- The Indentured Servant
- The Devotee

CHILDREN'S STORIES/NURSERY RHYMES

- Huckleberry Finn
- Jack from *Jack and the Beanstalk*

THE MIRROR

While the Innovator is charming, sexual, carefree and not goal-oriented, the Innovator's Mirror, the Crusader, is motivated by undertaking crusades that are exciting, adventurous and worthy of their efforts and talents. As the Mirror, the Crusader demands to chase the 'big, hairy, audacious goal' or set their sights on a mountain so large that it takes everyone's breath away. The Crusader is most likely to take over when the Innovator is bored or between helping people in crisis.

While the Innovator's self-image is one of being easygoing, caring and practical, the Innovator's Mirror is driven, ambitious and thrill-thirsty and wants to see and live the fruits of their success. The Mirror will want to see the house, the car, the clothes and the partner as a reflection of their efforts. The Crusader has a clear picture of what life will be like, what the life partner will look like, where they will live, how much they will earn and the level of respect they will receive and from whom. If this clear, yet unconscious, life vision doesn't get communicated to the Master, the Innovator will pay a high emotional price, working harder and harder yet never feeling satisfied with their achievements.

As the Mirror matures, the Crusader provides the Innovator with energy, stamina, focus and a surprising eye for detail. When integrated into the personality, the Crusader gives the Innovator vision, passion, energy, principles and the ability to inspire virtually anyone to join a righteous crusade.

The young Crusader Mirror provides the Innovator with constant self-criticism about virtually everything from their hair, voice and clothes through to their job, intelligence and manner of interacting with others. The Crusader is an unforgiving and relentless Mirror yelling loudly in the Innovator's mind at every turn. For the young Innovator this often leads to low self-esteem until the Master grows stronger and louder and learns to discipline or drown out the Mirror, or the Mirror grows up.

UNDERSTANDING INNOVATORS

Innovators best manage themselves by:

- Taking time to plan ahead and set agendas and priorities, rather than always taking things as they come
- Accepting that people are as important as functions and that most people need to understand why initiatives are being taken
- Disciplining themselves to be on time for meetings and deadlines
- Being organized

As team members, Innovators make the best contribution when:

- They are trouble-shooting and problem- solving
- They have complex issues/problems to solve
- They are in a deadline-driven environment where the situation needs a cool and calm head

I'm staggered by the question of what it's like to be a multi-millionaire. I always have to remind myself that I am.

Bruce Willis
Actor

When managing Innovators:

- Always provide a clear, hard deadline
- Explain why an initiative needs to be taken and the exact role you want them to play
- Don't expect them to automatically focus themselves on the right actions

How Innovators will act during meetings:

- Will listen and watch what is going on until they perceive the discussion is going round in circles and will then step in
- Will be calming in heated or difficult meetings
- Will want to know what the group is solving
- Will easily lose interest and sidetrack the discussion if not managed

Personality strengths that help the Innovator to further their development:

- Excellent at creating thinking outside the box
- Excellent in times of crisis
- Excellent at solving problems: big, small, vague or complex

Acting with courage

I don't feel like I am very courageous. I just do what needs to be done to get the job done. I can quickly assess a situation and solve the problem at hand using the tools available. I am very good in a crisis and as a first aid officer in a previous job, I was able to handle very nasty situations that had others passing out and throwing up. I just saw that a colleague was hurt and I was the one that needed to be there for him. No big deal. I just needed to get the job done.

Personality weaknesses that can stand in the way of the Innovator's development:
- Tends to see people as cogs, rather than people
- Can wind down and sleep in times of low stress
- Has great difficulty understanding why others are feeling the way they are

Opportunities for the Innovator to develop:
- Needs to keep the big picture in mind
- Needs to reconnect and allow passion back into their lives
- Needs to discipline themselves to read and learn before a crisis occurs

Threats to the Innovator's development:
- Can lose connection – feel life is pointless and enter into self-defeating behavior
- Can get distracted, experimenting and never getting anywhere
- Can get bogged down and develop skills that are learned only through personal experience, not based on best practice

WHEN NEGOTIATING WITH INNOVATORS

The effective communicator is able to align their narrative and the point they are wanting to make with the leadership style of the audience. That is, they use the same language, approach and behavior with the leadership style of the person they are presenting to.

When negotiating with Innovators, the way you position information is very important. Innovators are attracted to messages centered on two main themes that are most convincing to them: *'Show me that this will solve the next problem that comes up'* and *'Show me this is practical.'*

'Show me that this will solve the next problem that comes up'

There are two groups who access their C1 and P1 by nature, the Innovators and the Analyzers. This segment makes up 36 per cent of the general population. When negotiating with this group:
- Present the 'here and now' and how well the organization is able to respond quickly to whatever situation arises
- Present your argument in terms of new opportunities, new ideas, new projects and in all the divergent pieces of the organization

- Present your information through pictures, captions, simple flow charts and graphs
- Do not present abstract ideas or concepts or spatially-based dynamic models
- Emphasize experiential learning where they can set the pace
- Mention any links to the Internet
- Deliver your information in gulps
- Be aware that they will often not delineate between the different pieces if they all arrive together; for example, if a dividend arrives at the same time as a court summons, the dividend will be tarred with the same brush
- Be aware that they see vision as ungrounded and largely a waste of time
- Provide immediate answers, immediate results and immediate priorities because they withstand very low levels of delayed gratification
- Do not deliver too much strategy and not enough action

'Show me this is practical'

There are two groups who access their P1 and I2 by nature – the Innovator and the Change Agent. This segment makes up approximately 12 per cent of the general population. When negotiating with this group:

- As a leader, demonstrate decisive leadership with an open mind and high energy
- As an aside, explain, predict or control nature, cycles and reality
- As a leader, anticipate trends and proactively manage the situation
- Demonstrate competence and constant improvement, and that the leadership has a focus on this
- Be aware that they are highly critical of themselves and everyone else
- Do not be inconsistent which they read as deceit
- Deliver a strong argument rather than just rely on the credibility of the person making the statement – the rationale for the argument must be logically pieced together step by step
- Make their interaction with the organization be a learning experience for them
- Provide constant reassurance that their leaders do have the competence to achieve the objectives; this counteracts their own constant self-doubt that failure is just around the corner
- Present your point without typos, grammatical errors or logistical oversights because under stress they become perfectionists

Leadership Styles

- Communicate in compact, short, logical statements – they respond badly to 'waffle'
- Provide the rationale for every initiative to satiate their search for the 'why' of the situation
- Provide communication with graphs, models, icons and pictures

FAMOUS INNOVATORS

- Benjamin Franklin (US Founding Father)
- Benny Anderson (Singer, ABBA)
- Bruce Willis (Actor)
- Elvis Presley (Singer)
- Gerry Harvey (Australian Retail Giant)
- Harrison Ford (Actor)
- Hugh Grant (Actor)
- Katy Bates (Actor)
- Keanu Reaves (Actor)
- Kevin Spacey (Actor)
- Kim Dae-jung (Former South Korean President, Nobel Peace Prize winner)
- Kofi Annan (Former UN Secretary-General)
- Layne Beachley (World champion surfer)
- Meg Ryan (Actor)
- Mel Gibson (Actor)
- Samwise Gamgee (Character, Lord of the Rings)
- Sir Peter Cosgrove (Australian Governor General)
- Thomas Edison (Inventor)
- Tom Hanks (Actor)
- Tony Fernandes (Founder, Air Asia)

THE INNOVATOR AT WORK

The Innovator balances structure with spontaneity and has an excellent ability to intellectually process data or ideas. They work efficiently and always to a plan, although it may not always be written down. The Innovator can be relied upon to get things done. Once a plan is in place they become highly enthusiastic, productive and very conscientious. The Innovator can adapt what they have seen elsewhere and apply this vision to their situation. Their strength is in creating the right process.

They are extremely cooperative, willing to contribute and very supportive of others, especially if they are as efficient as the Innovator. They like to take responsibility for a team, to organize activities and to solve problems.

Innovators cope well with change. They love new ideas and are happy to adopt them as long as there's a problem to solve. They are often more flexible in thought than in deed.

They resolve conflict by finding a solution or workable plan if someone becomes angry the Innovator will use logic to justify their position. They will not usually become angry in response, except in extreme cases, where they can purge built-up anger on someone who is unlikely to fight back.

Innovators are mostly tolerant of others as long as they are efficient, friendly and want to achieve. They are generally highly determined individuals who expect the same level of determination and creativity from those around them.

They are not motivated simply by the desire to be successful and can be considered self-paced rather than competitive. They are more interested in experimenting than point scoring. Their confidence soars when they are showing their ability to solve problems laterally.

As leaders, they enjoy new ideas and new initiatives. They are organized, structured and keen to keep people working efficiently while making time to listen. Often their judgement may be clouded by their desire to keep things systematic.

They are quick-witted, enthusiastic communicators and are renowned for their clever use of puns. They will generally sense how their listeners respond to them and seek their feedback. Innovators love spontaneity both at work and at home. They enjoy surprises and 'spur of the moment' decisions.

Innovators are very loyal to people until they are crossed. They are extremely sensitive but are selective as to when they show it. They are generally optimistic; they may, however, become depressed or bored if there is not enough urgency. They like it when there are problems to solve.

They have a good memory for solutions and how to deal with people, but don't easily retain facts. They are unlikely to exaggerate and will deceive only if they feel they have been deceived. An Innovator has an excellent ability to negotiate.

An Innovator is a formidable problem-solver, organizer and performer during times of crisis, and can mobilize entire teams with unquestioned authority.

LEADERSHIP STYLE OF THE INNOVATOR

Each Neuro-Rational Type, due to its combination of thinking functions, has a different leadership style. These leadership styles are a function of the center of focus of the Neuro-Rational Types, and tend to be expressions of the underlying world view of the personality.

The Leadership Style of the Innovator

Situation	Explanation
1. The leader's modus operandi	Forges consensus through participation
2. The style in a phrase	'What do you think?'
3. Underlying emotional intelligence competencies	Collaboration, team leadership and communication
4. When the style works best	To build buy-in or get consensus, or to get input from valuable employees
5. Overall impact on climate	Positive

A ground-breaking survey of 3871 executives selected from a database of more than 20,000 executives[1] found distinct leadership styles which consistently appear in organizations. Daniel Goleman (2000) attributes these different leadership styles to different emotional intelligences. Each leadership style has a different impact on the work environment and on organizational performance. The most effective leaders use a variety of styles, choosing the appropriate style, timing and intensity to manage each situation.

The leadership style identified by Goleman's research that is most closely aligned to the profile of the Innovator is the *Democratic* style.

The research suggests that the Democratic style has a highly positive impact on corporate climate. The primary focus of the Democratic style of leadership is in collective decision-making and action (a P1- and I2-based approach).

Some attributes of this style are:

- **Consensual decision-making.** By spending time finding out the opinions and ideas of other people, the Democratic leader builds trust, respect and commitment from the workforce.

- **Flexibility.** Since employees have a say in the decisions that affect their goals and how they perform their work, flexibility and responsibility are both encouraged.

---

1 Survey was originally analyzed by Kelner, S., et al. (1996).

The Democratic Style

Daniel Goleman (2000) describes the actions of a leader with a Democratic style. She was a principal of a Catholic school which had to be closed when enrolment diminished.

She took the view that the problem was for everyone to solve, and she saw herself as the leader of that problem-solving process. Rather than 'awfulising' or evaluating, she simply threw herself into the situation, was present from moment to moment and spontaneously solved all the thousands of problems, big and small, that came across her desk. She held repeated meetings with staff, and later parents and the community. First, she explained the situation and listened while they talked. Then in true Innovator problem-solving style, she asked for their ideas and solutions. After two months of much talking, consulting and listening, it was clear to all that the school should close and the children be transferred to another Catholic school in the district. All proceeded calmly and methodically, which demonstrated the strengths of the Innovator.

Goleman contrasts this with another school that had to close. This principal did no consulting at all, but just made the announcement. His action was met by protests, litigation and negative media attention.

As we have seen, the Innovator is a natural leader in a crisis or in a situation where there is no ideal outcome.

- **High morale.** Listening to the concerns of the workers allows the leader to know what to do to keep morale high.
- **Realistic.** People operating in a Democratic system tend to be very realistic about what can and cannot be accomplished since they have a say in setting their own goals and the standards of success.

The Democratic style does not work well when the employees are not competent or informed enough to offer sound advice. In times of crisis consensus is totally inappropriate.

The Democratic style should be used when a leader is uncertain about the best direction to take and requires new ideas and guidance from able employees. It is also useful in generating fresh ideas for executing a vision, even if that vision is strong.

SCHOOL OF STRATEGIC THOUGHT

The natural differences are not limited to leadership styles alone; they also extend to a natural inclination towards different strategic thought. These differences have been researched by Mintzberg, Ahlstrad and Lampel (1998). For the Innovator, their approach to strategy emerges as people (acting either individually or collectively) come to learn about a situation as well as their organization's capability to deal with it. It is the learning school of strategy formation.

THE GENIUS OF THE INNOVATOR – PROBLEM-SOLVING

The Innovator's Genius is their ability to effectively solve problems that are complex, undefined and constantly changing. They are excellent at managing large groups of people in high-stress, dangerous or crisis situations. The Innovator is practical and creative, and can solve anything 'on the hop'. The Innovator is the natural leader when the 'right' emergency action is needed and there is no time.

Buckingham and Clifton (2001, p. 112) call this the restorative *theme of strength*. The Innovator simply loves solving problems, and indeed, finds them energizing.

Buckingham and Clifton (2001) describe how this Genius is manifested:

- This person enjoys the process of problem-solving and naturally analyzes the symptoms first, then identifies the problem, then finds a solution.
- Each problem-solver will have their own preference for practical, conceptual, or personal problems, and for familiar or new situations.
- All problem-solvers enjoy bringing things back to life, be it a person, thing, process or company. Saving things give them a real sense of satisfaction.

Leadership Styles

Chapter 16

The Change Agent
An In-Depth Look at the Change Agent

If you don't know what you are doing, darling, do it neatly.

Advice given to the author by his mother during his early maths experience at school

What we've got to thank Change Agents for:

- Systems and practices suitability
- Leadership credibility
- Alignment of what we say and do
- Philosophy
- Sociology
- The Stone Masons
- Buddhism
- Strategic thinking

THE CHANGE AGENT PROFILE

The price of wisdom is above rubies.

Job 28:18

OVERVIEW

The Change Agent's mind is able to see the big picture and the sequential order of activity required to achieve a given outcome. By nature they think in terms of flow charts. Although they usually feel most comfortable supporting the leadership rather than taking a high profile, they have no hesitation in stepping up to the line and outlining the most efficient way of achieving the desired outcomes if the leadership seems to be hesitating.

Even though Change Agents are rational and calm, they are ambitious and driven to achieve whatever goals they have set themselves. All their activity must be another step towards achieving their objectives and must be focused on learning about a new topic as well as the 'how to' of the topic so that the knowledge becomes a capability. For the Change Agent, work is work and play is work. Every day they expect to get closer to the planned outcomes.

Regardless of their training or level of professional development, this type likes systems and systems thinking. This can mean computer systems; information systems; or geological, engineering, organizational or agricultural systems. The mind of the Change Agent is instantly able to see where the system is failing to produce the required output and what needs to be done to put it right.

The Change Agent is particularly good at the development of effective strategies that require the construction of a series of actions to achieve a stated outcome that takes into account potential contingencies.

Very emotionally detached, the Change Agent rarely gives positive feedback to those living or working with them. Others sometimes think of them as removed or distant and sometimes find it difficult to understand why they run hot and cold.

> **Our prime purpose in this life is to help others. And if you can't help them, at least don't hurt them.**
>
> *Dalai Lama*
> *Spiritual leader of Tibet*

Leadership Styles

> *Any intelligent fool can make things bigger, more complex, and more violent. It takes a touch of genius – and a lot of courage – to move in the opposite direction.*
>
> Albert Einstein
Physicist

> *I feel deeply and passionately about many things but don't seem to show it. When I was young I avoided giving offence by masking my feelings and I took that into adulthood. Now when I look back I feel sad and wish I had dramatized my emotions for my own family, especially my pleasure when they did beautiful things for me that really touched me deeply. I said thank you in my own quiet way but it must have always disappointed them.*

FOCUS OF ATTENTION

Change Agents are brilliant at strategic systems thinking and inventing. This means that without even having to think about it too hard, they will instantly see why the system isn't working and what can be done about it. At their best, Change Agents are contemplative, independent, discerning, capable, unifying, strategic and insightful.

KEY CHARACTER DRIVERS

There are three key Intelligences that drive the Change Agent:

C2 – Vision

P1 – Logic

I2 – Heart

THE SUBTYPES

Each of the eight types is made up of three Intelligences. The Change Agent has C2 Vision, P1 Logic and I2 Heart. As we adapt to our life circumstances we tend to favor one of the three. This subtly changes the personality and gives rise to subtypes. All Change Agents will be able to relate to all three of the subtypes at some time in their life.

I don't go by the rule book. I lead from the heart, not the head.

Diana Spencer
Princess of Wales

THE VISIONARY CHANGE AGENT

The Visionary Change Agent focuses on the future. They will often have thoughts that are totally unrelated to what they are processing. Their ability to use their imagination allows them to plan long-term. It's the irrational leap that makes discovering brand new processes or ways to solve problems possible. The Visionary Change Agent may appear confusing to those around them – at work, they will be structured and conservative and at play, they will be vigorous and spontaneous. The Visionary Change Agent lives between the ideal and the practical worlds, and is constantly travelling between the two.

THE CONTROLLING CHANGE AGENT

The Controlling Change Agent will want to see projects through from beginning to end, has a healthy sense of humor, is balanced, analytical and even-handed. They will be self-disciplined and stable. The Controlling Change Agent will want loose ends tied up.

Their logic will suppress their spontaneity unless they are relaxed. The Controlling Change Agent will suppress their vision until they are tired or under the influence of alcohol. This structure will also control their natural mood swings and keep them stable and emotionally balanced.

THE SENSITIVE CHANGE AGENT

The Sensitive Change Agent will be very perceptive to how others are feeling – a true empathizer, putting people first at all costs.

They do not want their opinions to offend and so often suppress their thoughts. They will not necessarily need to tie up all the loose ends, but rather constantly stay focused on the emotional pulse of the person or people they are with.

The Sensitive Change Agent will tend to be totally different when they are with people than when they are by themselves. By themselves, they will be organized, task oriented and structured. With others they will tend to be the social glue, heading off conflict and often working hard to keep the peace.

LEADERSHIP STYLES RELATED TO THE CHANGE AGENT

When people discuss leadership styles, many of the characters they use will fall into the same category as the Change Agent, much the same way that there may be fifty-seven species of fern but regardless of the species, it still belongs to the fern family.

By way of example, some of these are:

- The Engineer
- The Builder
- The Schemer
- The Ambassador
- The Diplomat
- The Go-between
- The Patriarch
- The Parent

CHILDREN'S STORIES

- Little Red Riding Hood

THE MIRROR

While the Change Agent is strategic, that is, bringing the desired future into reality by creating systems that align with the vision and engaging the team to use them, the Change Agent's Mirror, the Energizer, is constantly criticizing the Change Agent for not getting enough done, not achieving, not articulating their position and not being particularly intelligent. The Mirror Energizer is the loudest of all the Mirror Masters and constantly wants to be heard. The Mirror Energizer is always ready for a fight.

The Change Agent's Mirror Energizer will always want to have their say. Terse comments to coffee shop staff about the quality of the food or service, sharp words of criticism about low performing or unattractive people, quips about hair style, weight, ethnicity, laziness, heritage, religion or acumen made by Change Agents are evidence of their Mirror.

Mirror Energizers are very strong, verbal and one-eyed. They can be opinionated, vindictive walking arguments, ever ready to tip their frustration, anger and opinions

Many African leaders refuse to send their troops on peace-keeping missions abroad because they probably need their armies to intimidate their own populations.

Kofi Annan
Secretary-General of the United Nations

over anyone who is within earshot. The young Mirror Energizers love to spend their energy on physical activities, dancing, sport, running community causes or events or driving themselves hard. As they mature, the Mirror Energizers learn how to focus this energy in a constructive way and provide energy to the Change Agent.

When fully integrated into the personality, the Mirror Energizer balances the Master Change Agent's strategic focus and detached approach to life with unlimited passion, clear judgement and unqualified loyalty to those they love.

UNDERSTANDING CHANGE AGENTS

Change Agents best manage themselves by:

- Disciplining themselves to value the loyalty and passion of their team as much as their functional contribution
- Learning to control their sharp tongue – the cutting remarks and the closed-door comments
- Learning to manage their frustration with constant changes to the brief or situation
- Learning to appreciate that while changing systems may make the organization more efficient in the long term, in the short term it will cause drama, confusion and inefficiency
- Learning to sandwich negative evaluations or feedback between encouraging statements

As team members, Change Agents make the best contribution when:

- They are able to trouble-shoot systems, organizational structures or processes to enhance efficiency and reduce user frustration
- New models, paradigms or approaches are required
- They can head up a team looking at new prototypes
- The brief is broad, even vague, but the outcome is specific

---

We must use time wisely and forever realize that the time is always ripe to do right.

Nelson Mandela
South African statesman who was released from prison to become the nation's first democratically elected president in 1994

When managing Change Agents:

- Clearly structure any interaction with them, exploring why you want to meet, what you want to cover, and the logical meeting structure you have chosen
- Rather than ad hoc feedback, wait until formal reviews or agreed times and then provide the feedback, starting with their role and working back to specific incidents or cases
- Request that they keep you in the loop either in writing or verbally and on an agreed and regular basis

How Change Agents will act during meetings:

- Will enjoy exploring new models, abstract ideas/philosophy
- Will see instantly where systems are not working and will make practical suggestions as to how they should change
- Can be confrontational and appear aggressive if other team members have not thought through their ideas

I'm always wiser after I've walked away from a discussion. I seem to need reflective time alone for the penny to drop, so it's important for me to try to remember to say, 'I'll get back to you'.

Personality strengths that help the Change Agent:

- Can integrate the impractical vision with practical structures
- Can understand complex conceptual models
- Can integrate people with systems

One of my most successful projects, as a teacher and Change Agent, was when I had the vision to benefit 1000 students in one event. I handpicked the staff, trained and encouraged them, and then supported their efforts. It all came together and we shared the great feedback and celebrated at the end.

Personality weaknesses that can stand in the way of the Change Agent furthering their development:

- Prone to low self-esteem because their visionary ideas are not practical and not valued by themselves
- Find it difficult to understand why people are feeling a particular way
- Can't help it; they are change agents – even when they don't want to be

Leadership Styles

I enjoy a good conversation, sharing ideas and so keep having small dinner parties. But I'm constantly disappointed by them. Instead of enjoying the cut and thrust of opinions, I usually find myself watching out that everyone is comfortable and no one's feelings are getting trampled on and that everyone's opinions are heard. I don't get a chance to be heard myself. Lately I've joined some groups dedicated to discussion where I don't feel responsible for anyone else's welfare and I'm joining in rather than watching them.

Opportunities for Change Agents to develop:
- Need to get in touch with the passion of life
- Need to learn how to change vision midway
- Need to see people as 'alive' – not just objects

Threats to Change Agent's development:
- Can become bored and mechanical if there is no crisis
- Can reach a 'block' when a project's parameters are changed
- Can turn everything and everyone in life into a machine which can then turn around and impersonally run them over

WHEN NEGOTIATING WITH CHANGE AGENTS

The effective communicator is able to align their narrative and the point they are wanting to make with the leadership style of the audience. That is, they use the same language, approach and behavior with the leadership style of the person they are presenting to.

When negotiating with Change Agents, the way you position information is very important. Change Agents are attracted to messages centered on two main themes, which are most convincing to them: **'Show me that you are willing to do what it takes to make the vision happen' and 'Show me this is practical.'**

'Show me that you are willing to do what it takes to make the vision happen'

There are two types who access their C2 and P1 – the Change Agent and the Planner. This segment makes up 15 per cent of the general population. When negotiating with this group:
- Minimize any activity that is not contributing to the future objective or vision of the organization

- Be aware that they have high expectations about what can be achieved and is often disappointed with the time required to reach milestones
- Be aware that they tend to fix a particular objective, milestone or vision in their mind and not update it – even when the situation or environment changes
- Provide a clear plan to achieve the clear vision, and demonstrate that there is order and organization, together with systems, processes and guidelines
- Be aware that they are idealistic by nature and want to see the organization striving to achieve as close to perfection as possible
- Demonstrate that the organization is responding to future trends, new markets, potential crises and staff trends
- Present market positioning and strategic analysis
- Present with models, abstract charts, ideas, themes and concepts

'Show me this is practical'

There are two groups who access their P1 and I2 by nature – the Change Agent and the Innovator. This segment makes up approximately 12 per cent of the general population. When negotiating with this group:

- As a leader, demonstrate decisive leadership with an open mind and high energy
- As an aside, explain, predict or control nature, cycles and reality
- As a leader, anticipate trends and proactively manage the situation
- Demonstrate competence and constant improvement, and that the leadership has a focus on this
- Be aware that they are highly critical of themselves and everyone else
- Do not be inconsistent which they read as deceit
- Deliver a strong argument rather than just rely on the credibility of the person making the statement – the rationale for the argument must be logically pieced together step by step
- Make their interaction with the organization a learning experience for them
- Provide constant reassurance that their leaders do have the competence to achieve the objectives; this counteracts their own constant self-doubt that failure is just around the corner
- Present your point without typos, grammatical errors or logistical oversights because under stress they become perfectionists
- Communicate in compact, short, logical statements – respond badly to 'waffle'

Leadership Styles

- Provide the rationale for every initiative to satiate their search for the 'why' of the situation
- Provide communication with graphs, models, icons and pictures

FAMOUS CHANGE AGENTS

- Abraham Lincoln (Former US President)
- Albert Einstein (Scientist)
- Angela Merkel (Chancellor of Germany)
- Buddha (Spiritual Leader)
- Charles Darwin (Scientist)
- Dalai Lama (Spiritual leader)
- Diana Spencer (Princess of Wales)
- Dianne Wiest (Actor)
- Hippocrates (Philosopher)
- Jim Rohn (Author, Entrepreneur)
- Johnny Depp (Actor)
- Joseph Banks (Botanist)
- Judi Dench (Actor)
- Julia Roberts (Actor)
- Karl Marx (Philosopher)
- Leonardo da Vinci (Artist)
- Marie Curie (Scientist)
- Max Weber (Sociologist)
- Nelson Mandela (Former South African President)
- Rene Descartes (Philosopher)
- Sir Isaac Newton (Mathematician)
- Socrates (Philosopher)
- Thomas Jefferson (Former US President)

CHANGE AGENTS AT WORK

Change Agents thrive on generating new ideas and concepts and are able to picture their vision very clearly. Their strength lies in creating ideas and plans, and they are most productive once a game plan has been established. They have an excellent ability to think issues through. They are very determined and controlled and will want to have a vision to work towards. They will not be openly competitive but will certainly work longer and harder than most to achieve their vision.

Change Agents can be very disciplined and expect the same from others. They work efficiently and to a plan, systematising everything they can. They are highly tolerant and patient with people as long as they are efficient and want to achieve. They enjoy people who have vision.

As leaders, they like structure, discipline and organization. They are easily able to provide their staff with an understanding of the organization's vision but probably will not see it necessary for routine work. They willingly contribute to making a team work together or getting a project organized. They are extremely supportive of staff, care about them as individuals and take responsibility for making their team feel positive and enthusiastic about their work when they themselves are excited by the vision. They are excellent delegators and have the skill of matching tasks with people. They can easily identify potential in people and can also be strict when required especially if they suspect incompetence or laziness.

Change Agents are very loyal as long as people fit in with their vision. They are mostly respectful of others. Generally they are able to see people for what they are and will often not enjoy being around highly opinionated people.

They resolve conflict by facing people in the direction of their vision and encouraging them to find a workable solution. They don't like people to be unhappy so they will seek to find solutions to any conflict to ensure everyone is happy. If someone is angry with them they will both feel the impact of the emotion and use logic to justify their position. Seldom will they become angry in response, but when they do they tremble with rage. They will often appear to look blank.

Change Agents cope well with change as long as it is heading somewhere. A Change Agent will want everyone to be happy about any changes that are being considered. If under stress, they work through the experience. They will most likely escape into their vision, check everyone is coping and then generate a way to solve the stress. Change Agents are both analytical and objective. Their internal conflict lies between cold hard logic and wanting people to be happy. They are more zany than spontaneous, and like the bizarre and oddball. They enjoy outrageous and illogical humor. They can easily see a person's weaknesses and may play on them.

They can become depressed or bored if they are unable to express their vision, or if this vision is not valued by friends or work colleagues. They are generally optimistic if they are being shown support. They are mostly balanced, stable individuals, although at times they may be influenced by the company they keep. They may deceive where necessary to achieve their plans or visions.

A Change Agent has an excellent understanding of the negotiation process and can gauge their opponents' thoughts and personal weaknesses and use them to their advantage. A Change Agent is most formidable when working long and hard to achieve their vision, organizing large teams in crisis situations and creating order from chaos.

> My physical environment is very important to me. I am not happy unless the place where I live is pleasant and comfortable. I like it to be harmonious rather than glitzy. I like to have several places for

relaxation, eating, work with hobbies, so that I have choices depending on how I feel. And it is a must to have plants somewhere and music.

THE CHANGE AGENT'S MIRROR IN THE WORKPLACE

At work, the Change Agent's Mirror – the Energizer – is critical, energetic and driven and this explains the Change Agent's energy and determination. When angry about someone's behavior, the Change Agent will criticize the behavior, the system or the situation in a diplomatic way. When the Master Change Agent is tired, inebriated or overly stressed, however, the same trigger will see the Energizer use the situation to destroy the person by a personal attack on their intentions, capability and intellectual capacity.

At home, the Mirror Energizer is argumentative, fickle and frustrated. Partners find young Mirror Energizers vindictive, aggressive and insensitive – waiting for the moment that their partner is at their weakest to attack with their judgement of the situation. This judgement invariably includes a pronouncement of someone's stupidity. At home, the Mirror Energizer will adopt soapboxes and stand on them at every opportunity.

LEADERSHIP STYLE OF THE CHANGE AGENT

Each Neuro-Rational Type, due to its combination of Intelligences, has a different leadership style. These leadership styles are a function of the center of focus of the Neuro-Rational Types, and tend to be expressions of the underlying world view of the personality.

A groundbreaking survey of 3871 executives selected from a database of more than 20,000 executives[1] found distinct leadership styles which consistently appear in organizations. Daniel Goleman (2000) attributes these different leadership styles to different emotional intelligences. Each leadership style has a different impact on the work environment and on organizational performance. The most effective leaders use a variety of styles, choosing the appropriate style, timing and intensity to manage each situation.

The leadership style identified by Goleman's research that is most closely linked to the profile of the Change Agent is the **Pacesetting** style.

The research suggests that the Pacesetting style has a negative overall impact on corporate climate. The primary focus of the Pacesetting style of leadership is on setting

---

[1] Survey was originally analyzed by Kelner, S., et al. (1996).

The Leadership Style of the Change Agent

Situation	Explanation
1. The leader's modus operandi	Sets high standards for performance
2. The style in a phrase	'Do as I do, now'
3. Underlying emotional intelligence competencies	Conscientiousness, drive to achieve, initiative
4. When the style works best	To get results from a highly motivated and competent team
5. Overall impact on climate	Negative

a high standard and doing things better and faster. This has a number of ramifications as a leadership style.

These are:

- **Performance standard.** The Pacesetting leader sets an extremely high performance standard and exemplifies these standards. There is an obsessiveness about doing things better and faster.

- **Feedback.** Poor performers are quickly highlighted and more is demanded from them. If they do not adjust and improve, this form of leadership seeks to replace them with people who can. No feedback is given on how people are doing unless the Pacesetter jumps in and takes over when they think that people are lagging.

- **Guidelines are rarely clearly articulated.** Others are expected to know what to do. An underlying thought process is, 'If I have to tell you, you're the wrong person for the job.' Thus work becomes about second-guessing the leader, while people also feel that they are not trusted to work in their own way or to take the initiative.

- **Work becomes task focused** and routine as flexibility and responsibility evaporate.

- **Commitment is reduced** because individuals have no sense of how their personal efforts fit into the big picture.

The Pacesetting Style

> Daniel Goleman (2000) tells the story of Sam, a competent technician who was made leader of an R&D team in a pharmaceutical company. Following the Pacesetting style, he made himself a model of excellent practice, helping the team when necessary. His team members were competent and the project was completed in record time.
>
> While the Change Agent leader is confident that everyone in their team is competent, everything is fine.
>
> But Sam was promoted to manager of the whole division and when he felt unsure that his team was competent, he took over and micro-managed the details. He ended up bogged down and ineffective as a leader.
>
> When the Change Agent's confidence in his team members' competence is broken, they reassess everything the person has done historically, to Energizer whether the lapse of competence is episodic or more widespread. They may test the person's competence by verbally grilling them, micro-managing them or by demanding reports detailing process and outcomes.
>
> The Change Agent needs to remember that competence is just one element in a highly functioning team. There are many examples of highly functioning teams that have low personal competence but high organizational capability. This is achieved through effective communication, team synergy, and the application of the many 'soft skills' that make teams tick.

Despite these drawbacks, the Pacesetting style does work well when all the employees are self-motivated, highly competent, and need little direction or coordination. Given a talented team to lead, the Pacesetting approach gets the task accomplished.

Furthermore, it is extremely appropriate during the entrepreneurial phase of a company's life cycle.

SCHOOL OF STRATEGIC THOUGHT

The natural differences between Neuro-Rational Types are not limited to leadership styles alone; they also extend to a natural inclination towards different strategic thought. These differences have been researched by Mintzberg, Ahlstrad and Lampel (1998). For the Change Agent, the environment is the central actor in the strategy making process. The environment presents itself as a set of general forces, and the individual must respond to these factors or be 'selected out'. This is the environmental school of strategy.

THE GENIUS OF THE CHANGE AGENT – SEEING CONGRUENCE

The Change Agent's Genius is about seeing congruence. This Genius lies in their ability to bring the people, the processes and the vision all into line. This congruence is the basis of good organizational development skills. This means checking that the vision is relevant and understood by the team, checking the processes are practical and are able to support team members, and that these practical processes are followed. While practical, Change Agents have the ability to think conceptually, with abstract ideas or philosophies that are complex and ungrounded. Their Genius is the ability to bring abstract vision to concrete reality.

Buckingham and Clifton (2001, p. 115) explain that rather than a skill that can be learned, this is a 'distinct way of thinking, a special perspective on the world'. This type of thinking follows the following process:

- The strategist sees patterns in an apparently complex situation.
- The patterns prompt the person to think of possible actions.
- They then play out in their head a number of scenarios in turn, each time asking, 'what if…?', considering possible results and potential problems.
- Next, the strategist selects the path which is most likely to lead to success, avoiding conflict, confusion or failure.
- The chosen path becomes their strategy, and they act according to their plan.

Probably my worst quality is that I get very passionate about what I think is right.

Hillary Clinton
Former US Secretary of State

Leadership Styles

Leadership Styles

Planner

Chapter 17

The Planner
An In-Depth Look at the Planner

You cannot depend on anybody. There is no guide, no teacher, and no authority. There is only you – your relationship with others and with the world – there is nothing else.

Krishnamurti

What we've got to thank Planners for:

- Risk management
- Large-scale engineering projects
- Computer programming
- Beautiful photography
- Institutions
- Political and environmental stability
- Clear lines of responsibility
- The completion of thankless and dangerous tasks

Leadership Styles

THE PLANNER PROFILE

Being a husband is for me as big a priority as being a father.

Roger Federer
Professional tennis player

OVERVIEW

The Planner's mind is structured and visionary. These opposites create a person with a clear vision and the discipline and structure to achieve it. Regardless of their training or level of professional development, the Planner is super-dependable and likes to be a respected contributor to the community and a pillar of society.

Very emotionally detached, Planners are inflexible when discussing plans, directions, approaches and logistics. If they are not given warning, however, they can cope with flexibility and ambiguity, and perform brilliantly 'on the hop'. This seems contradictory, but is achieved because they flip to their Mirror.

Planners tend to get one vision in mind and be totally inflexible with regard to either the vision or its implementation. This can sometimes mean that the Planner is committed and focused on implementing visions that are no longer relevant.

Planners enjoy the very best quality in things and particularly enjoy collecting anything that will appreciate in value.

Planners are very focused when there is a clear vision, executing enormous mind over matter, suppressing unwanted emotions and disciplining themselves and the people around them. They will follow the systems to the letter of the law. Any shortcutting or variance from the approved process will be quickly stopped and the perpetrator reprimanded. The Planner's way is the right way and they will want an audit trail to demonstrate compliance. This character trait makes them good inspectors.

While Planners see themselves as dependable and respectable, if they have no vision and no plan to follow, they freewheel and become obsessed with experiencing life. This means experiencing every possible form of physical sensation including the tasting of every kind of food and wine, flying, boating, fishing, canoeing, partying and holidaying. All this activity subsides when the Planners are once again inspired with a new vision and plan and set about implementing it.

FOCUS OF ATTENTION

The Planner is brilliant at steadfastly working in a stable and controlled way towards achieving a goal. They focus on creating stability in their own lives and the lives of those for whom they are responsible while managing the risks associated with any given endeavor. At their best, Planners are faithful, protective, responsible, effective planners, principled, explorative and honorable.

KEY CHARACTER DRIVERS

There are three key Intelligences that drive the Planner:

C2 – Vision

P1 – Logic

I1 – Data

THE SUBTYPES

Each of the eight types is made up of three Intelligences. The Planner has C2 Vision, P1 Logic and I1 Data. As we adapt to our life circumstances we tend to favor one of the three. This subtly changes the personality and gives rise to subtypes. All Planners will be able to relate to all three of the subtypes at some time in their life.

THE VISIONARY PLANNER

The Visionary Planner is future centered, often with visions that are not logically connected to their current line of thinking. Their creativity allows them to plan long term and imagine the future. It's the irrational leap that makes it possible to discover brand new processes or ways to solve problems. Because their vision is uncontrollable, it will conflict with the structure and order of their logic. The Visionary Planner may appear confusing to those around them because at work they will be structured and conservative and at play they will be vigorous and spontaneous.

> *Managing risk is critical because if you can be certain you've covered off the risks and integrated them squarely in your plan, you can put your heart and soul into the project with confidence that you won't be sideswiped from a blind spot down the track.*

Leadership Styles

THE CONTROLLING PLANNER

The Controlling Planner will want to see projects through from beginning to end, will have a healthy sense of humor, and be balanced, analytical and even-handed. They will be self-disciplined and stable. They will want loose ends tied up. Their personal self-control will suppress their vision unless they are relaxed, or until they are tired or under the influence of alcohol. Their structured mind will also control their natural mood swings and keep them stable and emotionally balanced.

THE WISE PLANNER

For the Wise Planner, the researching of information is far more important than following the process or coming up with ideas of their own. They would prefer to wait and obtain all the facts before making a decision. For the Wise Planners, all the ends do not have to be tied up. They will always want to know the facts supporting opinions. They enjoy reading and going to libraries, researching and learning about everything.

LEADERSHIP STYLES RELATED TO THE PLANNER

When people discuss leadership styles, many of the characters they use will fall into the same category as the Planner, much the same way that there may be fifty-seven species of fern but regardless of the species, it still belongs to the fern family.

By way of example, some of these are:

- The Savior
- The Messiah
- The Attila
- The Avenging Angel
- The Mad Scientist
- The Samurai
- The Serial Killer
- The Spoiler
- The Patriarch
- The Progenitor
- The Parent
- The Adonis
- The Emperor
- The Leader
- The Ruler
- The Chief

CHILDREN'S STORIES/CHARACTERS

- The Little Engine That Could
- Bill Steam Shovel (from Mr Squiggle)

> *We're busily wrecking the chances for future generations at a rapid rate of knots by not recognizing the damage we're doing to the natural environment, bearing in mind that this is the only planet that we know has any life on it.*
>
> *Prince Charles*
Duke of Cornwall

THE MIRROR

While the Master Planner is structured, logical, detail oriented and inflexible, the Planner's Mirror Master – the Diplomat – is lateral, passionate, intuitive and infinitely flexible. This means that while the Planner appears to be rigid and unmoving on most issues because they argue in an unyielding way, their final behavior often speaks of spontaneity and varies according to the opportunity at hand.

The Mirror Diplomat is a relatively quiet Mirror and often finds it hard to make itself heard over the volume of the Master Planner. This means that the Planner usually misses the insight offered by the Mirror.

At home, the Mirror gives softness to the Master Planner and motivates spontaneous romance, a fantastic sense of humor, an interest in family and a desire to emotionally engage family and friends in events and good times.

The young Mirror Diplomat is flirtatious, game playing, ruthless, deceitful and ambitious. As the Mirror matures, however, we see this behavior develop into an acute understanding of politics and an ability to see and act on opportunities.

When the Mirror is fully integrated into the personality, it balances the Planner's formidable strength, clarity, vision and process with humor, flexibility, an understanding of how to engage people in strategic action and a non-judgemental acceptance and warmth for all people.

> *When the vision is clear, necessary and big enough to be challenging, with a clear deadline and set of outcomes, reasons why it works, and reasons why it's worth it, I get a great sense of determination for conquering the impossible.*

UNDERSTANDING PLANNERS

Planners best manage themselves by:
- Remembering to be flexible and open to change
- Disciplining themselves to listen to those with poor reasoning and thinking skills
- Valuing all team members and the roles they play
- Giving positive feedback – face-to-face with staff
- Controlling their angry outbursts

As team members, Planners make the best contribution when:
- They can manage and plan a project from concept through to implementation
- Difficulties can be confronted head on and dealt with rationally
- Resources and timeframes are defined and information is complete
- Consistency is required

When managing Planners:
- Constantly encourage them to be flexible and not locked into one vision
- Encourage them to encourage their team members – help them give positive verbal feedback
- Remind them of the valuable role each team member plays
- Ensure all your key resources to them are written down in a structured format

I certainly want loose ends cleared up. In a meeting that's great, finalising the decision with a clear owner of who will action what deliverables when. In the social setting I'm really having to nip myself to just let it go.

How Planners will act during meetings:
- Planners don't like ambiguity or deception so often play the role of 'keeping the bastards honest'
- Once the vision is established, Planners will want specifics agreed upon – who, what, when, where and how
- They will be polite but not sensitive to the foibles of other team members – they will play blunt politics

- Will want the purpose of the meeting clearly defined with a clear agenda and timeframe
- Will easily lose interest and sidetrack the discussion if not managed

Having the agenda for a meeting, document or whatever is critical to having the interaction useful. Decisions and information are not meaningful in and of themselves. They're only meaningful in terms of how it fits into the tasks and directions. So having a meeting without an agenda is like a ship in a stormy sea landing on a beach, delivering nothing of any value to the right place except by fluke.

Personality strengths that help the Planner to further their development:
- Can balance the future vision with immediate practicalities
- Very structured, analytical and task-oriented
- Excellent at maintaining complete systems

Personality weaknesses that can stand in the way of the Planner's development:
- Can get very stressed juggling between vision and implementation
- Can often misread people and intentions
- Can be inflexible if midpoint change is required

Opportunities for Planners to develop:
- Need to learn how to be able to change track midpoint
- Need to learn how to reinject passion and meaning into projects
- Need to learn how to read people more accurately

Threats to Planner's development:
- Can 'close down' and refuse to budge off the agreed plan, even when change is required
- Can get bored and uninterested in their own life and try to create interest in risky activity
- Can misinterpret situations so badly that they can become ostracized or marginalized

WHEN NEGOTIATING WITH PLANNERS

The effective communicator is able to align their narrative and the point they are wanting to make with the leadership style of the audience. That is, they use the same language, approach and behavior with the leadership style of the person they are presenting to.

When negotiating with Planners, the way you position information is very important. Planners are attracted to messages centered on two main themes which are most convincing to them: *'Show me that you are willing to do what it takes to make the vision happen'* and *'Show me this idea is accurate with concrete data to support your position.'*

'Show me that you are willing to do what it takes to make the vision happen'

There are two types who access their C2 and P1 – the Planner and the Change Agent. This segment makes up 15 per cent of the general population.

When negotiating with this group:

- Minimize any activity that is not contributing to the future objective or vision of the organization
- Be aware that they have high expectations about what can be achieved and is often disappointed with the time required to reach milestones
- Be aware that they tend to fix a particular objective, milestone or vision in their mind and not update it – even when the situation or environment changes
- Provide a clear plan to achieve the clear vision, and demonstrate that there is order and organization, together with systems, processes and guidelines
- Be aware that they are idealistic by nature and want to see the organization striving to achieve as close to perfection as possible
- Demonstrate that the organization is responding to future trends, new markets, potential crises and staff trends
- Present market positioning and strategic analysis
- Present with models, abstract charts, ideas, themes and concepts

'Show me this idea is accurate with concrete data to support your position'

There are two types who access their P1 and I1 – the Planner and the Analyzer. This segment makes up 39 per cent of the general population.

When negotiating with this group:

- Prefers not to practise and instead prefers to get started
- Likes to see a logical and sensible approach to solving problems and crises
- Enjoys reading about and using tools, IT, equipment and machinery
- Will not read between the lines and instead needs all implicit information to be articulated before it is considered
- Likes information to be complete and comprehensive before a final decision is needed
- Prefers to read information rather than talk through issues
- Likes communication with in-depth analysis, charts, tables, graphs, concrete examples, photographs and details

FAMOUS PLANNERS

- Bill Gates (Founder, Microsoft)
- Billy Joel (Musician)
- Bing Cosby (Actor)
- Darth Vader (Character, Star Wars)
- Dustin Hoffman (Actor)
- George Bush (Former US President)
- Harry Truman (Former US President)
- Humphrey Bogart (Actor)
- J.D. Rockefeller (Businessman)
- Jack Nicholson (Actor)
- Madeline Albright (Former US Secretary of State)
- Morgan Freeman (Actor)
- Prince Charles (Prince of the UK)
- Richard Nixon (Former US President)
- Roger Federa (Tennis player)
- Russell Crowe (Actor)
- Sigmund Freud (Founding Father of Psychoanalysis)
- Sir Edmund Hilary (Explorer)
- Sir Winston Churchill (Former British Prime Minister)

PLANNERS AT WORK

A Planner is analytical, logical and has creative vision. However, their talent for creative vision is usually suppressed by a strong sense of logic. They tend to have two definite minds one very practical, and one focused on the creative world. Their greatest challenge is understanding these two opposite sides of their thinking. They balance a desire to be illogical and zany with being logical and conservative.

They are highly disciplined individuals, with a willingness to be consistent. If they are consistently required to suppress their creativity over a long period of time, they may become depressed or bored for no apparent reason.

Planners tend to exaggerate only when storytelling or sharing their vision. A Planner will be most motivated when they have a clear plan to write or follow. They have an excellent ability to process and can see a project from beginning to end. At work, their energy and enthusiasm will increase when they have a clear understanding of the overall organization's direction.

They will seek to understand their responsibilities within an organization and knowing these, will take them very seriously. If the parameters are vague, they will take these responsibilities less seriously.

They are more confident when they know a system and how it works, and their loyalty to structure and accepted procedures is foremost.

They are keen to achieve but never at the expense of others. They will achieve legitimate power through providing logical and factual solutions and strong leadership.

A Planner does not play games, preferring everyone to work together to achieve the vision. A Planner is highly disciplined and expects the same level of discipline from others. They are tolerant of others but become frustrated by an unstructured and undisciplined approach.

When confronted with aggression, they will tend to look at statements issued rather than at the individuals involved, but will match the intensity of the aggression. A Planner will sometimes cope with stress by escaping into their own world. They enjoy escaping from reality and a voyage into their world of creativity relieves tension.

They do not cope well with changes in course, unless they are driving the change themselves. It is important that at all times they are able to visualize the end result.

As leaders, Planners are very structured and logical. They will seek to share an organization's vision with staff and ensure they can achieve it. They will delegate only when job responsibilities are clear and understood. A Planner is determined and will work methodically to achieve a specific goal, often becoming impatient with others who do not have a similar discipline.

Planners have an exceptional memory for facts and are always willing to offer analytical and factual interpretations to problems. A Planner is calm, sincere and stable with periods of zaniness to contradict their normal behavior. They will

Leadership Styles

> *Your most unhappy customers are your greatest source of learning.*
>
> *Bill Gates*
> *Microsoft Founder*

mostly appear set in their ways and conservative; however, their creativity will often generate periods of spontaneous rebelliousness and sometimes perceived offensive behavior.

A Planner is at their most formidable when creating long-term strategies or when implementing operational procedures.

THE PLANNER'S MIRROR IN THE WORKPLACE

At work, the Diplomat Mirror will express itself in humor, a willingness to change track when new opportunities present themselves and an almost involuntary involvement in the politics of the organization.

Perhaps the best contribution of the Mirror at work, for Planners in a leadership position, is the Mirror's insistence that their employees are genuinely engaged in understanding, supporting and implementing the strategic direction.

The Mirror Diplomat is also responsible for the willingness of the Planner to move jobs and take career advancement opportunities, even if it means moving to another company, city, profession or country.

THE LEADERSHIP STYLE OF THE PLANNER

Each Neuro-Rational Type, due to its combination of thinking functions, has a different leadership style. These leadership styles are a function of the center of focus of the Neuro-Rational Types, and tend to be expressions of the underlying world view of each personality.

A groundbreaking survey of 3871 executives selected from a database of more than 20,000 executives[1] found distinct leadership styles which consistently appear in organizations. Daniel Goleman (2000) attributes these different leadership styles to different emotional intelligences. Each leadership style has a different impact on the work environment and on organizational performance. The most effective leaders use a variety of styles, choosing the appropriate style, timing and

---

1   Survey was originally analyzed by Kelner et al. (1996).

The Leadership Style of the Planner

Situation	Explanation
1. The leader's modus operandi	Mobilizes people towards a vision
2. The style in a phrase	'Come with me'
3. Underlying emotional intelligence competencies	Self-confidence, empathy, change catalyst
4. When the style works best	When changes require a new vision, or when a clear direction is needed
5. Overall impact on climate	Most strongly positive

intensity to manage each situation.

The leadership style identified by Goleman's research that is most closely linked to the profile of the Planner is the *Authoritative* style.

The author's experience supports the insightful research reported by Goleman. The Authoritative style is the most effective leadership style as it drives up every aspect of corporate climate. The primary focus of the Authoritative style of leadership is vision, either for a team or the wider organizational collective. This has a number of beneficial ramifications as a leadership style as follows:

- **Role focus.** The Planner is focused on the role and the team.

- **Clarity.** The visionary (strong C2 element) nature of the Authoritative leader generates motivation because people come to see clearly how their work fits into the larger vision of the organization.

- **Inspire commitment.** Their visionary focus allows them to frame the individual tasks in the context of the overall vision (I1 articulated vision). Therefore, people can see how their work matters and why it is important. It brings significance to the employee's daily activities and so increases their sense of commitment.

- **Strong standards.** With a strong sense of vision, leadership can define standards that underpin the overall objectives. This assists all decision-making and creates confidence in those decisions.

- **Feedback.** In providing feedback, the single objective is whether the

The Authoritative Style

Daniel Goleman (2000) relates the tale of Tom, director of marketing in a floundering chain of pizza restaurants.

In the Authoritative style of a Planner, he assumed the leadership role that had been missing in the company.

His clarity and specificity of thinking showed him that the real objective was to supply their customers' need for convenient-to-get pizza. This should be the bottom line. Managers should be encouraged to use their creativity to make their pizzas convenient. This became part of their mission statement.

The finances of the company were turned around by the clear vision of the Authoritative leader.

Managers used their imagination to find new convenient places to sell their pizza, and they began to guarantee faster delivery times.

The leader specified the desired outcome and the team rose to the challenge with the freedom to respond however they wished. Such is the strength of the Authoritative style of leadership.

---

performance has furthered the vision (assisted by I1). Therefore, determinates of positive or negative feedback are fixed and not subject to whimsy.

- **Standards.** These are clear and stated up front, as are the rewards for performance.
- **Flexibility.** It is encouraged, as the desired result is stated and the specific methodology is not articulated. These leaders encourage others to take calculated risks, and give freedom to innovate and experiment. The Planner leader creates stability, which allows the team members to move out of their lower selves and use their noble qualities.

The Authoritative style works well in almost any business environment. But when a company is 'adrift' and a new course needs to be charted it is most effective.

This style is not effective when a leader is working with a team of experts or peers who are more experienced. In these circumstances they may see the Authoritative leader as pompous or out-of-touch. Furthermore, if the leadership style becomes overbearing, then it can undermine effective teamwork.

SCHOOL OF STRATEGIC THOUGHT

The natural differences are not limited to leadership styles alone; they also extend to a natural inclination towards different strategic thought. These differences have been researched by Mintzberg, Ahlstrad and Lampel (1998). For the Planner, strategy formation is a cognitive process that takes place in the mind of the strategist. Strategies emerge as the strategist filters the maps, concepts and schemes shaping their thinking.

THE GENIUS OF THE PLANNER – PLANNING

The Planner's Genius lies in their ability to 'see' what is ahead and to prepare for it now. This means creating the right systems, anticipating the problems, researching all relevant data and ensuring blind panic is turned into beneficial and useful planning. They also understand the importance of every team member playing a central yet different role. Because the Planner likes their world to go to plan, they plan everything very thoroughly.

In order to maintain a sense of stability and control, they set up processes and structures for all aspects of their life. When they plan, they break large projects into a series of short-term tasks, with dates, time lines, and specific and detailed items. Others may be surprised by the time and effort the Planner gives to their organization, routine and detailed planning, but this is how they can be totally reliable and disciplined, creating a sense of certainty about making the plan come together (Buckingham et al., 2001).

Chapter 18

The Analyzer
An In-Depth Look at the Analyzer

*When all is said and done,
there has been more said than done.*

What we've got to thank Analyzers for:

- Objectivity
- Order and organization
- Rational argument
- Curiosity
- Specialist technical knowledge
- Written records
- Audit trails

THE ANALYZER PROFILE

Never speculate; never endorse beyond your surplus cash fund; make the firm's interest yours ... concentrate, put all your eggs in one basket and watch that basket; expenditure always within revenue; lastly, be not impatient, for, as Emerson says, 'No one can cheat you out of ultimate success but yourself.'

Andrew Carnegie

OVERVIEW

The Analyzer's mind is highly intellectual, analytical and detailed, with an excellent memory for facts. This personality has an outstanding ability to analyze situations and has a calm and detached approach to life. Analyzers are not judgemental, are slow to anger and are naturally intrigued by money, scorecards and balance sheets. They have an inbuilt fascination with the game of life.

Regardless of their training or level of professional development, the Analyzer likes order and organization. Their mind naturally separates their life into different compartments. The way they interact with a colleague at work and at home therefore can be quite different, with work issues kept at work and leisure issues kept for leisure time.

Very self-sufficient emotionally, Analyzers love excitement, activity and crisis. The Analyzer's core competency lies in the ability to break any situation into bite-sized pieces that can be addressed. A complex project, for example, may be broken into strengths to gain leverage from and weaknesses to be addressed, or it may be broken into short-, medium- and long-term issues. Even in the midst of a terrible crisis, the situation is still just a situation that needs to be tidied up.

FOCUS OF ATTENTION

Analyzers are brilliant at sorting out mess: minimizing tax, systemising contracts, structural analysis and categorizing detailed information. At their best Analyzers are self-reliant, controlled and detached; they master systems, and are holistic, expert and wise.

KEY CHARACTER DRIVERS

There are three key Intelligences that drive the Analyzer:

C1 – Spontaneity

P1 – Logic

I1 – Data

THE SUBTYPES

Each of the eight types is made up of three Intelligences. The Analyzer has C1 Spontaneity, P1 Logic and I1 Data. As we adapt to our life circumstances we tend to favor one of the three. This subtly changes the personality and gives rise to subtypes. All Analyzers will be able to relate to all three of the subtypes at some time in their life.

THE SPONTANEOUS ANALYZER

Although the Spontaneous Analyzer is able to follow through with projects, their spontaneity will always be pulling them away from structures and procedures. They will like new projects, new people, new thoughts and new ideas. They will probably be good with their hands, hop from topic to topic in conversation and have a witty, albeit dry, sense of humor. This spontaneity will sometimes conflict with their logic.

THE CONTROLLING ANALYZER

The Controlling Analyzer will want to see projects through from beginning to end and will have a healthy sense of humor, be balanced, analytical and even-handed. They will be self-disciplined and stable. They will want loose ends tied up. Their logic will suppress their spontaneity unless they are relaxed.

THE WISE ANALYZER

For this subtype, the researching of information is far more important than either following the plan or coming up with ideas of their own. They would prefer to wait and obtain all the facts before making a decision. For the Wise Analyzer, all the ends do not have to be tied up. They will always want to know the facts supporting opinions. They enjoy reading and libraries, researching and learning about everything.

LEADERSHIP STYLES RELATED TO THE ANALYZER

When people discuss leadership styles, many of the characters they use will fall into the same category as the Analyzer, much the same way that there may be fifty-seven species of fern but regardless of the species, it still belongs to the fern family.

By way of example, some of these are:

- The Spy
- The Double Agent
- The Sleuth
- Sherlock Holmes
- The Warrior
- The Crime Fighter
- The Gambler
- The Midas
- The Miser
- The Private Investigator

CHILDREN'S STORIES/CHARACTERS

- Brains (*The Thunderbirds*)
- Robin (*Batman and Robin*)
- Bert (*Ernie and Bert*)

THE MIRROR

While the Analyzer is structured, analytical, detached and focused on the detail, the Analyzer's Mirror Master – the Coach – is idealistic, optimistic, passionate and committed to bringing the best out in people and creating a better future. As a Mirror, the Coach is usually encouraging, motivating and future-centered. However, this Mirror will ask the big hard questions of the Analyzer, such as 'What value am I really adding? Is this environment at home or at work supporting the individuals I care about? Is this hard work really amounting to anything? Am I supporting my family? Am I genuine, ethical and fair? And what have I tangibly created recently?'

At home, the Mirror will take a deep and real interest in family members and will spend hours of time worrying about the issues they are facing and walking beside them as these issues are resolved.

Young Coach Mirrors are quiet and often get marginalized by the control-focused Master Analyzer. When this happens, Analyzers have no sense of the important emotional role those close to them play in their lives and they treat them as objects to move and manage, rather than people to value, learn from and admire.

If I stopped making records or performing, I'd probably still be famous for a while being me. But I'd rather have something to show for myself.

Kylie Minogue
Australian pop star

As the Coach Mirror matures, it becomes more assertive and insists the Analyzer be more generous with time, money and affection.

The Mirror Coach will insist that all resources earned and hoarded by the Analyzer go towards helping family and friends.

When the Coach Mirror is integrated into the Analyzer profile, it gives the structured and detached Analyzer a caring and nurturing side, personal passion and the desire and ability to create a better future.

UNDERSTANDING ANALYZERS

Analyzers best manage themselves by:

- Disciplining themselves to keep an eye on the bigger picture – where are we headed and why are we doing this?
- Remembering that people are not cogs. They need to understand why they are doing things and they need to be valued for their contribution; not being fired is not good enough
- Remembering that tasks, budgets and people are interconnected; if action is taken in one area the emotional/financial fallout will bleed into other areas

As team members, Analyzers make the best contribution when:

- They can work on specific elements of a project and report back to the group with the outcomes
- They don't have to manage complex people issues
- They are dealing with specifics rather than vague concepts
- They are auditing/checking/receiving or analyzing data

Never speculate, never endorse beyond your surplus cash fund, make the firm's interest yours ... concentrate, put all your eggs in one basket and watch that basket; expenditure always within revenue; lastly, be not impatient, for, as Emerson says, 'no one can cheat you out of ultimate success but yourself'.

Andrew Carnegie
American Industrialist

When managing Analyzers:

- Check that their activity is in line with the wider vision and ensure they refresh their focus regularly
- Encourage them to encourage their team. They won't do it by nature
- Ensure anything you want to communicate to them that is important is written down
- Insist on face-to-face meetings so that things can be discussed – otherwise everything will be done by email

How Analyzers will act during meetings:

- Will need ideas/feelings/reactions to be said, in order for them to be taken on board and will want clear decisions
- Will want specifics/real practical information, sequentially presented; keep it short, relevant and stay on topic
- Will want realism about resources and timeframes
- Will want to see continuity, only changing the segments that are not working

Personality strengths that help Analyzers to further their development:

- Consistent and reliable
- Able to make order from chaos
- Excellent cool heads in a crisis

Personality weaknesses that can stand in the way of an Analyzer's development:

- Inability to work without a clear structure
- Can lose heart and connection with people
- Can lose energy and interest when there is no pressure

I don't believe in pessimism. If something doesn't come up the way you want, forge ahead. If you think it's going to rain, it will.

Clint Eastwood
Actor

Opportunities for Analyzers to develop:

- Need to look at the big picture and keep activity focused on the important rather than the urgent tasks
- Need to develop their ability to deal with ambiguity
- Need to learn how to value and empathize with others

Threats to the Analyzer's development:

- Can't see the big picture
- Will freeze when faced with ambiguous situations
- Can treat people like machines and destroy their spirit

WHEN NEGOTIATING WITH ANALYZERS

The effective communicator is able to align their narrative and the point they are wanting to make with the leadership style of the audience. That is, they use the same language, approach and behavior with the leadership style of the person they are presenting to.

When negotiating with Analyzers the way you position information is very important. Analyzers are attracted to messages centered around two main themes which are most convincing to them: *'Show me this idea is accurate with concrete data to support your position'* and *'Show me that this will solve the next problem that comes up.'*

'Show me this idea is accurate with concrete data to support your position'

There are two types who access their P1 and I1 – the Analyzer and the Planner. This segment makes up 39 per cent of the general population. When negotiating with this group:

- Prefers not to practise and instead prefers to get started
- Likes to see a logical and sensible approach to solving problems and crises
- Enjoys reading about and using tools, IT, equipment and machinery
- Will not read between the lines and instead needs all implicit information to be articulated before it is considered
- Likes information to be complete and comprehensive before a decision is needed
- Prefers to read information rather than talk through issues
- Likes communication with in-depth analysis, charts, tables, graphs, concrete examples, photographs and details

Leadership Styles

'Show me that this will solve the next problem that comes up'

There are two groups who access their C1 and P1 by nature, the Analyzers and the Innovators. This segment makes up 36 per cent of the general population. When negotiating with this group:

- Present the 'here and now' and how well the organization is able to respond quickly to whatever situation arises
- Present your argument in terms of new opportunities, new ideas, new projects and in all the divergent pieces of the organization
- Assume a very short attention span
- Present your information through pictures, captions, simple flow charts and graphs
- Do not present abstract ideas or concepts or spatially-based dynamic models
- Emphasize experiential learning where they can set the pace
- Mention any links to the Internet
- Deliver your information in gulps
- Be aware that they will often not delineate between the different pieces if they all arrive together; for example, if a dividend arrives at the same time as a court summons, the dividend will be tarred with the same brush
- Be aware that they see vision as ungrounded and largely a waste of time
- Provide immediate answers, immediate results and immediate priorities because they withstand very low levels of delayed gratification
- Do not deliver too much strategy and not enough action

FAMOUS ANALYZERS

- Clint Eastwood (Actor)
- David Beckham (Soccer player)
- Dr Laura Schlessinger (Radio talk show host)
- George Washington (former US President)
- Idris Harding (WWI Code Breaker)
- Ingvar Kamprad (Founder, IKEA)
- James Bond (Movie character)
- Kevin Costner (Actor)
- Kylie Minogue (Singer)
- Mark Webber (Former Formula 1 driver)
- Mike Wallace (Game show host)
- Nicole Kidman (Actor)
- Sandra Day O'Connor (Supreme court justice)
- Vince Lombardi (Football player)
- Warren Buffet (Investor)

ANALYZERS AT WORK

Analyzers are practical and productive individuals. They are conscientious and can be relied upon to complete tasks systematically. They are dedicated and responsible, and are cooperative and supportive as long as others are working within the accepted guidelines. They tend to be critical of others whom they suspect may be working against those guidelines.

The Analyzer does not want to play power games or create friction, and is accomplished at gaining the maximum personal benefit from organization-based infrastructure. Their tolerance is generally high as long as people are doing their best and are not trying to challenge procedures, and they respect those who understand and follow those procedures.

They approach tasks in a methodical manner, and once started on a project will persist until it is completed. They accept change willingly as long as there is a point to the change. New ideas and projects appeal to them but they become frustrated if there is no structure or plan to follow. Their challenge is to achieve set goals.

An Analyzer will want to exert influence over illogical or unstructured people. They are very disciplined, especially with themselves, and their expectation will be that staff and colleagues are similarly disciplined. They will not naturally delegate, but will want 'to do it right themselves'.

They do not enjoy competition in the workplace. Their motivation lies more in achieving specific tasks than competing with others. They are more likely to compete with themselves by setting their own performance criteria and then striving to achieve these expectations.

The Analyzer needs to be able to see their own success rather than feel it. They often aspire to being a small cog in a big wheel rather than a big cog in a small wheel. They are much more interested in the here and now than the future so will tend to take the vision of others and make it practical.

An Analyzer has an excellent ability to process complex, detailed data. Once a project is started they will persist until it is completed. They approach tasks in a methodical and patient manner. They will memorize facts and figures with no difficulty.

Associate with men of good quality if you esteem your own reputation; for it is better to be alone than in bad company.

George Washington
(former US President)

Leadership Styles

They enjoy being able to store information and retrieve it efficiently. An Analyzer is willing to supply facts and provide analytical solutions and lateral suggestions. As their name suggests, they are excellent at analysis.

The Analyzer copes with stress in the same way they cope with everything else. They will consider the facts, analyze them and take a logical course of action. Their ability to think laterally enables them to find solutions to problems.

They tend to resolve conflict by focusing on the task and what needs to be achieved, rather than the individuals involved. Again, their skill for providing lateral solutions and ideas enables them to dissipate conflict effectively. Their judgement can be relied upon because it is balanced and even-handed.

An Analyzer is generally quiet and unassuming. They have a calming effect upon others and can be relied upon to bring stability to those around them.

Relaxation for an Analyzer, however, is often a high-energy, high-stress activity. At play, the Analyzer will show their competitive side, pitting their physical prowess against the opposition. Analyzers enjoy sport and make good team members.

They are most confident when they understand exactly what is happening around them. As a leader, they will be firm but fair. They will create rules and procedures and ensure others adhere to them. They are capable of reprimanding or dismissing staff.

An Analyzer has a practical, down-to-earth communication style. They will systematically discuss facts and topics and will tend to keep the discussion balanced and in perspective. An Analyzer will have an excellent ability to spell, punctuate and edit. Their written and verbal communication will be structured and information based.

Despite a keenness for structure, an Analyzer can be spontaneous. They will enjoy starting new projects but will insist on working to an ordered and structured timetable.

What you see is what you get with an Analyzer. They are unlikely to deceive or exaggerate. An Analyzer is principally a conservative and loyal individual. They don't respond well to being pressured, preferring to work at their own pace. They have an excellent eye for detail. They are often able to highlight issues that others may overlook.

Analyzers are at their most formidable when they are sorting, categorizing, analyzing and problem-solving.

THE ANALYZER'S MIRROR IN THE WORKPLACE

At work, the Analyzer's Mirror – the Coach – can be seen in patient listening, reflective and supportive comments given during tough times, support for the underdog and an interest in creating an inclusive and supportive work environment where everyone is respected, valued and allowed to reach their potential.

LEADERSHIP STYLE OF THE ANALYZER

Each Neuro-Rational Type, due to its combination of Intelligences, has a different leadership style. These leadership styles are a function of the center of focus of the Neuro-Rational Types, and tend to be expressions of the underlying world view of the personality. The most effective leaders use a variety of styles, choosing the appropriate style, timing and intensity to manage each situation.

The leadership style most closely aligned to the profile of the Analyzer is the *Tactical* style.

The author's research suggests that the Tactical style has a positive overall impact on corporate climate. The primary focus of the Tactical style is on accurate and verifiable information. This has a number of ramifications as a leadership style.

These are:

- Employee's **insight is highly valued,** and the Tactical leader is a keen interviewer.
- **Individuals are included** in bringing about the strategic plan on a 'need to know' basis.
- Tactical leaders enjoy making many small decisions that keep the business functioning smoothly (P1 and C1 interaction).
- Being neither pushy nor a fast mover, pushy people and sometimes fast movers are ignored or removed. The Tactical leader will make up their mind for themselves (strong P1 element).
- **Feedback is minimal.** The Tactical leader will brief individuals or small teams, but tend not to let everyone know what is happening. Since employees do not know the corporate vision, this lack of communication can create a political environment.

> *It takes 20 years to build a reputation and five minutes to ruin it. If you think about that, you'll do things differently.*
>
> *Warren Buffet*
> *Investor*

The Leadership Style of the Analyzer

Situation	Explanation
1. The leader's modus operandi	Act based on accurate and verifiable information
2. The style in a phrase	'Prove it'
3. When the style works best	In highly technical or specialized environments
4. Overall impact on climate	Positive

This form of leadership may lead to confusion and procrastination as key decisions are held up and bottlenecks are created.

Key performers may leave because decisions take too long and they do not feel particularly valued by the leader.

Tactical leadership works well in highly technical or specialized business environments when the people being led are professionally autonomous and work in self-managed teams. It can also work where individuals are isolated and require infrequent briefings.

Despite these drawbacks, the Tactical style does work well when all the employees are self-motivated, highly competent, and need little direction or coordination. Given a talented team to lead, a leader using the Tactical approach gets the task accomplished. This leader tends to be highly respected by their employees. While they may feel unsure of the direction of the company, workers know that they will have a high degree of job security if they are polite, reasonable, and put forward informed and logical arguments to corporate issues.

SCHOOL OF STRATEGIC THOUGHT

The natural differences between Neuro-Rational Types are not limited to leadership styles alone; they also extend to a natural inclination towards different strategic thought. These differences have been researched by Mintzberg, Ahlstrand and Lampel (1998). For the Analyzer, the simple informal steps of the design school become an elaborate sequence of steps represented by the planning school of strategic thought. It focuses on formal procedure, formal training, formal analysis, and lots of numbers. When you produce every component part as specified, assemble them according to the blueprint, strategy will result.

THE GENIUS OF THE ANALYZER – CREATING ORDER

The Analyzer's Genius lies in their ability to create order, systems and stability. This means keeping a calm head in emergencies, grounding new opportunities or settling down situations, people and teams when there is too much ambiguity. It means being analytical. In transition, the Analyzer creates clarity and certainty.

Buckingham and Clifton (2001, p. 86) describes the behavior of the person using this strength as follows:

- When they are presented with someone's theory, their reaction is to demand proof.
- The only acceptable truth is based on objective facts.
- They see themselves as objective and dispassionate, because data is value free. Others recognize their logic and intellectual rigor.
- As they analyze, they look for patterns, causes and effects in relation to the proposition or situation and so reveal any flaws in the other person's argument or the real facts of the situation.

Leadership Styles

Chapter 19

The Energizer
An In-Depth Look at the Energizer

RULE #1: 'With your partner in life - appear interested.'
Warren Clarke

What we've got to thank Energizers for:

- Clarity
- Search for truth
- Energy
- Enthusiasm
- Getting things done
- The 'Devil's Advocate' position
- Stamina
- Determination

OVERVIEW

No matter what people tell you, words and ideas can change the world.

Robin Williams
Actor

The Energizer's mind is fast, efficient, clear, certain and razor sharp. It can remember details and likes to keep discussion concrete, ideas practical and tasks specific. It is driven by a constant desire to complete large amounts of work. While quality is important, Energizers enjoy following efficient systems that enable them to do two days' work in one day. Constantly changing, refining and improving systems is an annoyance to Energizers who would prefer to 'get on with it' rather than spend two days refining a system that could save one day's work.

Regardless of their training or level of professional development, the Energizer likes working quickly and efficiently in an area of personal interest where they are recognized and rewarded financially. Their passion is being able to successfully complete projects where all the key stakeholders are happy and there is written acknowledgement of the contribution made by the Energizer or their team.

Very emotionally passionate, Energizers see strong relationships as being central to achievement and will protect those they are responsible for, defend those they respect and confront those they believe are wrong. They believe in the importance of institutions like the church, schools, and the legal system. They do not, however, have an abiding trust in their leaders and so constantly ask the hard questions to 'keep the bastards honest'. They often join social clubs or groups and conduct community work because they enjoy meeting new people and doing the right thing.

An Energizer has great clarity with regard to their opinions on most issues and likes to put their case forward even if the topic doesn't come up. They are energetic, enthusiastic, focused and quick working and have an excellent eye for ensuring all the details are right and the ends are tied up.

Energizers have a natural interest in commerce and the process of making money. They are natural small business owners and tend to find themselves in charge of logistics organization, be it for sales, weddings, charity balls, fundraising or banquets. Energizers thrive on activity, deadlines, logistics, organizing teams, and multi-tasking.

FOCUS OF ATTENTION

Energizers are brilliant at building and maintaining customer loyalty because they genuinely want the right outcome for the customer and go the extra mile in making sure the customer is not only happy but wants to do further business with them. At their best, Energizers are obedient, loyal, enthusiastic, driven, entrepreneurial, motivational, enlivening and cathartic.

KEY CHARACTER DRIVERS

There are three key Intelligences that drive the Energizer:

C1 – Spontaneity

P2 – Passion

I1 – Data

THE SUBTYPES

Each of the eight types is made up of three Intelligences. The Energizer has C1 Spontaneity, P2 Passion and I1 Data. As we adapt to our life circumstances we tend to favor one of the three. This subtly changes the personality and gives rise to subtypes. All Energizers will be able to relate to all three of the subtypes at some time in their life.

THE CREATIVE ENERGIZER

The Creative Energizer will enjoy new ideas, thoughts and solutions and will be able to adapt other people's concepts, designs and processes to support their objectives. They will lose interest in old projects and people quickly, wanting instead to constantly meet new challenges. They are quick minded, witty and enthusiastic for the latest thought.

THE POWERFUL ENERGIZER

The Powerful Energizer will have strong opinions about most things and will

---

If you feel you have a film that's valid, you stick your ass on the line.

Nick Nolte

Actor

want issues resolved. They are keen to succeed and want to outperform people's expectations.

At times they will tend to soapbox their ideas even though others may not wish to hear. Certainly one of their greatest challenges is to voice their opinions and ideas in such a way as not to offend their audience and not tread on emotional toes. The Powerful Energizer will be excellent for creating change and will not be daunted by negative feedback. It is recommended, however, that they find themselves an intuitive person they can trust, and be guided by their ability to read other people's reactions, and therefore know when they are going too far.

THE WISE ENERGIZER

For the Wise Energizer, the researching of information is far more important than either following the plan or coming up with ideas of their own.

They would prefer to wait and obtain all the facts before making a decision. For the Wise Energizer, all the ends do not have to be tied up. They will always want to know the facts supporting opinions. They enjoy reading, the Internet, researching, and learning about the world.

LEADERSHIP STYLES RELATED TO THE ENERGIZER

When people discuss leadership styles, many of the characters they use will fall into the same category as the Energizer, much the same way that there may be fifty-seven species of fern but, regardless of the species, it still belongs to the fern family.

By way of example, some of these are:

- The Bully
- The Hedonist
- The Gourmet
- The Chef
- The Critic
- The Examiner

- The Mediator
- The Arbitrator
- The Liberator
- The Anarchist
- The Journalist

- The Revolutionary
- The Political protester
- The Non-conformist
- The Scribe

CHILDREN'S STORIES/NURSERY RHYMES

- Basil Brush
- Oscar the Grouch

- Mr Squiggle
- Miss Piggy

THE MIRROR

While the Energizer is dedicated to fast-paced, fast-talking, argumentative action, the Energizer's Mirror Master – the Change Agent – looks for the strategic intent of the activity and is motivated by learning new capabilities, that is, the 'how to' of the 'what'. This thirst for new capabilities often draws the Energizer to projects that will teach them new skills even if the projects seem strangely unrelated to the Energizer's current skills, interests or preferences.

As a Mirror Master, the Change Agent is constantly critiquing the behavior and pointing out the inconsistencies of the spontaneous and energetic Energizer. This constant questioning demoralizes the Energizer who, in response, learns to ignore the constant criticism and usually adopts the attitude of think less and do more.

At home, the Mirror Change Agent is cunning and strategic, pointing out to the Energizer's friends and family the inconsistencies between what is said and done, and what is promised and forgotten, providing interpretations for inconsistent behavior.

The young Mirror Change Agent is strong and speaks rarely but when they do speak, they do so with great authority, which puts the Master Energizer off balance. The Mirror Change Agent focuses on truth, honesty and teasing out weaknesses so they can be dealt with strategically. The Mirror is not interested in keeping the peace if the Energizer is speaking rubbish.

As the Mirror Change Agent matures, they learn that not all inconsistency is bad, not everything can be solved in advance and that passion rather than logic is OK.

When fully integrated, the Master Energizer's passion, energy and focus on action are balanced by the Mirror Change Agent's strategic outlook and philosophy, drive to learn new capabilities and ability to align all action with the vision and genuine needs and wants of the people involved.

UNDERSTANDING ENERGIZERS

Energizers use their personality to best manage themselves by:
- Learning to be more sensitive with reprimands, requests and feedback
- Disciplining themselves to confirm the bigger picture before they get started on the operation at hand
- Disciplining themselves to see the value in people with whom they disagree
- Disciplining themselves to slow down for people who need more time to think things through

As team members, Energizers make the best contribution when:
- A team needs to be rejuvenated and re-energized
- A 'roll up the sleeves and get started' approach is required
- Vast amounts of activity are required, and outputs are needed
- Things need to be brought to a head
- There is clarity, unity, purpose and direction, and the Energizer is given the OK to make things happen

When managing Energizers:
- Provide clear and written feedback, both positive and negative, on their activity
- State specifically what behavior you want to see and what you don't want to see
- Provide feedback 'on the spot' or immediately after the meeting
- Give negative feedback in short two-minute sessions
- Write down feedback on reports given – positive and negative
- Always be pacey, to the point and specific

How Energizers will act during meetings:
- Will tend to shoot from the hip and polarize their support very quickly
- Will want clear decisions made and outcomes from the meeting
- Will argue their point passionately and creatively
- Will want public recognition for the work they do
- Will be insensitive to the feelings of others
- Will praise those they feel have done a good job
- Will not want complexity, vagueness or sluggish thoughts

Personality strengths that help the Energizers to further their development:
- Ability to drive new projects
- Can drive a team hard
- High achiever
- Never miss a deadline, never late
- Very focused on doing what it takes to achieve the goal

Personality weaknesses that can stand in the way of the Energizer's development:
- Misreads people
- Can 'burn out' themselves and others
- Fractures world into 'good' and 'bad'
- Can be very insensitive
- Can be too egocentrically linked to outcomes

Opportunities for the Energizer to develop:
- Needs to keep deadlines and expectations in perspective
- Needs to learn how to relax
- Needs to see the continuum, not the poles
- Needs to learn how far to push people

Threats to the Energizer's development:
- Can create needless conflict
- Can create enemies
- Can become too political
- Can provoke people to revolt

WHEN NEGOTIATING WITH ENERGIZERS

The effective communicator is able to align their narrative and the point they are wanting to make with the leadership style of the audience. That is, they use the same language, approach and behavior with the leadership style of the person they are presenting to.

When negotiating with Energizers the way you position information is very important. Energizers are attracted to messages centered around two main themes

---

I wouldn't say I invented tacky, but I definitely brought it to its present high popularity.

Bette Midler
Singer-songwriter, actress, comedian, author,
producer, activist

which are most convincing to them: *'Show me how this can help us get some quick wins'* and *'Show me this idea is the best way forward.'*

'Show me how this can help us get some quick wins'

There are two types who naturally access their P2 and C1 functions – the Energizer and the Diplomat. This segment makes up 36 per cent of the general population. When negotiating with this group:

- Present constant initiatives that will give the organization the edge
- Demonstrate new ideas, business ventures and people as an indication that the leadership is doing a good job
- Exhibit how the organization has taken advantage of the opportunities created by shifts in the market (for example, competitors failing)
- Show evidence that the organization is responsive to market trends
- Show fast activity that secures 'quick wins'
- Use strategies that are grounded and that last no longer than a few years
- Show clear milestones, responsibilities and target dates for achievement
- Be prepared to convince them on every point
- Be aware that they consider the credibility of the presenter as important as the message itself
- Demonstrate passion, success and drive

'Show me this idea is the best way forward'

There are two types who access the P2 and I1 functions by nature – the Energizer and the Crusader. This segment makes up approximately 37 per cent of the general population. When negotiating with this group:

- Do not show indifference, lack of passion, coldness or apathy
- Sell the benefits of new ideas particularly if these benefits can be quantified
- Keep the discussion tangible and concrete with specifics
- Do not present intuitive and unproven concepts, models, abstract ideas, hunches, intuitions or possibilities
- Show that there is a valid code of conduct and that there is a right and wrong way of doing things
- Show that leaders are approaching tasks the RIGHT way
- Demonstrate that you are following the rules, respecting the status quo, paying taxes, doing jury duty and being fair

- In your communication, be precise, passionate, action-oriented and respectful of institutions and roles/positions
- Demonstrate that their leaders are strong yet approachable, and will protect those within their responsibility
- Articulate goals, set milestones and show that these goals are achieved
- Demonstrate that the leadership is passionate to do whatever it takes to keep the energy and focus maintained

FAMOUS ENERGIZERS

- Bette Midler (Actor, singer)
- Danny DeVito (Actor)
- Dr Seuss (Author)
- Eddie Murphy (Actor)
- Edith Piaf (Singer)
- Goldie Hawn (Actor)
- John Burley (Author)
- Julie Andrews (Actor)
- Justin Bieber (Singer)
- Kramer (TV character, Seinfeld)
- Madonna (Singer)
- Nick Nolte (Actor)
- Robbie Williams (Singer)
- Robin Williams (Actor)
- Russell Brand (Actor, comedian)
- Sir Richard Branson (Founder, Virgin Group)
- Stephen Hawking (Scientist)
- Tina Turner (Singer)
- Tom Cruise (Actor)
- Will Smith (Actor)

THE ENERGIZER AT WORK

At work, the Energizer's Mirror can be seen in the constant questions regarding how the behavior of others either aligns or doesn't align with their personal philosophy, their past behavior or the project objectives. It is the Energizer's Mirror that makes the quiet sarcastic remarks about double standards, faulty processes and flawed strategy. The Mirror Change Agent is also constantly looking for opportunities to learn new skills and capabilities and understand systems or organizations at all levels.

LEADERSHIP STYLE OF THE ENERGIZER

Each Neuro-Rational Type, due to its combination of Intelligences, has a different leadership style. These leadership styles are a function of the center of focus of the Neuro-Rational Types, and tend to be expressions of the underlying world view of the personality.

A survey of 3871 executives selected from a database of more than 20,000 executives found distinct leadership styles. Daniel Goleman (2000) attributes these different leadership styles to different emotional intelligences. Each leadership style has a different impact on the work environment and on organizational performance. The most effective leaders use a variety of styles, choosing the appropriate style, timing and intensity to manage each situation.

The leadership style identified by Goleman's research that is most closely linked to the profile of the Energizer is the *Coercive* style.

The author's experience supports the insightful research reported by Goleman. In most situations, the Coercive style has the most negative overall impact on corporate climate. The primary focus of the Coercive style of leadership is on extreme top-down decision-making. It is focused on achieving the immediate results at all cost (a strong P2 element).

Some of the characteristics of this leadership style are:

- Coercive leaders **demand immediate compliance** with orders, but do not bother explaining the reasons behind them. If they are not followed, then the leaders tend to resort to threats.
- Rather than delegating authority, they **seek tight control** of any situation and monitor it studiously.
- **Feedback is minimal**. If given at all, it tends to focus on what people did wrong rather than what they did well. By rarely using praise and freely

The Leadership Style of the Energizer

Situation	Explanation
1. The leader's modus operandi	Demands immediate compliance
2. The style in a phrase	'Do what I tell you'
3. Underlying emotional intelligence competencies	Drive to achieve, initiative, self-control
4. When the style works best	In a crisis, to kickstart a turnaround, or with problem employees
5. Overall impact on climate	Negative

The Coercive Style

Daniel Goleman (2000) gives an example of a CEO who was brought into a failing company because of his reputation for turning companies around.

He proceeded to do the cost cutting and firing that was long overdue, and the company was momentarily saved.

But because of the aggressive, belittling, abusive personality of the Coercive leader, morale suffered. Most of the senior staff left or were fired and people only reported good news for fear that the CEO would 'shoot the messenger' of bad news. In the end, the board had to fire the CEO and find another person to rescue the company.

The Energizer has to remember that 50 per cent of the population do not care about outputs – they're only interested in the process. So if you get the job done at the expense of the relationship and the respect of 50 per cent of the team, it is too high a price to pay. They will all 'dig in' on the next project. So slow down, connect with people and remember that whereas a broom doesn't mind sweeping the floor, the person behind the broom does. And sometimes let them do it their own way in their own time.

criticizing employees, they start to erode people's spirits and the pride of satisfaction they take in their work.

- **Flexibility and responsibility are lost**. Since the decisions are made from the top, flexibility and creativity die and people feel so disrespected that responsibility evaporates.
- This style does **not give feedback** building the individual's sense that their job fits into a grand, shared mission.

Despite these drawbacks, the Coercive style is beneficial in extreme circumstances, such as during a turnaround or when a hostile takeover is looming. It can be used to break failed business habits and shock people into new ways of working. But the long-term impact is detrimental if another style of leadership is not used once the emergency has passed.

SCHOOL OF STRATEGIC THOUGHT

The natural differences between Neuro-Rational Types are not limited to leadership styles alone; they also extend to a natural inclination towards different strategic thought. These differences have been researched by Mintzberg, Ahlstrand and Lampel (1998). The Energizer proposes a model of strategy that seems to attain a fit between internal capabilities and external possibilities. It equates to the design school, and is the home of the SWOT approach (Strengths, Weaknesses, Opportunities and Threats).

THE GENIUS OF THE ENERGIZER – ENERGIZING AND TURNING TALK INTO ACTION

The Energizer has the Genius of turning talk into action by focusing on what can be done NOW to get things on the road. That is, the Genius of the Energizer is in the application of their energy and activating projects with energy.

Buckingham and Clifton (2001, p. 84) describe the Energizer's behavior as follows:

- Their focus is on action, getting things started, getting things done.
- They are impatient with analysis and debate and once a decision is made they cannot wait to start. The absence of detail does not slow them down.
- This person learns by experience. They act, look at the result and learn from it. This is a reactive rather than a proactive stance.
- They believe we are judged only by what we actually do.

SECTION 3

The Quest For Personal Focus

Personal Focus

The Quest For Personal Focus

So far, on your quest, you have discovered that when you were born the Universe gave you a special gift. 'Special' because it was just for you — it had your name on it. 'Special' because it was a gift whose very purpose was to allow you to be special. 'Special' in a way that can mean success in all the areas of your life that really matter to you.

We call this gift from the universe your Leadership Style.

It is time now to help you unwrap this gift and use it to become all that you were born to be. You can do this by developing personal FOCUS:

- **F:** Fight the good fight
- **O:** Operationalize your attributes
- **C:** Courageously examine yourself and your life
- **U:** Use a master's strategy
- **S:** Strive to manage your energy

Personal Focus

***Success is a science; if you have the conditions,
you get the results.***

Oscar Wilde (1884 - 1900) Letter 7, March - April 1883

Chapter 20

F: Fight The Good Fight

Success is a natural consequence of applying your natural gift in a focused way. It is the birthright of every living person. It is our right and responsibility to succeed. But if this is the case, why do so few of us get there?

Well, as the saying almost goes, most of us are looking for success in all the wrong places.

Dr S. Blotnick, a United States psychologist and the author of the book *Getting Rich Your Own Way*, tracked literally thousands of high school students who wanted to be millionaires. Twenty years later, only a handful of them had succeeded. In his study, Dr Blotnick verified what modern and ancient speakers, authors, philosophers and mentors have been saying for more than 4000 years.

Firstly, he discovered success is not a matter of luck! While a few individuals in the group had won the lottery, they had also lost the money again.

Secondly, he found that no 'get-rich-quick' schemes had worked. Instead, those who **only** focused on getting rich failed without exception because their heart, mind and soul were not in the endeavor. (As you can imagine, 'get-rich-quick' schemes are usually devised by minds dominated by C1 which is not known for its critical thinking and follow through.)

Dr Blotnick found that having a clear vision wasn't enough if it stood without hands-on activity, and neither was simply living one day at a time with faith that things would slowly improve (because usually, they don't).

He discovered that strategically manoeuvring and playing the corporate game (summarized in the old saying, 'It's not what you know or who you know, but what you know about who you know') only worked for a while. He found that this approach usually ended in tears because eventually everyone finds their match and is beaten in the game of politics.

He found that knowledge alone didn't get people there (there are plenty of broke people with photographic memories), and neither did an understanding of people (psychiatrists have one of the highest rates of suicide).

THE MILLION DOLLAR ANSWER

Instead, he discovered that those who had become happy millionaires had achieved it by becoming masters in their chosen area. As masters, they had successfully risen above the rest and had become leaders in their field. As masters, they could charge a premium for their work, because they added more value to the marketplace than others did and they were recognized for it financially.

Dr Blotnick chronicled success in financial terms, but using this formula for success yields far greater returns than just money. It is true that if you become a master you will reap financial rewards, but your soul and spirit will also reap priceless dividends. One essential stepping stone to joy is to become a master in a field about which you are personally passionate. This truth profoundly affected Karl Marx who called this phenomenon 'praxis'. This inspired him to develop a philosophy where people were encouraged to find intrinsic reward in the work they undertook rather than just the extrinsic financial reward. While his communist philosophy had some rather glaring flaws, it has this strong element of truth in it which has inspired countless millions of people the world over.

It is also a cornerstone of Greek philosophy. Socrates wrote, 'Concern yourself less with what you have than with what you are, so that you can become as excellent as possible.'

Money is one way society acknowledges a master. But money is the result of mastery-based joy and not the cause of it. As the Biblical writer asks, 'What is the value of gaining the whole world if you have to say goodbye to your true self?'

The Stoics had a term for the external things in life they believed they couldn't control. These were matters to which they believed we should feel 'indifferent'. In contrast, issues regarding our own personal development and the mastery of how we deal with these matters of indifference were considered matters central to our very existence.

Only by learning how to master a skill or discipline in the external world can we apply this internally and become integrated and whole. As the US business philosopher Jim Rohn says, "Become a millionaire not just for the money, but for what it will make of you."

This is a profound truth that is largely overlooked in contemporary Western society where most of us are focused on making a quick dollar and retiring — and where society almost celebrates anyone who manages to avoid doing the hard yards and yet still hits the big time financially. Life is not about the retirement. Life is about learning, climbing and mastering.

Life is about becoming a master in a field of endeavor that feeds your soul with the richness of creative expression and fills your heart with passion and your spirit with hope and freedom.

BUT, HOW DOES A MASTER BECOME A MASTER?

First of all, a master has fully accepted and understood his or her own personal strengths and weaknesses. Masters have also acknowledged and valued their universal gift and know that their area of mastery is built on this gift. In other words, they have successfully navigated the first transition in life from oblivion to awakening.

Secondly, they have learnt from a master who has taught them the ropes. By this I mean that they have learnt the master's strategy in the area they wished to specialize in and master themselves.

Thirdly, they have adapted the strategy of this mentor/master to suit themselves, to suit their personality and their preferences.

Finally they have added to this body of knowledge something of themselves — something unique that sets them apart from the rest of the pack.

Bryce Courtney is an excellent storyteller who draws on his unique experience in Africa to give depth, meaning and a unique flavor to his stories.

Molly Meldrum brings his unique approach to relationship-building to music journalism and while Richard Branson is a seasoned business person, he brings his unique vision and creative flair to everything he does.

The first three steps towards mastery outlined above are taken in the Focus stage (which is what we cover in this section). The final step, of adding a little of yourself, is also one of the tasks in the Mastery stage. Experiencing this kind of mastery is indescribable and connects us to infinite wisdom, power, energy and passion.

It's worth the effort.

BUT WHY WOULD I BOTHER MAKING THE SECOND TRANSITION FROM AWAKENING TO FOCUS?

Awakening is a wonderful stage to experience. In this phase our eyes are opened and we discover the true laws of cause and effect. But while this is an essential stage in the journey, if we get stuck in this stage, life can begin to lose its magic. Once we understand how we can win the game at work, with relationships, financially and physically, it is very tempting to turn everything in life into a game or a competition. As the years pass, relationships stop being an authentic exchange of two souls and instead become a competition of strategies and manipulation. At work, the politics within politics, the games within games, the deception behind the deception get to the point where you don't even know what is true any more.

The life paradigm at this stage is simple. Life is a game. At this stage, the objective of life is to win. The problem with this paradigm is that it is so two dimensional and shallow that eventually the soul, heart and mind get terribly, terribly bored.

One cause of depression is simply chronic boredom. One reason so many people have wrung out every last bit of interest in their lives is because they are only playing the game of life on one very dull level. Once they know they can play the game and win, they really must get ready to move on. To not do so will mean the guaranteed death of the real essence of who they are.

There is nothing more tragic than a mature adult 'stuck' at this level. Interaction with them brings a mixture of emotions including a sense that you are simply a pawn in their game, a sense that they are not committed in any way and an overriding gut warning that you need to be very careful. I heard this described to me by one senior executive as 'being slimed'. And it is true that whenever you have spent time with someone 'stuck' in this stage you leave the interaction feeling 'slimy'.

The key to moving to the next stage is to learn how to focus your internal energy on achieving genuine results rather than on simply winning the game. It is also about expressing the genuine and authentic essence that is really you. It's about moving from seeing peers and colleagues as the enemy and instead seeing them as worthwhile human beings who can make a powerful contribution to your objectives without your manipulation. It is also about developing honest self-insight based on unsolicited comments from colleagues who value your authentic contribution.

YOU WILL NEVER REACH YOUR FULL POTENTIAL BY YOURSELF

You will only reach your full potential if you can harness the capabilities and commitment of others — the third stage. Without this skill you will at best be a lonely island and at worst be loathed for the very things for which you should be praised.

Your ability to create, motivate and inspire teams is directly linked to how well you navigate and master your ability to focus. Do this badly and you will never really understand what people mean by teamwork.

Many of the senior teams with whom I work in the corporate sector are made up of individuals who have not navigated this stage well. The result is a group of individuals 'sort of' reporting to each other. This is not teamwork. If you ask individual team members about the value of the team, they draw a blank and instead talk about how the team really stands in the way of their own ideas and initiatives.

Failure to successfully master this third stage means that these team members are stuck in the Awakening stage and are forever sentenced to playing their sad games to a cynical audience which claps the latest tactic or manipulative comment. As tragic as this sounds, this probably sums up about two-thirds of all dysfunctional boards and senior executive teams.

THE FIRST STEP IS ALWAYS THE HARDEST

The very first step in the transition from the second to the third stage is to begin the process of becoming personally committed to being a master in a chosen field.

LET'S DO THIS THING

Take a few minutes to write down six milestones that you would like to achieve or areas of endeavor you would like to master. These areas may be as diverse as becoming an effective parent, experiencing an overseas trip or getting a promotion. It can be something that you want, something that you want to become, something that you want to own, something you want to experience, something you want to know or a role or task that you want to master.

Now select the milestone or area that will most draw on the gift given to your thinking profile. These are outlined in Appendix One. This is an ideal area of mastery to begin to focus on as you read the suggestions outlined in the following chapters.

YOUR MISSION IF YOU CHOOSE TO ACCEPT IT

The third level of development, Focus, requires you not only to acknowledge your gift, but also to focus on developing it and becoming a master in this area. At this stage you struggle and learn how to balance your own personal achievement with the contribution made by fellow team members or peers.

This stage gives you the opportunity to learn how to manage the personal impulses, selfishness and addictions that are the natural consequences of the functions or energies that your mind uses naturally. The Focus stage teaches you how to manage your internal world of feelings, emotions, thoughts and distractions.

This self-management is essential because your external world mirrors your internal world. For example, if you have low self-esteem, who is the rest of the world to disagree? If you manipulate others, they will in turn manipulate you. You can only inspire and manage others to the degree to which you can inspire and manage yourself. You can only understand others to the degree to which you understand yourself. You must master your internal world if you are to master your external world with any permanence.[1]

---

1 It is true that the selfish, manipulative and unevolved can get ahead. But it is usually only because they have a team behind them cleaning up the emotional mess they have caused and ironing out the drama they have created. And without exception the value they add will be in the application of their gift. When they are applying their area of mastery they will inspire followers once again. The problems will have emerged when they have ventured away from their area of mastery and have confused mastery with natural brilliance and have decided that being an expert in one area qualifies them in every conceivable area. These folk are locked into difficult lives of constant battle, disharmony and disappointment.

To manage yourself effectively you will require a strategy — a personal strategy that builds on your strengths, balances up your weaknesses and builds the intellectual strength and discipline required by a master.

MEET THE MOST POWERFUL STRATEGIST OF ALL TIME

With this in mind, I would like to introduce you to the greatest strategist of all time. He is the master's mentor and the great-great-great-great-grandfather of all strategic thinkers — the Supreme Chinese Warlord and master strategist, Sun-Tzu. If you apply the strategies this warlord can give you about managing yourself you will achieve true mastery in a fraction of the time it would take you to achieve it by trial and error.

These are some words inspired by Thomas Cleary, one of the principal translators of Sun-Tzu:

SUN-TZU WAS A BRILLIANT STRATEGIST WHO CAN HELP YOU FIGHT THE GOOD FIGHT

The Art of War

Written 2600 years ago, Sun-Tzu's *The Art of War* remains one of the most well-respected and influential books of strategy in the twenty-first century. Modern Eastern politicians and executives alike have studied it as intensely as military leaders and strategists for nearly three millennia.

Virtually overnight, post-war Japan transformed its feudal culture to effective corporate and political cultures through applying strategies from this ancient classic. You could easily argue that this example perfectly demonstrates the power of Sun-Tzu's dictum that to win without fighting works best. Having the objective of invincibility, *The Art of War* is the perfect study for corporations to win in an increasingly competitive marketplace. Its core teaching is this: to win without battle, and it is equally applicable to interpersonal, interorganizational and international conflicts, competition and strategy within politics, corporations and the military. The insight available through this book is an unassailable strength through the understanding of the politics, psychology and mechanics of conflict.

The *Art of War's* derived power is tempered by a profound humanism undercurrent giving the book a distinctly Taoist flavor. This book of war is also one of peace. Above all, it is a fundamental tool for dealing with conflict, strategy and resolution.

But how can the writings of Sun-Tzu help you to become a master? The answer lies in wisdom that is known by every spiritual movement, psychologist and parent in the world and that is that the only person who stops you from becoming a master is *yourself*. You stand in the way of your own success. Let me explain.

The three functions that your mind naturally accesses are your strengths. These functions represent your identity as you have come to know and love yourself. But look at those other three functions that are not nearly so familiar. This unfamiliar 'other' personality is underdeveloped. For example, if you naturally access your C1 lateral thinking, P1 logic and I1 information functions, your self-identity will be built around the C1, P1, I1 Analyzer (Master) personality. This familiar character will fall within your self-identity comfort zone. But not nearly as familiar are the functions that you don't naturally access. In this case these would be the C2, P2 and I2 functions (the Coach personality). This character that sits unacknowledged in your mind is your Mirror.

BARBARA'S MIRROR RAN HER LIFE!

One of the best personal employees I've ever had the pleasure to work with, Barbara, once said to me, 'I keep going to succeed, but just when I'm about to start doing really well, someone in my head says, What on earth do you think you're doing? You can't do that. What's a little country girl like you doing trying to succeed in the big city?' Where did that voice come from?

It came from that other unfamiliar and underdeveloped part of Barbara called her Mirror. To move forward, Barbara had to learn how to apply the strategies and discipline of Sun-Tzu to put her true Master back in the driving seat of her life.

Like Barbara, we all have two sides to our character. One side is familiar and gifted and the other (our Mirror) is unfamiliar and undeveloped.

The Art of War suggests that while true personal power is only achieved when these opposites are integrated (at the fifth level of development which is called Integration), the period of time before this, the first four levels of development, is flat out internal war.

Have you ever noticed that as you focus on trying to achieve, your underdeveloped Mirror often speaks louder than your true Master does? This self-sabotage is powerful and holds us all back from being the masters we were born to become.

So as it turns out, we are often our own worst enemies.

To succeed we must form an alliance with our Mirror. Believe me, to do this you have to be incredibly focused. Your Mirror wakes up with you every day and will put forward any number of reasons why you can't possibly succeed. He or she experiences your successes and failures and knows your best kept secrets. He or she says the things to you that no one else would be game to say.

EXPLORING THE MASTER AND MIRROR

I first met Maria when she was in her early twenties. Thin, intelligent and charming, she wore the latest fashion with style and grace. She could keep her own in academic discussions and was bright enough to have had missed a year of school and attended university a year early. She was balanced, attentive and successful ... or so it seemed.

But there was another side of Maria. With a little alcohol or stress Maria would change from being logical and controlled into being vindictive and aggressive – verbally attacking people, especially those she loved, destroying prized possessions and even physically attacking her partner. When the damage had been done Maria would flip back to her old self and apologize and try to clean up the mess. It was as if Maria had two completely different personalities, and it was as if each of these personalities was completely independent with opposite positions on virtually everything. Maria was confused. She knew that she had to do something about the situation if she was to keep her husband and her family. Until recently scientists would have been at a loss to know what was creating this apparent split personality but now new research may be able to give us some answers.

Maria's situation might seem extreme but the idea of each of us being made up of two autonomous personalities isn't unique to Maria and it isn't new.

The ancient Central American Indians, the Maya Lenca, talk about each of us having two distinct personalities: a Master or Hero personality and a Mirror. Jung's concept of individuation requires us to integrate the rejected side of ourselves, which he describes as our shadow. Many Eastern and Middle Eastern philosophies emphasize the importance of integrating the Yin and the Yang – the two opposite parts of us.

But while the concept is clear, the application of the concept into our daily lives is a little less accessible. In the past ten years excellent research has been conducted in this area, firstly to identify the nature of the two personalities and then to discover how they impact on our lives.

Perhaps some of the best research in this area has been conducted by Frederic Schiffer MD, a US-based psychiatrist and researcher. His groundbreaking work into dual-brain psychology published in his book *Of Two Minds* by Simon and Schuster in 1998, documents the existence of two distinct personalities in all of us regardless of our mental and emotional health, and the impact on our life of having these two distinct personalities. He details case after case where, like Maria, individuals of all

Personal Focus

different personalities, backgrounds, education levels and emotional maturity go through a process of discovering and beginning the process of integrating the two personalities that reside within them. The stories are both surprising and inspiring. In his own words;

*The aim of dual-brain therapy [**working with your Mirror - my words**] is to mend the archaic, destructive ideas and emotions of the mind on the troubled side [**Mirror**] to teach it that it is safer and more valuable than it learned during some traumatic experiences, and to help it appropriately grieve and come to terms with its actual losses and disappointments so that it can appreciate its abundant gains — to teach patients how to recognize and listen for the mind in their troubled hemisphere, and then how to speak to it — out loud! I show patients also how to strengthen their more mature minds [**Master**] and, most importantly, how to improve the relationship between the two.*

While the focus of Schiffer's work was on the process of discovering the identity, behaviors and emotions associated with both personalities, the NeuroPower Framework allows users immediate access and insight into both their Master and Mirror profiles and outlines the process for healing and integrating them for personal growth, success, balance and creativity.

When I work with large corporations wanting to increase the level of output from their employees I explain the interaction between the Master and Mirror using a matrix that plots the current level of Master and Mirror satisfaction. This in turn gives us a broad idea of our current level of capacity. All the motivation and will in the world does not help us achieve our personal or corporate objectives if we do not have the personal capacity to achieve them.

THE ROLE OF THE MASTER (WHAT YOU WANT)

The Master controls our self-identity (who we think we are), our language, our image (how we see ourselves) and our wish list (our wants). In the West we are all employed for the value we bring to the marketplace – that is, the skills, capabilities and attitudes of our Master. The Master is our hero, able to achieve almost any task it is given. If our Master is getting what it wants, it is enthusiastic and talks highly of the situation. Society is only interested in our Master.

THE ROLE OF THE MIRROR (WHAT YOU NEED)

Our Mirror, however, expresses itself through our behavior. If our Mirror is getting what it needs, we stay; if not, we leave. Our Mirror, regardless of our Master's effort to keep it in the closet, longs for expression and takes any opportunity to make itself heard.

Personal Focus

HOW EMPOWERED IS YOUR MASTER? (WHAT YOU WANT)

To clarify what you want, start the exercise by focusing on your Master. What is your Master's leadership style? Does your current situation enable you to use this leadership style? Score out of 10 the degree to which the situation (job, task or relationship) enables your Master to develop your leadership style, take risks and apply its knowledge.

HOW SATISFIED IS YOUR MIRROR? (WHAT YOU NEED)

Now score out of 10 the degree to which the situation (job, task or relationship) addresses the specific focus of attention for your Mirror. For example, as a Change Agent your Energizer is looking for tangible rewards, clear recognition, and the ability to make an immediate difference and to have some fun.

When you have a score out of 10 for both your Master (Want) and Mirror (Need) multiply them for a 'best guess' figure, which represents your current capacity in percentage terms.

The intersection of our scores will place us into one of the matrix's four quadrants; trapped incompetent, short-term performers, transient moaners or long-term performers. An example of how this 'best guess' plotting works is detailed in Appendix Three, as is an in-depth explanation of the matrix's four quadrants.

APPLYING THE INSIGHT FROM THE CAPACITY MATRIX AT WORK

Leaders, managers and supervisors find this framework provides them with a very powerful way to increase the capacity of their workforce by attending to their employees' wants (which they can articulate) and their employees' needs (which they cannot articulate because their Mirror cannot speak).

APPLYING THE INSIGHT FROM THE CAPACITY MATRIX IN LIFE

This method of analysis also holds true for friendships, marriages, partnerships, projects and hobbies – any activity requiring your focus. For example, in your marriage you could be a short-term moaner or in a friendship you may be a trapped incompetent.

In my experience, many leaders, managers and high performing individuals in all walks of life report that understanding their Master and Mirror was an important plank to achieving personal performance, satisfaction and stability.

Earlier I introduced Maria's situation. With an understanding of her Master (in her case a Change Agent) and her Mirror (in her case an Energizer) the stage is set to

Personal Focus

explore what her Energizer is needing but not getting. If the issue is the relationship, the Energizer is kept carefully under wraps until the controlling Change Agent is drunk. Only then can the Energizer come out of hiding and express the frustration of not getting the praise, excitement, recognition, intensity and reward it wants. An understanding of the Master and Mirror enabled focused exploration of these issues, which lay below the conscious mind of the Change Agent.

Each of us works very hard to carefully craft an image that aligns with our ideal selves. This image is our Master leadership style. This Master tries to control every aspect of the way we represent ourselves to the world. This Master also creates a pressure cooker for our Mirror who is trapped in our skin and just waiting for the Master to lose control. This internal battle causes many of the internal conflicts we all feel. This internal conflict often spills over into the outside world in spontaneous outbursts or uncontrollable behavior. We are employed for the skills of our Master – we get fired for the behavior of our Mirror. We get married for the better – the worse is often the Mirror.

To understand personality, it is absolutely critical to understand the role both the Mirror and Master play, and to personally and intimately know both characters. This takes good mirroring from friends, family and colleagues and requires the individual to develop the ability to self-observe.

One of the most frustrating and irritating aspects of the Mirror is that while everyone else in the world seems to be able to see your Mirror, at first you often won't be able to see it yourself.

I am sometimes employed to work with dysfunctional boards where Mirrors are dominating proceedings. When I can see that the individuals' Masters are brilliant and mature but the Mirror is less mature and holding court, I sometimes video the session for later viewing. The looks on the faces of the Masters when I show them the Mirror are of complete disgust. They have no idea that they personally behave the way they do. Their Master has no visibility of their Mirror. And without the video they simply will not believe the feedback from associates. They have to see it to believe it.

APPLICATION: So what can we do?

The seven steps to effectively working with your Master and your Mirror

1. Observe the Mirror in action – how old is your Mirror?

The first step is to recognize, observe and experience the Mirror. If the Mirror is a child it will have a tendency to awfulize and catastrophize events and see the worst in everything and everyone. It does this because it expects the old situation to be repeated and to create certainty. This often becomes a self-fulfilling prophecy.

2. Create an outlet for your Mirror and open negotiations

If you are high in I1 (Analyzers, Planners, Energizers and Crusaders), your Mirror will express itself through conversation with a trusted friend, family member or counsellor. If you are high in I2 (Coaches, Diplomats, Change Agents and Innovators), your Mirror will express itself through the written word. (Automatic writing and personal journals are very powerful.) The key is to express the Mirror's point of view and then have the Master seriously assess it and either dismiss it or integrate it into its position. For all Mirrors a powerful technique is to have the Master or counsellor talk directly to the Mirror with explicit instructions about how the Mirror must behave.

3. Strengthen your Master

Your Master is your own internal hero. This hero needs to be strengthened into being a healthy leader who can guide and parent your Mirror. The Master needs to be strong enough to listen to the Mirror's concerns and emotional troubles without being dragged down into them.

To be effective the Master needs to be more grounded, more evolved, more responsible and less impulsive. Achieving this requires that the Master receive support, encouragement and training. Ironically the Master will only be at its strongest when its adult Mirror joins it. Our true strength is only achieved when the Master has worked with the Mirror and the two work as a team.

4. Challenge the Mirror's assumptions

The Mirror is absolutely convinced that whatever trauma it has received will be repeated. When this doesn't happen the Mirror becomes even more anxious, knowing that the inevitable has simply been delayed and probably amplified (an accumulation of dammed-up disaster is building).

The Master must carefully and systematically assess if the Mirror has a good point or not. When healthy, the Mirror is a powerful and insightful ally that helps us make powerful and insightful decisions. The job of the Master is to determine if the Mirror is talking truth or gibberish.

5. Talk to your Mirror

To convince your Mirror to change is no different than persuading someone else to change – your Master, counsellor or therapist will need to use the same techniques. But successful persuasion is based more on the credibility of the persuader than the strength of the argument. The Master must be patient, polite, gentle and caring. The Master must be able to convince the Mirror that it cares, it understands and it can cope.

6. Manage the relationship between the two characters

Your Mirror and your Master have a special relationship, which, like all relationships, follows some principles. (This internal relationship is often reproduced externally with partners, family and friends.)

> *a. Firstly, they influence each other.* If we cannot see that, it is because we have not developed the ability to observe the Mirror in action. When we come out of discussions, for example, wondering why we said some things that we don't even believe – the Mirror has shown itself. We need to develop very keen insight into the Mirror, ways for it to be valued and to express itself so that it doesn't need to show up in uncontrollable outbursts.

> *b. Secondly, we need to look at the nature of the Master/Mirror relationship and determine where it sits in the continuum of cooperation-antagonism, dominance-submission, parent-child and success-failure.* What you want is a loving and trusting relationship between the two which might start as parent (Master) and child (Mirror) but which moves

towards a collegial relationship of mutual understanding and respect.

c. Thirdly, the nature of the relationship will be influenced by the relative power of the Master and the Mirror. It is the job of the Master to ensure that it keeps ultimate control regardless of the payoffs. The Master is the hero not the victim or the paranoid Mirror.

7. Manage your life so that the Master gets what it wants and the Mirror what it needs

Your Master wants challenges, risk-taking to expand its comfort zone, new ideas, education, courses and 'great big hairy audacious goals'. This needs to be balanced with your Mirror that needs to be nurtured, persuaded into any change and reassured at every step of the way. The task of the individual is to balance the activity of life so that both characters are catered for rather than wildly swinging from satisfying one to satisfying the other with one always unhappy and offside and ready to ambush the other.

Ultimately we want a constructive adult relationship based on mutual respect and harmony that can integrate the two opposing wisdoms in such a way that we get Integrity with Courage, Diplomacy with Honor, Inspiration with Wisdom and Enthusiasm with Discernment.

THE LAW OF AVERAGES

In my experience, regardless of what you do, things seem to go well about one in every ten times. One time out of ten you will succeed for no given reason — you just happen to succeed. It's almost as if the universe wants to say, 'Remember this? This is success.'

Statistically that means that on average if you try ten times a day, odds are you will succeed at least once. It also means that you have to try fifty times a week to win once a day. This strategy is a passive 'Fire, Ready, Aim!' strategy.

When we resort to this life strategy we usually decide that 'There's nothing we can do to improve our chances' and sooner or later we decide that success is just too hard! It is at this point that we close our minds and say goodbye to our dreams and aspirations and become sad and lonely disconnected souls in a sea of like-minded mediocrity. Our Mirror takes control and it's all down hill from there.

SUN-TZU'S PREPARATION PHASE

Insight is the first step and you already have that!

Sun-Tzu says the first preparation you need to do is, 'Know yourself (your Master), know your enemy (your Mirror) — 100 battles, 100 victories.' He says that if you know yourself and apply the right strategy, the odds of success rise from 10 per cent to 100 per cent!

Our personal wars are won or lost according to the quality of insight we have at hand. Sun-Tzu's term was 'the estimates'.

This 'estimates phase' has been conducted for you already by the Quest profiler. Using this tool, you have carried out a thorough audit of your greatest assets (your mind, spirit and soul). With this information you have successfully traversed the first transition from Oblivion to Awakening. You are aware of your strengths and weaknesses and have spent time learning how to make the most of your strengths and balancing up your weaknesses.

You also know your universal gift, which in Celtic mythology is like your own Excalibur sword. You will use this gift to cut down your barriers to success and put yourself back in touch with why you are on this mysterious planet.

So far, you are travelling well. If you have completed the profiler and know your universal gift, give yourself a tick! You are now ready to take Sun-Tzu's next piece of advice.

Step Two: Without vision, the people perish (proverbs)

Sun-Tzu emphasizes that you must have an incredibly clear vision of where you are headed and know how this vision connects to your day-to-day work. It is impossible to *focus* if your vision is a *blur*.

This vision needs to be a clear image in your mind's eye of what you are here on earth to do. To achieve this clarity, some people participate in a 'vision quest', where they sit in nature for a day or two, and ponder the question, 'What on earth am I doing?' or as Napoleon Hill would say, 'What's my major, definite purpose?'

While using the mind's vision or C2 function is natural for about 25 per cent of the population (in fact they probably dream up so many visions that their challenge is to select just one and stick with it), what about those of us who do not naturally access our C2 function?

Well, here are three practical exercises to get the C2 unblocked.

Personal Focus

Creative Vision Hint No. 1: Create a dream board

Take a large piece of cardboard and a pile of magazines, then cut out and paste on your dream board any images or photos from the magazine that picture something you would like to do, be or have. This process is a little like an imagination 'jogger' or vision oracle. Every time you see this board it will refocus you on your long-term vision.

Creative Vision Hint No. 2: Ask a visionary

If you are low in the C2 vision function, you may prefer to talk to someone who's high in vision. Explain that you are looking for a personal vision and you wondered if they could give you some ideas. When they describe a vision that resonates with you, write it down and imagine it along with them. You don't have to be high in C2 to be able to adopt a clear picture of the future that appeals to you.

Creative Vision Hint No. 3: Let yourself dream

Another suggestion is to create time to let yourself dream about how life could be. The best time to dream is after 11 o'clock at night. When you let yourself dream, imagine living, doing or owning your dream. Feel what it's like; smell what it's like. Daydream as if you are really there. Give yourself permission to use your imagination and really live the experience in your mind and heart.

If you really want to build the power of your imagination read *Awaken the Giant Within*; Anthony Robbins uses some very powerful Neuro-Linguistic Programming (NLP) techniques which will help you dream like a pro.

The key here is to give yourself permission to use your imagination or vision to imagine various options for your future. Notice how you feel when you are doing this. The objective is to keep going until you find something that inspires, motivates and captures your passion. Don't assume that the first idea that comes into your mind is the best one. Sometimes it may take you three months of daydreaming for you to stumble across your life purpose!

Remember that the C2 function is not instantly airborne. It takes time to take off and time to land. That's why the Maya Lenca people from Central America call this function or energy 'Eagle energy'. So don't try to do the exercise in ten minutes — leave yourself at least an hour and preferably two or three so that you can relax into the stream of ideas and thoughts.

Daydreaming is an art form practised by today's leaders to inspire tomorrow's followers.

Step Three: Set and focus on your goals

This is the shortest paragraph on goal setting ever written.

Once you've focused your vision, your next step is to break this broad life vision into goals.

Your goals should be specific, measurable, ambitious, realistic and tangible (SMART). When your goals are set following this formula they are smart. Remember that each of us has been given exactly the same amount of time. The difference between being highly effective and just wasting your allocation of time is what we do with it.

The key is to focus on what you want to be, have or become, and not waste your time and effort on anything else. This is one of the major points of difference between those who break through and become masters and those who are left forever striving. Learn how to quieten your mind so that you can focus on just one task at a time.

I work with one of Australia's greatest business strategists, Susan Nixon. I have seen her create clear paths forward for some of Australia's largest public and private companies. If I present her with a document for her to look through she has an extraordinary ability to block her mind of absolutely everything and superfocus on the one task she has selected to complete. In that time she trains 100 per cent of her intellectual capacity and energy on one project with astounding results.

In his book *The Spiritual Path to Complete Fulfilment*, Philip Harris suggests that one-pointedness is when one's mind is held steadily on a given task or topic for a length of time (pp 54–55).

He adds that when stimulation and attention from outside the mind are reduced the mind becomes clearer, sharper and steadier. This state, also known as 'optimum experience' or 'flow', is the state that becomes second nature to the unconscious competent master.

When Einstein said that we only use around 10 per cent of our brainpower, he was referring to our inability to focus or concentrate. I work with many senior executives who are so busy multi-tasking, with dozens of balls in the air, that they are unable to do anything well.

Your ability to achieve your goals is directly proportional to your ability to narrow your focus and concentrate all your intellectual and personal energy by aligning your heart, mind and soul.

Only when you can FOCUS every ounce of power and intellectual ability will you start to see your SMART goals materialising. Wimp out on this and as the old saying warns, **you will be a Jack of all trades but master of none.**

Practical exercises to help you develop your ability to focus are clearly outlined in Pier Tsui-Po's excellent book called *Super Focusing*.

Chapter 20 Checklist

1. Focus on clarifying your gift in life. How do you currently use this gift in your life?
2. Write down six milestones or objectives you would like to achieve. Make absolutely sure you want these things because if you apply the principles outlined in this book, you will achieve them.
3. Identify your alter ego or Mirror character. What is its characteristics? Ask your partner or close friends if they have ever seen this character in you, and what it is like.
4. Write down the three things that stand in the way of you achieving your objectives, and decide if you are willing to give these things up or fight them to achieve your objectives. When you complete this exercise you have defined the battleground.
5. Re-examine your strengths and weaknesses – be realistic about your failings and your potential.
6. Clearly visualize your objectives. See them, feel them, experience them so that they become real to you – as real as your current reality. Try creating a dream board, asking a visionary and letting yourself dream.
7. Focus your goals by making them SMART, that is, Specific, Measurable, Ambitious, Realistic and Tangible.

Personal Focus

Conviction is worthless unless it is converted into conduct.
Thomas Carlyle

Personal Focus

Chapter 21

O: Operationalize Your Attributes

DEVELOP YOUR PERSONAL CODE OF CONDUCT

Once you have specific goals that you wish to achieve, the next step is to clarify your personal code of conduct. These are the behaviors that you want to encourage in your life. Those with a loose code of conduct have an inability to effectively manage their own behavior and the results of that behavior. Instead, they tend to 'make it up as they go along' and as a result end up spending a lifetime tidying up the confusion they have created both in their own minds and in the minds of the people with whom they work.

These are your life principles or what Steven Covey would call your 'true north'. Without a behavior compass which can face you true north, you can very quickly get lost in life and tossed around in the undercurrents of other people's agendas and objectives.

As the saying goes, 'If you are not achieving your own objectives, you are probably achieving somebody else's'.

What you do speaks so loudly,
that I cannot hear what you are saying

The Greek philosopher Epictetus believed our code of conduct should particularly focus on the four areas over which we have personal control, namely:

- Our judgement and opinions
- Our desires
- The things we are attracted to and move towards, and
- The things that we dislike that we move away from.

I usually encourage people to distil their code of conduct down to six fundamental behaviors. Of course, this task becomes much easier when you are aware of your strengths, weaknesses and universal gift.

Enacting these behaviors is absolutely essential to developing a solid character which people can trust and which achieves results. It is also an area that has been

Personal Focus

widely researched by those wanting to quantify key behaviors demonstrated by effective leaders. As discussed earlier, the path to becoming a powerful leader of others is predicated by becoming a powerful leader of yourself.

The following pages are a composite list of all the attributes that have been identified by the different authors as important leadership behaviors. Choose just six key behaviors or attributes from this list. These are the behaviors on which I suggest you focus during the next three months.

The following table was adapted from one compiled by Dave Ulrich, Jack Zenger and Norm Smallwood in the book *Results Based Leadership* (pp8 – 13) ©1999 President and Fellows of Harvard College.

Personal Focus

Dimensions	Exemplar Behaviors or Actions To what extent do I do the following?
SET DIRECTION	
Appreciate external possibilities	• Contemplate life and perceive new possibilities.[a] • Have the capabilities to form networks beyond your comfort zone.[b] • Commit personal resources to improve your productivity. • Consistently provide clear personal direction. • Demonstrate vigorous environmental concern.
Orientate towards the future	• Show a strong passion in creating a vision.[c] • Communicate tangible vision, values and strategy.[d] • Develop a pathfinding mission.[e] • Circumscribe and act on your personal core values.[f] • Act from a set of inspiring core values and beliefs.[g] • Adopt a strategic mindset. • Lay hold of the future through assessing it, technology, foresight, conceptual flexibility, vision and strategic alignment, and by enhancing your personal image.

a. Kanter, R., 'World-Class Leaders: The Power of Partnering' in The Leader of the Future, ed. Frances Hesselbein, Marshall Goldsmith, and Richard Beckhard (San Francisco: Jossey-Bass, 1995), pp89–98.
b. Ibid.
c. Schein, E., 'Leadership and Organizational Culture' in The Leader of the Future, Hesselbein, Goldsmith and Beckhard, pp59–70.
d. Yeung and Ready, 'Developing Leadership Capabilities of Global Corporations'
e. Covey, S., 'Three Roles of the Leader in the New Paradigm' in The Leader of the Future, Hesselbein, Goldsmith, and Beckhard, pp149–160.
f. Fitz-enz, J., survey, Saratoga Institute, 1997
g. Heskett and Schlesinger, 'Leaders Who Shape and Keep Performance-Oriented Culture' in The Leader of the Future, Hesselbein, Goldsmith, and Beckhard, pp111–120.

Personal Focus

Dimensions	Exemplar Behaviors or Actions To what extent do I do the following?
SET DIRECTION (CONT.)	
Transform vision into action	• Bring into line performance with the vision.[h] • Develop and communicate a shared vision.[i] • Bring others on board to attain a future outcome. • Change strategy into results. • Motivate a common purpose. • Develop a climate suitable for success.
MOBILIZE INDIVIDUAL COMMITMENT	
Build collaborative relationships	• Have a love for others. • Have the capacity to be independent, but also to work with others.[j] • Be able to offer support and encouragement more than just judgement, criticism and evaluation.[k] • Encourage collaboration by promoting mutual goals and enhancing trust.[l]
Share authority and control	• Show a willingness and capacity to share authority and control.[m] • Listen to others more than tell them.[n] • Have a willingness and capacity to include others and encourage participation.[o] • Wield authority with dignity.[p]

h. Blanchard, K., 'Turning the Organizational Pyramid Upside Down' in The Leader of the Future, Hesselbein, Goldsmith, and Beckhard, pp81–88.
i. Kouzes, J., and Posner, B., The Leadership Challenge: How to Keep Getting Extraordinary Things Done in Organizations (San Francisco: Jossey-Bass, 1995).
j. Handy, C., 'The New Language of Organizing and Its Implications for Leaders' in The Leader of the Future, Hesselbein, Goldsmith, and Beckhard, pp3–10.
k. Blanchard, K., 'Turning the Organizational Pyramid Upside Down' in The Leader of the Future, Hesselbein, Goldsmith, and Beckhard,
l. Kouzes, J., and Posner, B., The Leadership Challenge: How to Keep Getting Extraordinary Things Done in Organizations (San Francisco: Jossey-Bass, 1995)
m. Schein, E., 'Leadership and Organizational Culture' in The Leader of the Future, Hesselbein, Goldsmith and Beckhard.
n. Heskett and Schlesinger, 'Leaders Who Shape and Keep Performance-Oriented Culture' in The Leader of the Future, Hesselbein, Goldsmith, and Beckhard
o. Schein, E., 'Leadership and Organizational Culture' in The Leader of the Future, Hesselbein, Goldsmith and Beckhard.
p. Heskett and Schlesinger, 'Leaders Who Shape and Keep Performance-Oriented Culture'

Personal Focus

Exemplar Behaviors or Actions	
Dimensions	**To what extent do I do the following?**
MOBILIZE INDIVIDUAL COMMITMENT (CONT.)	
Share authority and control (cont.)	• Empower and engage others.[q] • Encourage others to do their best.[r] • Empower others through sharing authority and information.[s] • Adopt a series of different approaches in order to get the best out of everyone. • Create opportunities for people to contribute their greatest personal abilities on behalf of the team.
Manage concentration	• Manage your energy and change other people's physical state.[t] • Articulate yourself to touch the hearts of others.[u] • Create emotions through engendering...[v] – Confidence in scared people. – Confidence in self-doubting people. – Activity where there has been hesitancy. – Strength where there has been weakness. – Capability where there was ineptness. – Courage where there was cowardice. – Optimism where there was pessimism. – Conviction where there was equivocating.
ENGENDER ORGANIZATIONAL CAPABILITY	
Develop infrastructure	• Exhibit formal leadership skills of integrating, planning activities of different projects, and resourcing them all. • Develop ad hoc leadership cadres as required within each project.[w]

q. Covey, S., 'Three Roles of the Leader in the New Paradigm' in The Leader of the Future, Hesselbein, Goldsmith, and Beckhard.
r. Yeung and Ready, 'Developing Leadership Capabilities of Global Corporations'
s. Kouzes, J., and Posner, B., The Leadership Challenge: How to Keep Getting Extraordinary Things Done in Organizations (San Francisco: Jossey-Bass, 1995).
t. Blanchard, K., 'Turning the Organizational Pyramid Upside Down' in The Leader of the Future, Hesselbein, Goldsmith, and Beckhard,
u. Heskett and Schlesinger, 'Leaders Who Shape and Keep Performance-Oriented Culture' in The Leader of the Future, Hesselbein, Goldsmith, and Beckhard
v. Bardwick, J., 'Peacetime Management and Wartime Leadership' in The Leader of the Future, Hesselbein, Goldsmith, and Beckhard, pp131–140.
w. Bridges, W., 'Leading the De-Jobbed Organizations' in The Leader of the Future, Hesselbein, Goldsmith, and Beckhard, pp11–18.

Dimensions	To what extent do I do the following?
ENGENDER ORGANIZATIONAL CAPABILITY (CONT.)	
Develop infrastructure (cont.)	• Bring into line and ensure the congruence between desired future and strategy.[x] • Actively communicate a wide range of information to those participating in bringing out my vision. • Provide encouragement and resources required for continuous improvement.[y] • Create enthusiastic support for my goals.
Use diversity as a source of leverage	• Exhibit tolerance of diversity in performance, values and standards. • Find the strength of team members as a source of strength and not fear.[aa] • Integrate the abilities and perspectives of different cultures, sectors and disciplines. • Effectively resolve conflict and focus on common cause.[bb] • Advocate partnering and collaboration as the optimal modes of behavior.[cc] • Use people completely, regardless of their race, gender, ethnic origin or culture.
Arrange teams	• Develop self-managing project teams.[dd] • Use different opinions and ideas to cross-fertilize and bring out the best from one another.[ee] • Choose the most talented individuals available. • Provide specific and frequent feedback that assists in improving team performance. • Develop the team even during a period of financial loss.

x. Covey, S., 'Three Roles of the Leader in the New Paradigm' in The Leader of the Future, Hesselbein, Goldsmith, and Beckhard,
y. Fitz-enz, J., survey, Saratoga Institute, 1997
aa. Drucker, P. F., 'Toward the New Organization,' Leader to Leader 2, no. 3 (1997): pp6–8.
bb. Kanter, R., 'World-Class Leaders: The Power of Partnering'
cc. Fitz-enz, J., survey, Saratoga Institute, 1997
dd. Bridges, 'Leading the De-Jobbed Organization'
ee. Kanter, R., 'World-Class Leaders: The Power of Partnering' in The Leader of the Future, ed. Frances Hesselbein, Marshall Goldsmith, and Richard Beckhard (San Francisco: Jossey-Bass, 1995),

Dimensions	To what extent do I do the following?
ENGENDER ORGANIZATIONAL CAPABILITY (CONT.)	
Create human resource systems	• Maintain the organizational culture. • Create your desired culture. • Have the abilities to critically assess cultural assumptions.[ff] • Act as an initiator of cultural change.[gg] • Consciously contribute to a proactive and constructive work culture.[hh]
Assist change occurring	• Make change occur and operate as a change agent in your own life.[ii] • Show the emotional strength required to manage the anxiety arising from change.[jj] • Act as a catalyst and manager of strategic change.[kk] • Look for opportunities by confronting and challenging the status quo. • Innovatively approach the status quo. • Experiment with risky approaches. • Learn from mistakes and successes.[ll] • Continuously try to find simpler ways to realize objectives. • Seek opportunities contained within change rather than looking for excuses to avoid change. • Start the change process rather than responding to external pressures for it. • Rigorously question the status quo. • Utilize the opinions and ideas of other people to change.

ff. Schein, E., 'Leadership and Organizational Culture' in The Leader of the Future, Hesselbein, Goldsmith and Beckhard,
gg. Yeung and Ready, 'Developing Leadership Capabilities of Global Corporations'
hh. Fitz-enz, J., survey, Saratoga Institute, 1997
ii. Schein, E., 'Leadership and Organizational Culture' in The Leader of the Future, Hesselbein, Goldsmith and Beckhard,
jj. Ibid.
kk. Yeung and Ready, 'Developing Leadership Capabilities of Global Corporations'
ll. Kouzes, J., and Posner, B., The Leadership Challenge: How to Keep Getting Extraordinary Things Done in Organizations (San Francisco: Jossey-Bass, 1995).

Personal Focus

Dimensions	To what extent do I do the following?
DEMONSTRATE PERSONAL CHARACTER	
Practise what it is that you preach	• Live the values of your personal code of conduct.[mm] • Lead others by example.
Have and develop a positive self-image	• Create a strong personal belief: exhibit self-confidence with humility.[oo] • Show high levels of perception and insight into the world and into interpersonal relationships and teamwork. • Show high levels of motivation to enable other group members to move through the pain of learning and change.[pp]
Have mental ability and personal charisma	• Maintain an open mind and extend yourself to others. • Be open to information from outside the current framework. • Vision new opportunities.[qq] • Look for new chances to learn. • Maintain integrity. • Develop a broad base of knowledge. • Develop insight by looking at things from different angles. • Approach mistakes as learning opportunities. • Stay receptive of criticism. • Maintain the ability to develop self-knowledge – try to process problems in new ways and attempt new things.[rr] • Face the challenge of improving yourself. • Deal appropriately with difficult, ambitious and contradictory circumstances. • Recommend consideration of counterintuitive alternatives.

mm. Heskett and Schlesinger, 'Leaders Who Shape and Keep Performance-Oriented Culture' in The Leader of the Future, Hesselbein, Goldsmith, and Beckhard
nn. Drucker, P. F., 'Toward the New Organization,' Leader to Leader 2, no. 3 (1997)
oo. Handy, C., 'The New Language of Organizing and Its Implications for Leaders' in The Leader of the Future, Hesselbein, Goldsmith, and Beckhard
pp. Schein, E., 'Leadership and Organizational Culture' in The Leader of the Future, Hesselbein, Goldsmith and Beckhard.
qq. Kanter, R., 'World-Class Leaders: The Power of Partnering' in The Leader of the Future, ed. Frances Hesselbein, Marshall Goldsmith, and Richard Beckhard (San Francisco: Jossey-Bass, 1995),
rr. Lombardo, M., and Eichinger, R., 'Learning Agility' working paper, Lominger, Minneapolis, 1997.

Once you have selected the six most important behaviors you intend to enact in your life you have only half finished the exercise! Your next task is to think through what the results of these behaviors will be and link them to the key objectives you have set yourself. For example, one of your selected behaviors might be to *focus my attention on my vision and keep the end in mind **so that*** I can reduce my wasted time and have the shed built by September. Add this 'so that' part of the statement to your selected attribute so that you can create very clear cause and effect statements with results that can be measured.

If you select a behavior for the sake of it that has no 'so that' result, you must drop the behavior because there is no point in having it on your list. You only want behaviors that are linked to results. This is because your purpose in all this is to achieve your objectives. If you simply select attributes or behaviors that are nice, while you may wind up a nice person you will probably not be a focused person who is systematically achieving their set objectives.

During the Focus stage of your life you need to learn how to be both a person of character and a yielder of great results.

The other way to benefit from this exercise is to list your six key objectives and link them with key attributes or behaviors with the words 'because of'. For example: I will have an excellent relationship with my son (result) ***because of*** my commitment to listen to him and spend at least four uninterrupted hours with him a week (attribute/behavior). I use this same exercise with boards and organizations wanting to develop their organizational culture. Without this link to results, desired organizational cultures can be inspiring and enjoyable places to work that don't achieve the set objectives and often meet financial ruin!

As an individual you have too little time and energy to be wasting it by focusing on behavior that is not aligned to an objective.

YOU MUST NOW LEARN HOW TO MANAGE YOUR ENERGY

Your personal energy is your most precious resource. If your life vision, goals and code of conduct are congruent or in alignment an amazing thing will happen. You will experience an explosion of internal energy.

Every misalignment blocks your personal energy and enthusiasm. When and where you are going, what you want and what you do don't line up, you can expect to be constantly exhausted and quickly disheartened by obstacles.

Instead, follow the advice of a 2600-year-old warlord (Sun-Tzu) and be proactive by spending the extra time to bring these three areas of your life into alignment.

Develop the discipline to spend the right amount of energy on the right things.

- Spend 30 per cent of your time on refining and updating your vision, code of conduct and goals;
- Spend about 30 per cent of your time doing the action that you've planned in your strategy (this is strategic activity);
- Spend about 30 per cent of your time doing life's housework: eating, sleeping and earning a living;
- Then you can spend the last 10 per cent of your time on just being, because at the end of the day, you are a human being, not a human doing.

This focus on alignment is the foundation of personal energy. If you are unsure if you are in alignment in these three areas ask someone with a C2, P1, I2 profile (the Change Agent). Their gift is to see alignment, or lack thereof in an instant. Their diagnosis is often brutal but always accurate.

The alignment of these three areas magnifies energy. Internal synchronicity is very powerful, but it is only as strong as its weakest link. If, for example, you have a clear personal vision, but your code of conduct is murky, there's a link in your chain missing and, therefore, an energy blockage. If your code of conduct and your vision are clear but you don't have specific goals, your energy will be blocked.

Think of a time in your life when you seemed to have boundless energy and I bet you had these three areas totally aligned and you felt as if you were able to draw pure energy straight from heaven (when you draw on heaven's energy you feel clearheaded, calm, optimistic, grounded and unstoppable).

Chapter 21 Checklist

1. Look at the Exemplar Behaviors or Actions tables and select six attributes or behaviors that will directly contribute to achieving your objectives.
2. Create a personal leadership statement with six complete statements. Use the structure 'Attribute' so that 'Result'. Alternatively, you can start with your desired results and use the 'because of' structure.
3. Audit your current allocation of time to check that you are spending 30 per cent on your vision, code of conduct and goals; 30% on taking action; and 30 per cent on doing life's housework. Are you spending 10 per cent on 'being rather than doing'? Because you should be.
4. Check out how aligned your vision, code of conduct (personal leadership attributes) and goals really are. Any lack of alignment here will drain you of energy and your ability to focus. Spend the time to bring these areas into alignment.

I am a life-enhancing pessimist.

J.B. Priestly 1884 - 1984
Instead of the Trees (1977)

Chapter 22

C: Courageously Examine Your Life

ANALYZE YOUR PERSONAL CHARACTERISTICS AND EXTERNAL TRENDS

With these three elements aligned Sun-Tzu turns his attention to the terrain, the trends and the countryside. He suggests that to succeed we need to fully consider our personal opportunities and threats.

There was a process developed in the 1970s that became very popular in business. It was called the 'SWOT analysis'. SWOT stands for Strengths, Weaknesses, Opportunities and Threats. Large companies used this process to decide how they could best move forward in a strategic way by promoting their strengths, trying to solve their weaknesses, maximising their opportunities and developing mitigation plans for their threats.

In the third millennium we call this process the 'CT scan' — strengths and weaknesses are the two sides of the one coin; they are CharacteristicS. If we integrate opportunities and threats, it also turns out to be two sides of the same coin — TRENDS. Every person in life has to work with their own innate personal characteristics and respond to the external trends in their world.

Take a minute to construct your own personal CT scan. Write down the key characteristics of your profile. Consider the three critical elements that sound most like you (your strengths) and least like you (your weaknesses). How would you describe these characteristics?

For example, if you are highly intuitive and empathetic to others this will make you a good listener but it will also mean that you will experience enormous internal turmoil when you have to take action that will hurt another person. If you see the latter point as a weakness and try to block it out you will also block out your strength. In this example, this sensitivity is simultaneously a strength and weakness and so is therefore a characteristic of your personality. (These are summarized for each thinking function in Section 1 - Your First Step In Your Life Quest.)

What this exercise should demonstrate to you is that there is no value in endlessly trying to reinvent yourself to try to become the ideal you. Your innate characteristics

Personal Focus

are your characteristics. You can either accept them or, if you do manage to change yourself, you end up swapping this set of strengths and weaknesses for another set of strengths and weaknesses.

In personal development, the suggestion that we all strive to become perfect is the greatest con of all time. My advice is to stop trying to change yourself and instead get on with using your characteristics to kick some goals. No matter how marvellous you become you'll have equally dodgy elements in your profile. In life, focusing on this red herring is a sure life waster.

It will be your activity that will create a new reality and success for you, not constantly trying to change yourself and living under the myth that you will be successful by becoming perfect. Even if you develop more strengths, if you are not careful, rather than celebrating them you will only be able to see your corresponding new weaknesses.

If we turn to the outside world for a moment, you must also consider the current opportunities and threats that are confronting your life, or as Sun-Tzu would say, the trends for the future. Remember that in every opportunity there is a threat and in every threat an opportunity. This means that you may be praying for an opportunity and when it presents itself to you, you may not be able to see it if you can only see the threat. Both opportunities and threats are TRENDS — two sides of the same coin. We must both behold the opportunity and beware the threat.

In NeuroPower workshops sometimes this is underlined when those with low self-esteem can easily list their weaknesses and threats and it takes someone else in the workshop to be able to turn these coins over and see the corresponding strengths and opportunities. When depression sets in we can only see the down side. But once we win the war, we only remember the high points. The key is to keep this natural tendency of selective amnesia in mind and discipline ourselves to constantly see both sides of the coin – not just the side facing upwards.

KEEP THE UPPER HAND

Your internal Master sees your strengths and opportunities; however, often your Mirror sees your weaknesses and threats. How you see life right now should give you an indication of who is winning the war.

It is OK to consult your Mirror but don't let them take over. When your Mirror takes control, not only does life become unbearably hopeless but also you will find that you have no energy and your actual hands-on abilities diminish.

The Maya Lenca people from Central America would describe this process as descending into the underworld and it is marked with anger, depression, cruelty and self-sabotage.

They believe there are many levels to this dark place so the simple advice is to steer clear and pull yourself out if you inadvertently fall in. As you befriend your Mirror you will discover how they can be healthily integrated into your life, but until then just be cautious.

UNDERSTAND THE POWER OF THE SEASONS AND LEARN HOW TO WORK WITH THEM RATHER THAN FIGHT THEM AND FAIL!

Sun-Tzu also suggests that we must learn how to harness the seasons of our lives. Realistically, everything has a season. We all have a life cycle because everything that lives, grows according to seasons, cycles or recurring patterns. This can be seen in the weather, business cycles, in relationships, property prices, political popularity, peace, fashion, and even the marketing, selling and packaging of products and services. In fact, I have chosen to illustrate these seasons by charting the launch of a new commodity-based product in a supermarket.

APPLYING PRODUCT LIFE CYCLE ANALYSIS TO YOUR LIFE (THE BCG OF LIFE[1])

You have probably noticed that when a product is first repackaged or displayed on the shelf in a supermarket it's usually packaged as 'new' or 'improved'. This launch is the first phase of the product life cycle. In marketing, this phase is called a *Question Mark* phase because despite all the consumer research in the world no one really knows if it will be successful.

The second phase of the product life cycle (*Rising Star*) sees the product starting to sell. During this phase the manufacturer starts spending money on production capacity and the distributor starts spending a lot more money on advertising.

The third step of the product life cycle is called the *Cash Cow*. At this third stage the manufacturer is selling more and making more money than they are having to spend on manufacturing the product and advertising it.

And then finally, in the last stage of the product life cycle the sales drop and the manufacturer can spend as much money on advertising as they want and the cost of the sales will be matched by the amount having to be spent on advertising and promotion. This is known as the *Dog* phase of the product life cycle.

These four phases of the product life cycle are reflected in every new product that enters the market.

These cyclical phases could be renamed: Spring for planting (Question Mark),

---

1   Adapted from the Boston Consulting Group matrix

Summer for growing and weeding (Rising Star); Autumn for harvesting (Cash Cow); and Winter for lying fallow or recuperating (Dog). Each activity you choose to undertake in life falls into one of the phases in this cycle. Understand them and you will succeed. Fight them and you will die of exhaustion.

In the West we tend to celebrate the Question Mark phase. All the Hollywood movies finish at the Question Mark phase, just when the story is about to get a bit more interesting. The Question Mark phase is marked by the emotions of excitement, enthusiasm, creativity and a sense of freshness and living on the edge. Profiles that are particularly high in C1 and C2 will be drawn to this stage. They are often known as starters not finishers.

But rather than living 100 per cent of your life in this phase which is what happens when you move city or swamp yourself in a brand new project, you want there to be a balance in your life. So everyone, even the C1 and C2 most dominant, need to have just a few projects in this phase. Everyone also needs to have at least one Rising Star project. The profile most naturally drawn to this Rising Star phase is the P2 I1. This profile just loves getting projects off the ground but loses interest the moment they evolve into Cash Cow.

The profile most drawn to the Cash Cow phase is the P1 I2. Cash Cow is about completing the task in a predetermined efficient way. The P1 I2 enjoys this and puts in place a stable and reliable TQM process to make sure the process continues to slowly evolve.

Finally, when a project hits the Dog phase, the mind completely switches off and we become robots wishing we were somewhere else. You need to divest yourself of these Dog projects before you become so brain dead that you need to prop yourself up with anti-depressants.

The point is that while each profile is drawn to a different stage of the life cycle and will feel 'at home' during that phase, we must learn how to motivate ourselves to be able to focus on all stages of the life cycle. If we just follow our whims we will miss out on three of life's seasons and become dark about the experiences life has presented us with and disappointed with the contribution we have had the opportunity to make.

For example, those attracted to phase one become peeved because they never achieve anything substantial — they will move on before the projects reach the Rising Star stage and amount to something.

Phase two folk become bitter and twisted because they spend a lifetime putting in all their energy on projects that somebody else reaps the results of with far less stress and energy when the project moves to Cash Cow just after they lose interest.

Phase three folk become cynical administrators who spend their lives cleaning up

Personal Focus

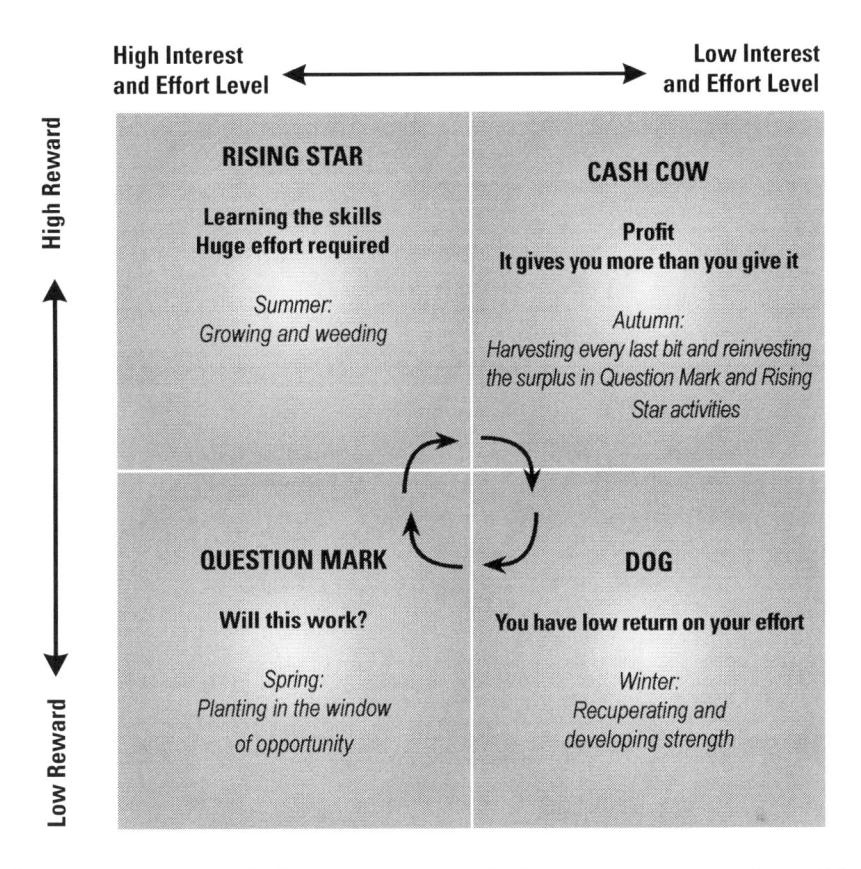

	High Interest and Effort Level ⟷	Low Interest and Effort Level
High Reward	**RISING STAR** Learning the skills Huge effort required *Summer:* *Growing and weeding*	**CASH COW** Profit It gives you more than you give it *Autumn:* *Harvesting every last bit and reinvesting the surplus in Question Mark and Rising Star activities*
Low Reward	**QUESTION MARK** Will this work? *Spring:* *Planting in the window of opportunity*	**DOG** You have low return on your effort *Winter:* *Recuperating and developing strength*

other people's messes and who never get the credit for having created anything of their own. Those stuck in phase four look back at their lives and just wish they could have another go and this time do something interesting.

The task is to learn how to manage your natural yearning to stay in the season naturally suited to your profile and instead balance the projects in your life across all four seasons realizing that most projects will pass through all four seasons within seven years anyway.

ANALYZE WHERE YOUR EFFORT IN LIFE GOES

This model enables you to analyze where your effort in life is going and the kind of return this effort is yielding.

Sun-Tzu suggests that we analyze and anticipate the return we will receive on the amount of effort we put in. To succeed, this return on investment must be strategically managed.

LET ME EXPLAIN

We start every new project with the Question Mark quadrant— we don't know how it's going to end up. It may succeed or it may fail.

Then as the project starts to build momentum we move into the Rising Star quadrant — that's where you're putting in enormous effort and you start to see some encouraging signs.

Then you move into the Cash Cow quadrant and you start to get a return. In fact, you are getting more out of the project than you are putting in.

Then finally you move into the Dog phase at the end of the cycle where the activity gives you so little reward you lose more than you get.

If you were to analyze your life now, in which quadrant do each of your activities fit? You need at least a few Question Mark activities because these are your future. How many of your activities would fall into the Rising Star category because you are going to have to put a lot of energy into them to get them moving? Is there a Cash Cow activity in your life? In which case you are going to need to make sure that you 'milk' the Cash Cow of energy and rewards and strategically invest that surplus into your Question Mark activities; is this a Dog activity? In which case you want to unload the activity as fast and responsibly as possible.

GIVE YOURSELF A ROUND OF APPLAUSE

This strategic approach to life won't work unless you have the self-discipline to give yourself rewards for keeping to the plan and staying focused on the right activity. When was the last time that when you achieved something significant you celebrated the success with something meaningful?

Rewards for the right strategic action make up for losing the right to not act strategically.

We tend to assume that one day in the future when we have achieved our vision, we will celebrate in style. It would seem that many of us believe that if we spend the first twenty years of our career working really hard, the next twenty years we can celebrate really hard. Trouble is, it doesn't quite work like that.

I've heard it said, 'Success is what you become while you're achieving your objectives.'

What you become! Not where you end up! So in the Focus phase we need to find ways of rewarding ourselves along the way and developing the commitment to discipline ourselves to focus on the right action.

Chapter 22 Checklist

Are you ready to develop a mastery strategy?

The four key questions of phase one — preparation.

Once these four questions are answered you are ready to learn how to create a strategy.

- **Question 1.** Do I have a clear vision that summarizes why I am here? What is my major definite purpose in life and does this link to clearly identified objectives?
- **Question 2.** Do I have a clear code of conduct that highlights specific behaviors and links these attributes to the specific outcomes that I am seeking?
- **Question 3.** Have I conducted a CT scan and had the confidence to see both sides of the coin? Have I really accepted that all my weaknesses are also strengths and all my threats are also opportunities and vice versa?
- **Question 4.** How do the various activities in my life fit into the life cycle, and do I have the right balance? Do the projects in my life fit into the Question Mark phase, the Rising Star phase, the Cash Cow phase or the Dog phase? And then finally, what reward strategy or system will I create for myself?

Once this analysis or the 'estimates phase' is complete you are ready to move to the strategy stage.

Personal Focus

I have a cunning plan.
Baldrick in Blackadder 2 (1987)

Chapter 23

U: Use A Master's Strategy

BUT WHAT IS STRATEGY?

The term 'strategic' is fascinating. At its simplest it means a plan. A strategic plan refers to the process of thinking ahead to create an effective series of steps which in turn creates a new reality. A strategy is born when someone realizes that things will go wrong if something doesn't change the course of events. This usually starts in their mind as an innocent question.

For somebody who is at the front line in a war, the strategic question might be 'I'm hungry — what are we going to have for lunch?' For the officers in charge of that soldier, the strategic question for them might be 'We need to get a good night's sleep, but where are we going to camp tonight?' For the senior officers, it might be 'What supplies will we need in two weeks' time?' For the general, the question might be 'Should we be in this war?'

So what is strategic for one might not be strategic for another. The questions and their corresponding action plans or 'strategies' will be different.

Therefore, what **you** see as 'strategic action' will depend on what you see as undesirable in your life and what you see as the inevitable course of events if action isn't taken.

One of the myths many people have is that they don't use strategies. Of course they do. We all have strategies for how we live in life. Even to not think about something is a strategy.

In sport or in chess we describe a strategy as a game plan. In business we describe a strategy as a business plan. To deal with emergencies, firms spend millions developing an emergency plan which outlines strategically what to do and how to do it if the unthinkable happens. But there are many more everyday examples of strategic planning.

When you go to McDonald's and have a burger, the way you are served, the questions you are asked and the way the burger is cooked are all according to a plan. In fact, if you were to look at every holiday you've planned, every event you've organized and every weekend you've managed to fit about three times more into than you thought possible, they will all have been strategically planned.

Every day you wake up, get dressed and have breakfast; you may be on automatic pilot, but you are following a series of activities that at some stage you will have thought out, followed and through trial and error refined.

Let me give you an example over a cup of tea.

EVEN THE SIMPLEST TASK REQUIRES THE IMPLEMENTATION OF A STRATEGY OR PLAN OF ATTACK

If you want to teach someone how to make a cup of tea and they've never even seen one before, you may start by imparting the following strategy. Firstly, show them what a cup of tea looks like (plant the vision in their mind). This is what they are heading towards. Then you may outline a step-by-step action plan.

Step one: you might say, 'Find a cup.'

Step two: 'Find a teabag.'

Step three: 'Boil the water.'

Step four: 'Put the teabag into a cup and tip the boiling water into the cup until it's filled to within a centimetre of the top of the cup.'

Step five: 'Take out the teabag and throw it away.' And hey presto, you've got your cup of tea.

REFINING THE STRATEGY

To improve this strategy by making the process faster, you might consider putting the kettle on the stove first while you get the cup and the teabag ready and save some time by multi-tasking. To refine it some more, you might consider the idea of sitting the wet teabag in a spoon (once you've jiggled the teabag). That way, when you throw it away, it won't drip all over the bench. And another way to improve it might be to drain the teabag in the teaspoon with the teabag string. These are little improvements to the broad strategy which were prompted by the questions:

'Is this taking too long?' 'How can I stop the teabag from dripping?' and 'How can I avoid putting a wet and soggy teabag in the rubbish bin?'

IGNORE THE NAGGING QUESTION TO YOUR OWN PERIL!

So a nagging question is the prompt that lets you know that you need a new strategy or need to improve your current situation. A question like this goes around and around in your mind. As the songwriter says: 'Like a never ending circle, like a wheel within a wheel.'

And usually the more internal anxiety you feel when asking that question, the more you need a new strategy or need to amend your current strategy.

ASK THE MILLION-DOLLAR QUESTION

What questions have you had running around in your mind lately that are causing you anxiety, and that you probably haven't made the time to focus on, because deep down, you don't like the answer?

How is my career going?

Is my primary relationship really working?

Is my job secure?

Will I have enough money for my retirement?

Do I spend enough quality time with the kids?

These are all great questions that would require you to either develop a brand new strategy or amend your current strategy. In other words, you can't answer these questions with a simple yes or no, good or bad. To be satisfactorily answered each question will need a clear vision, an analysis of the situation and a clear game plan of action.

SUN-TZU'S FIVE BASIC STRATEGIES FOR LIFE

In essence there are five basic strategies. Three of these are 'attack' strategies, and two are 'position' strategies. These are generic strategies. In other words, you'll be able to use these in any activity you choose to undertake. This is very 'big picture' thinking, and gives you an insight into how you can strategically approach any task.

Strategy #1— Frontal attack

The first type of attack strategy is called a 'frontal attack'. It seems to me that for most people 99.9 per cent of everything that they do in life seems to fall into this approach to problem-solving. But Sun-Tzu says, 'At all costs, avoid the frontal attack.' Only use the frontal attack strategy where you have a 3 to 1 advantage. If you've got three times the support, three times the insight, three times the wisdom or a 300 per cent advantage, you can try the frontal attack. But honestly, how often is this the case?

Strategy #2 — Fragment

The second strategy is called a 'fragment' strategy. This is where the focus is on one fragment or segment of the total war. You win in one corner.

If you're going to learn how to become an artist, don't paint a whole canvas. Instead, if you adopt a fragment strategy, begin by painting a plate and then slowly, only once you've mastered that task, do you go on to the next larger and more complex one. In sales it's often referred to as the 'foot in the door' strategy. It suggests that you only bite off what you can chew quickly and then swallow with no risk of choking.

Strategy #3 — Flanking

The third attack strategy called 'flanking' is where you shift the war zone. Your opponent may think you're going to fight on the mountain but you flank and fight in the valley. I use the flanking strategy all the time.

As an example, imagine that you want to get fit. You may not enjoy walking, but you may enjoy taking the dog for a walk. If you use your enjoyment of walking the dog to ensure you get fit, you're flanking. You may have heard the saying, 'Teachers teach until they've learned the lesson.' This is another example of flanking. Salespeople flank when they change the issue from the brand of a product to the color of the product.

So in summary I've just outlined the three attack strategies: the frontal attack, the fragment attack, and the flanking attack. I'll now outline the two positioning strategies.

Strategy #4 — Develop

The first is the 'develop' or 'wait and see' strategy. This is when you consciously find a way to stall and hold things up and in the meantime you use this time to find some allies, seek advice, or look for some way of being able to leverage from your strengths.

Procrastination of this nature is very strategic if you use the time to strengthen your defences.

Strategy #5 — Run/Retreat

The final positioning strategy is the run or retreat strategy. This is the scorched earth policy made famous by the Russians for wiping out Napoleon's and Hitler's armies.

This is where you say, 'I'm giving up. I'm resigning. I'm out of this relationship.' That's when you can see there is no way you can possibly win, so you cut your losses and run. Many people use this strategy when life becomes too overwhelming and they feel they can't cope any more.

HOW MANY OF THESE STRATEGIES DO YOU USE?

In my experience most people use only two strategies — attack and run. But Sun-Tzu says you should be using all of these strategies to get the result you want.

Every activity you undertake will use either one or a combination of these strategies. Your task is to make sure that you choose the strategy or combination of strategies that effectively keep your energy and focus up, and get the job done.

BECOMING A MASTER

Now interestingly enough, there is very little difference between a master and a novice who applies a master's strategy (once they've practised it a few times). Well, here's something to ponder for a moment — do you have any master strategies? The answer is, that each one of us has literally hundreds of master strategies that we use every single day of our lives.

You may have heard different speakers talk about, or read about your comfort zone. A comfort zone is where you have a particular task or activity sorted out, 'wired' or mastered. In your comfort zone, you have used a strategy so much that it has become a habit. Imagine how powerful you would be in life if your every habit had developed from a master strategy.

> *We are what we repeatedly do. Excellence,*
> *then, is not an act, but a habit.*
>
> Aristotle

YOUR OUTCOME IS ONLY AS GOOD AS YOUR STRATEGY FOR ACTION

I have heard of some fascinating strategies.

A guy in his forties was telling me the other day that when he was a teenager, he had a very effective dating strategy which involved him taking girls ice-skating. I asked, 'Why ice-skating?' He explained, 'Because with ice-skating you'd invite girls along and you'd have to hang on to them at first to take them around the skating rink. Soon enough, they'd fall over, and you'd have to take them home and warm them up with a nice cup of tea and a cuddle.' It seems this was a very good dating strategy for him!

Here's a simple little 'finding-a-car park' strategy. When you go into a car park and you're looking for a car space, people usually assume that you, 'Look for the free car space.' A good friend of mine, Victoria, taught me a simple strategy. She suggested that I stop looking for empty car spaces. Instead, she suggested that I look for shopping-laden people and follow those people, because they're going to lead me to a car that's about to leave. I use this strategy all the time and it really is an effective parking-the-car strategy that's saved me hours of driving around.

Some people have developed a powerful real estate strategy. How do you know that some places are going to move ahead? People will have strategies on it. Others have a speaking strategy, and all the millionaires have a moneymaking strategy.

BUT HOW DO YOU KNOW A STRATEGY WILL WORK FOR YOU?

Remember, strategies will only work for you when they leverage from your personal strengths and balance your weaknesses. Whenever you take a master strategy off the shelf, you will always have to amend it so that it becomes your own personal strategy.

THE POWER OF A METAPHOR

Another important part of any 'power strategy' is the metaphor. If you take Sun-Tzu's lead, you'll be seeing life as a war — a war waged within your own mind as you fight the entropy, laziness and the Mirror within yourself. Your fight is to be focused and disciplined to take the right action to achieve the objective.

How do you metaphorically describe your career, your relationship with your significant other or your role as a parent? How would you metaphorically describe your wealth creation plan? Tell me your metaphor and I'll tell you your outcome because one so significantly influences the other.

For your strategies to work you must choose the right metaphor.

THE BUILDING BLOCKS OF CREATING A MASTER STRATEGY

Here are four tips to take into account when developing your master strategies to achieve your desired outcomes.

1. When selecting a strategy, go to the top and find a master.

I'm amazed at how many people go to someone who has no idea, and copy his or her strategies. Why learn a new strategy from the bottom of the heap? You've got to learn it just the same; why not start at the top?

2. Don't restrict yourself to people who are still alive.

Sun-Tzu has been dead for 2600 years, yet his strategies have made military successes of some and millions of dollars for others. Books, stories and tapes are great sources of information for strategy. If you don't have time to read a book, listen to tapes. In other words, if you can't be a bookworm, be a tapeworm!

Remember, all wisdom that will change your life can be boiled down to a series of brilliantly conceived strategies that someone else will have learned the hard way.

3. Don't expect masters to know their strategies.

Many masters don't realize or appreciate what they know. Many people don't know how brilliant they really are. Remember that when you are in your comfort zone you

Personal Focus

will have converted your strategy into a habit. At this point it becomes second nature. You may ask a brilliant speaker, 'You're a sensational public speaker. How do you do that?' They may seriously have no idea. So you may have to watch and learn.

I've learned sales skills from one of the world's best salespeople. She is sensational. Yet, until I pointed out to her the strategy she was using, she wasn't aware of it. She'd incorrectly put it down to her bubbly personality and her ability to enjoy herself. Trainers call this phenomenon the 'unconscious competent'.

In other words, she applies her strategy brilliantly, without conscious thought.

4. At the beginning of a learning cycle, you don't know what you don't know.

(This is called the unconscious incompetent.) It's disheartening to realize that when you don't know what you don't know, you really don't know it. And people who don't know anything about something often end up appointing themselves experts because they know no better. Often these are the people who are very eager to teach you. Be warned.

Have you ever met somebody who has just started to play a musical instrument? They want to play it for everyone, don't they? It always amazes me. People who have just started on their journey in learning about a particular field of knowledge, be it theology, engineering, architecture, or gardening — they're experts. At this stage they are not at the point where they have even an inkling of what they don't know. Ironically, this stage of oblivion is often when we feel the most empowered, can think very clearly and are very articulate because we are not bogged down with the tensions, complications and competing influences of truth. Unfortunately, for every complex problem, there is a simple solution ... and it's wrong!

IF ONLY MASTERS REALIZED THAT THEY ARE UNCONSCIOUS COMPETENTS!

The first breakthrough in the process of learning a new strategy is when we get a glimpse of what we don't know and we feel the anxiety associated with an uncertain future. It can be a blow to the ego. But it's the essential very first step to learning something new. The Central American Indians call this stage the 'Oblivion'-to-'Awakening' transition. This is the very first step in the learning cycle of life.

Once we have taken this first step and made the first transition, we have an overwhelming desire to fill the gap and learn what we don't know. Only when we have found the strategy we intend using and our head is filled with the knowledge of the strategy are we fully awake and have become a conscious competent.

At this stage, we know what we know. But it also means that we have to watch

Personal Focus

ourselves every step of the way and use discipline and focus to follow the master's strategy. It also means that we have to consistently discipline ourselves because while we 'know what we know' we are only consciously competent. In other words, the moment we lose concentration and stop applying the strategy, we fall off the horse. hmm ...

Finally, we become the unconscious competent, which is the start of the mastery stage. It is when we are in our comfort zone and do things by habit without even thinking. As I've said, it's difficult, ironically, for a master to appreciate what they know. This is because it is so much second nature to them that they don't even think about it.

The short and long of these three stages is ... don't expect masters to be able to always communicate and teach their strategy. Sometimes you'll need to watch and identify that they are masters without any prompting from them.

HERE'S A BONUS ... STRATEGIES ARE 100 PER CENT TRANSFERABLE

Amazingly, if you are brilliant in one field, you can usually transfer the strategic wisdom of that knowledge to a totally different field and achieve outstanding results.

Why is it that such a large number of senior managers come from industries that have nothing to do with their current place of employment? Answer — because all the lessons and things that they learned in one industry, they transfer 100 per cent to another industry.

Edward de Bono makes the point in his book *Tactics* that if your industry can't solve a problem try asking someone outside your industry what they would do, because they will probably be able to solve it.

This works very effectively because the strategies that are used in one industry to solve problems are 100 per cent transferable to another industry. So if you're good at something, odds are it is going to be easy to apply this strategy to master another unrelated area.

If you've taken yourself from nothing to something as a gardener, you can use that same process to teach yourself how to ski. Sounds crazy, but it's true.

Strategies are about empowering you! Your personal strategies are fully transferable so you already have your own success formula. Your task is to learn how to dig into your own mind to find this personal strategy of yours and to use your highly developed focusing skills to apply it to achieve your SMART objectives.

Personal Focus

Chapter 23 Checklist

- Take time to identify your current strategies for achieving your SMART objectives. Will these strategies get you there or do you need to devise more powerful strategies?
- Do you need to find yourself a master in this area who can give you some fresh strategies to use?
- Are your strategies building on your strengths? Can you use an approach or strategy you've already mastered in one area, and transfer this strategy to a new area?
- Have you selected the right metaphor to support the implementation of your strategy?

Personal Focus

If we did all the things we are capable of doing, we would literally astound ourselves.

Thomas A. Edison

Chapter 24

The Six Keys to Unlocking Your Own Master Strategy

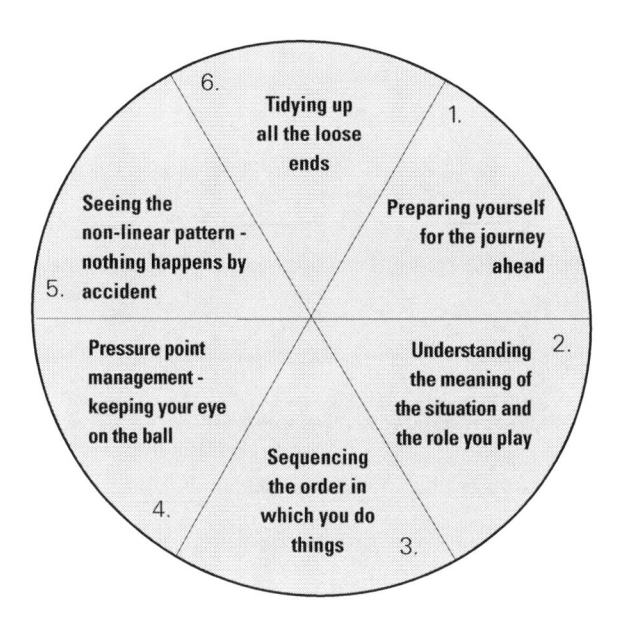

Wheel diagram with six segments:
1. Preparing yourself for the journey ahead
2. Understanding the meaning of the situation and the role you play
3. Sequencing the order in which you do things
4. Pressure point management - keeping your eye on the ball
5. Seeing the non-linear pattern - nothing happens by accident
6. Tidying up all the loose ends

Because strategy is at the heart of focused and effective activity, it is important that you understand the six keys to discovering your own master strategy. The right way to do this is to catch yourself using a strategy for a task that you would consider yourself to be a master of already.

STEP 1 - NOTICE HOW YOU PREPARE FOR THE TASK

Every master prepares before taking action. Let's say, for example, that you are a master at preparing a meal for a dinner party. What do you do to prepare for it? Do you imagine the people arriving? Do you imagine what sort of food they'd like? Do you imagine the conversation that evening? Do you imagine the season, and what's going to complement it? Do you imagine how hot it's going to be? What do you do to prepare yourself for the activity?

Effective preparation will ensure that your mind is ready to use the right functions for the task at hand. You can use this approach to prepare yourself for any task you undertake.

STEP 2 - NOTICE THE MEANING YOU ARE MAKING

The second element in creating a strategy is to notice how you see yourself in relation to the task. What role do you imagine yourself playing? Do you see yourself as a dancer, a coordinator, a leader or friend? If we go back to our example of preparing an evening meal, do you see yourself as an artist? Do you see yourself as the entertainment? Do you see yourself as the social glue? Do you see that your role is to coordinate the evening so that there are no clashes? Do you imagine that you're conducting an orchestra or that you're organizing traffic? Do you see that you're taking people on an exciting journey or settling them down? If you ask a master, they'll tell you the metaphor they use. Sometimes it will shock you, but this is often the fastest and most powerful way to know you are using just the right energy or function.

STEP 3 - NOTICE THE SEQUENCE

Now notice in broad terms, what sequence of events you follow. What tasks do you complete and in what order? This is the logical and relatively obvious part (this is what I described earlier with the strategy for making a cup of tea).

STEP 4 - NOTICE WHERE YOU PLACE YOUR ATTENTION; ON WHAT DO YOU FOCUS?

Fourthly, notice that when you are undertaking the activity there are key things you watch for as indicators of potential problems. This is a concept I call Pressure Point Management.

Pressure Point Management takes the view that a master can see the wood and the trees. The master knows intuitively that there are just a few key indicators that you watch for to give you an idea of how things are going. Manage these pressure points and you manage the situation or the event. This is about learning how to focus on the significant pressure points rather than trying to watch everything. As Confucius once said, 'If you emphasize everything you emphasize nothing.' If you focus on everything you lose focus.

For fourteen years I ran a public relations practice of around thirty staff. I discovered that it was impossible to know absolutely everything that was going on, but I could effectively manage the organization by focusing on just four pressure points.

The four pressure points were:
- The winning of new clients who came into the firm;
- The selection of new staff who were employed by the organization and the induction process of those new staff;
- Cash flow; and
- The professional time-to-billing ratio.

If I kept my finger on the pulse of these four key pressure points, I knew exactly how healthy the firm was. By effectively managing these four areas I could effectively manage the firm.

As another example, a good friend of mine works as a sister in a children's hospital. She says that when she sees a baby, if it's pink and it's making noise, she knows it's probably OK. But if it's not pink and it's not making noise, that child may have major medical problems. It may seem really simple, but when you think about it, a junior nurse may give less attention to a white, silent baby than a pink, noisy baby because at first glance they seem to be OK, even though the exact opposite holds true.

Pressure Point Management is being able to see the wood for the trees and knowing what is significant and where to put the focus of attention for maximum leverage and the best results.

Get this right and you're ready to move to Step 5.

STEP 5 - REALIZE THAT YOU DO NOTHING BY ACCIDENT

If there is a problem along the way, what do you do? How do you solve it? Where do you start? The health of your strategy is not based on whether or not it goes without a hitch but instead how quickly you can solve the problems that will invariably come across your path. But here's the spin — assume that everything you do as a master has a reason. A master does nothing by accident. This is part of the unconscious competent behavior that you exhibit as a master. You will be amazed at some of your unconscious strategies for solving some of the problems that emerge along the way.

Let me give you an example. Greg, the Managing Director of a small electrical firm, is a technician who works in the electrical field. For years he has worked solving electrical problems on industrial sites. When confronted with a problem the first thing he does before he starts work, is to simply wander around the site. For years he wasn't even aware that he did this.

The client will often say to him, 'Well, what are you going to do about it?' And he says, 'Let me go and get the tools and I'll make a start.'

Now Greg has a C1 lateral thinking, P1 logic and I2 empathy thinking profile. For

Personal Focus

him, the act of walking back to the car (which he unconsciously parks some distance from the building) gets his creative juices flowing and lets him intuitively think about the problem. So part of his unconscious strategy is to create some thinking time by walking back to the car. For Greg this works brilliantly. Without this time, solutions for him would be far more elusive. But why?

Did you know that unconsciously, when you're solving a problem, the best way your unconscious can really work on something is to empty your conscious mind and let it whir around without your conscious constraints. The best way to do this is to do something else. That's why becoming unbelievably obsessed with a problem and chasing it around and around and around your brain often doesn't work. Instead, you're best to clear your mind and do something else. For some people this means they play golf or tennis, or they undertake something totally unrelated because it's in consciously doing something else that your subconscious mind can solve a problem.

So Greg walks a block or more back to the car to get the tools he'll need and then walks back. This delay strategy has given him twenty to twenty-five minutes. A few months ago one of his workers asked, 'Why don't we just go in with the tools in the first place?' It was only when Greg realized that this was part of his master strategy that he was able to explain that his odd behavior was there for a reason. He was a master but until recently was unaware of this absolutely critical preparation component of his master strategy.

So as a master, assume everything you do, has a reason. You do nothing by accident. For Greg even parking away from the building and walking to and fro was no accident.

STEP 6 - TIDY EVERYTHING UP

Finally, take note of what you do to tie everything up. What's the finale? What do you do to make sure that things are resolved? What do you do afterwards, to unwind? The master always completes the cycle, tidies and prepares to move on to the next task.

A STRATEGY IS LIKE A PERSONAL ROAD MAP

Now that you've identified a specific sequence of activity in this area of mastery see this as a generic road map. It doesn't matter whether you apply this to sailing, golf, at work or home, this road map can navigate you through any situation. It is your own personal mastery strategy that leverages from your strengths and balances your weaknesses. And, if that's how you focus and apply yourself in one area, you'll be able to take that strategy intact and use it to master tasks that are completely unrelated.

You can use this road map to master painting a canvas or the house or how to play the violin, because it's your own master strategy for life. It is your learning strategy. Your mastery strategy. This is **your** strategy. Only a person with exactly the same Leadership Style has a learning strategy just like yours!

You may have heard the saying, 'Give a man a fish, and you give him a meal. Teach him how to fish, and you feed him for life.' By knowing your master strategy, you can take a fraction of the time to reach mastery in any chosen endeavor because you already have the master's road map.

People often realize that strategies can be applied in similar fields. If, for example, they've mastered football and then they want to learn soccer, they can see the link and they go about learning soccer in the same way that they learned football. Or if they're good at playing the flute and then they have to learn the piano, they automatically use the same strategies. But what they don't realize is that these same strategies can be used for every aspect in life, even in areas which are totally unrelated. The soccer player could use their strategy for learning how to play soccer to master the violin and vice versa, because every skill and insight or accomplishment begins by effectively using their mind.

It is almost as if every person reading this book, in their mind, has a little strategy which works brilliantly for them, and every time they've succeeded, they'll have used it. But, for whatever reason, it's invisible to them. If we can bring that invisible strategy into your consciousness, and you can use it as a conscious competent, you can take years off mastering new skills. You can triple your ability to be able to perform.

INDIVIDUAL STRATEGIES FOR LEARNING

Let's focus for a moment on individual strategies for learning. If you can imagine yourself as a child, you can get a better idea of how you can teach yourself. If you're high in C1, when you're learning something new, you'll tend to be hands on (kinaesthetic) so you will learn through action. If you're high in C2, you need to be able to imagine the whole scenario from beginning to end. So you need to begin with the end in mind and understand the big picture.

P1 uses a step-by-step hands-on approach. P2 uses a wait-and-see approach — first of all, you'll want to wait and you'll want to watch and you'll want to see who succeeds and who fails. Then you'll select the strategy that will give you the best chance of performing immediately. Often people who are high in P2 try it once, and if they don't excel, they drop out.

I1 will want to read and experience first hand whatever they are learning — they will need to see it and prove it for themselves to believe it.

I2 will want to read it and imagine it and won't take action until they feel comfortable.

I was giving this talk and an Analyzer (C1, P1, I1) person said to me, 'I love what you're saying, but it makes no sense to me. When I'm making a cup of tea, or parking a car, the strategies you use for both of these things are totally different. How can you say they're the same strategy?' Well, let me explain. If I know nothing about parking a car or nothing about making a cup of tea, the way I go about mastering the skill or learning this new information is going to be the same. The way I learn will be consistent.

THE AUTHOR'S LEARNING STRATEGY

I'll give you my personal learning strategy. As a Coach leadership style C2, P2, I2, I'm visionary, passionate and emotionally sensitive. So while my strategies will only work for about 24 per cent of the population, this discussion will give you an idea of how my strategy for learning to be a master works.

'What am I really trying to learn here?' The first step in my master strategy is scoping the task. I'll give you an example. One of the jobs I did to earn money when I was going through university was to train doctors how to play the piano in just three months.

It was a big claim and I charged good money for it. How could I do it? The answer is that I discovered that most people didn't want to learn how to play the piano at all. Instead, they just wanted to learn how to play one tune. One tune! That was easy. Particularly if I scoped it by saying, 'Would you like to be able to play like this?' They'd listen to my example and respond, 'Yes, I'd like to be able to play that tune just like that.'

Effectively, they were not really learning how to play the piano. They were learning how to play one tune on the piano. But as far as they were concerned, they were learning how to play the piano (a Fragment strategy).

So the first question I ask is, 'What specifically do I want to achieve? Do I want to learn how to make every type of tea or just one type of tea? Do I want to learn how to park every kind of car or just one car in one kind of parking spot?' For me, this has enabled me to master many specific tasks with great depth but absolutely no breadth.

The second step in my master strategy involves research.

When I want to collect as much information as I can on a topic and master a skill, I love to read books. I'll go to the bookstore, and I'll buy ten books on the one topic. I'll scan everything. And because I'm a C2, P2, I2, I can scan with ease.

When I scan I'll look for the headings. What I generally find is that all the books will tend to have the same sort of headings, because they'll broadly break a topic up

Personal Focus

Mind map

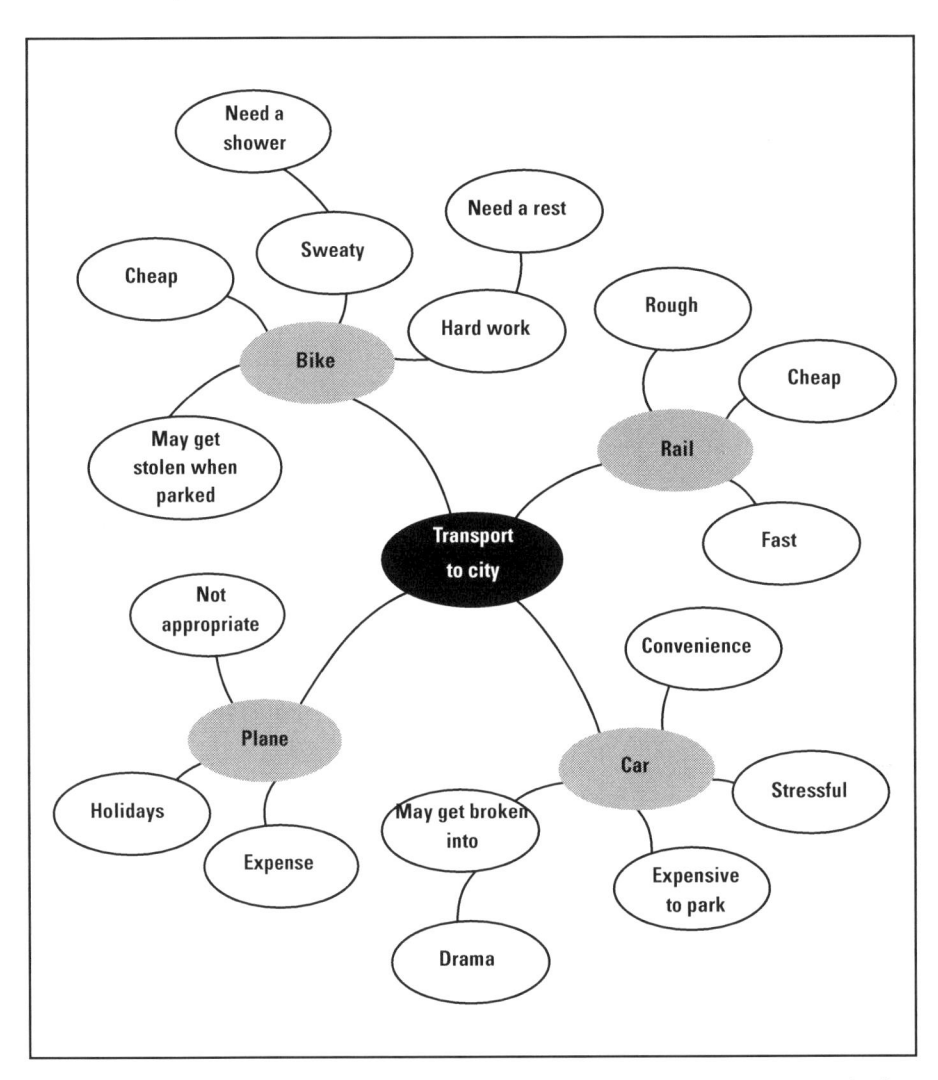

Transport to city mind map with branches:

- **Bike**: Need a shower, Sweaty, Cheap, Hard work, May get stolen when parked
- **Rail**: Need a rest, Rough, Cheap, Fast
- **Car**: Convenience, Stressful, Expensive to park, May get broken into, Drama
- **Plane**: Not appropriate, Holidays, Expense

into the same sorts of areas. When mastering any new area I want to learn the key areas to consider. When parking a car or being a brain surgeon or learning how to cook a new recipe, what are the things I need to consider?

If, for example, I was going to learn how to park a car, I might go to the Department of Transport or a defensive driving school and ask them for any relevant books they can give me. I might go to the library or hit the Internet and have a look at what they

Personal Focus

have on parking cars. I suck up all that information and I create for myself a mind map. After about ten hours of reading, this enables me to see the whole topic in one glance. This is very important for a C2, I2 like me.

Above is a mind map of transport to the city, graphically illustrating the process of 'seeing' the whole topic.

The third step in my learning strategy requires me to select a compatible author.

In other words, which of these books has a strategy that is compatible with my profile? To do this I'll look for the sort of language they use. If they list ninety-seven things that you need to do, and it's all very detailed, the author probably has an I1-dominated mind. But if they're saying, 'Broadly, this is what you look for ...' or 'This is how this task impacts those around you,' it means they're probably an I2. I'll look for an author with whom I can relate.

In reality you don't need to be able to psychoanalyze the author, or guess their profile. All you need to do is read it and if you relate to the book, then it means that, probably, they're a similar profile to you. That's why there are some books you can easily relate to while others just confuse you. Usually, you appreciate and relate to the books that are written by authors with profiles similar to yours.

Once I have identified the book to which I most easily relate, I make that book the benchmark. That book will form the backbone of my understanding about the topic.

My next task is to make the author's knowledge relevant to my environment and to my profile by creating an environment where I can practise. If it's a new topic that I am learning about, I might bring it up at dinner conversation to see whether or not all the ideas come together, or I might write something in my journal, put together an essay on it or write an article on it. It's in doing, speaking and creating that these ideas coalesce and begin to integrate with the knowledge I have already. Ultimately this is what creates wisdom.

Finally I test it, refine it, and start connecting this head knowledge into hands-on practice.

I refine it, test it, and refine it and test it, and refine it and ...

The topic about which I am learning and the skill set I am mastering is irrelevant. It's the way I learn that's important because for me that is consistent. These five steps summarize my master strategy for learning.

Chapter 24 Checklist

My challenge to you

My challenge to you is to find the personal strategy that's worked brilliantly and produced the best results in your life, because that's your master formula. Your master formula is probably going to have six steps.

1. You're going to have a way of defining the task and being specific.
2. You're going to have a process for collecting all the information.
3. You're going to create a map of understanding. (Now for me, that's a mind map with all the key elements. For you, it may be a list, or it may be something you put in your diary. It will need to be a map of understanding of some nature. Just discover what works best for you.)
4. You'll have to create a process, a sequence of tasks to get the job done.
5. You'll have strengths and weaknesses with this strategy, and you will need to have some way of being able to use your strengths and balance up your weaknesses. You will need to have a personal strategy for doing that.
6. You will have to break the sequence into milestones that fit with your vision. Check if it leverages your strengths and balances your weaknesses. And finally, commit yourself to the rewards that you're going to get for having achieved this task.

Personal Focus

There is no genius in life like the genius of energy and industry.

Donald Grant Mitchell

Chapter 25

S: Strive to Manage Your Energy

HOW WELL DO YOU MANAGE YOUR ENERGY LEVELS?

Even if you have accurate insight and the right strategy for both you and the situation, you will still need personal **energy** to be able to put that strategy into effect. Without boundless energy, even if you know exactly what to do, you will spend your life constantly trying to recuperate from the day-to-day slams that come your way while you watch your life float past as you give up once in a lifetime opportunities for all of a lifetime consequences.

In this chapter, we're giving you the formula for boundless energy so that you can put in place the master strategies to achieve your objectives.

THERE ARE FIVE KEYS TO PERSONAL ENERGY

The first key is to learn how to manage yourself. You may have read about personal entropy from Scott Peck in his book *The Road Less Travelled*. That's code for laziness. I heard the human race once described as resembling a shark, in that to survive, a shark needs to keep moving to force the water through its gills. So too we need to keep moving, learning, experiencing and growing to survive.

In fact, it's a full-on battle. On one side we have the part of us that wants to stay focused and committed to achieve the objectives we set ourselves and do the work that we were sent here to do. On the other side we have the part of us that just wants to sit around, usually trying to escape the hard work of reality with alcohol, sport or TV, watching gorgeous people and pretty much doing as little as possible.

Remember, Sun-Tzu suggests we know ourselves with some depth. The time has come for us to delve just a little deeper.

In life, we are all attracted to three fundamental things:
- Love and appreciation (we can't help it; we like people who like us)
- Money (whether we like it or not), and
- Energy

Of all those things, the one common denominator is **energy**.

We all gravitate towards activities that give us energy. We avoid doing the things that drain us of energy. Anything that really gives us a buzz, we enjoy. If the skills

Personal Focus

chart says you get energized by conflict, odds are, you'll be quite good at generating and resolving conflict, because you'll have been drawn to it and energized by it your whole life.

Conversely, if you get energized by looking at detail, facts and figures, then odds are, you'll have been drawn to that your whole life, so you'll have highly developed skills in that area. And that's why we can say with some certainty that if you're energized by an activity, it means you're probably going to have a high skill level in that area.

HOW MUCH OF YOUR LIFE ARE YOU DOING THINGS THAT EMPOWER YOU AND HOW MUCH OF YOUR LIFE ARE YOU DOING THINGS THAT DRAIN YOU OF ENERGY?

If your whole life is scattered with activity that de-energizes you, odds are, you're going to be de-energized or disempowered. Your activities will have effectively wrung the energy out of your life.

Here's a rule of thumb. For every one activity that zaps you of energy make sure that you have two activities that empower you. Plan your day by using a plus-minus-plus energy sandwich.

WE FEEL GOOD WHEN WE'RE DOING TASKS THAT GIVE US ENERGY, SO WHY NOT STRUCTURE YOUR LIFE ACCORDINGLY?

Too often, people focus on things that they can't do and that zap them of energy. Then when they are disempowered and not in a peak state, it's virtually impossible for them to perform at their best. In teamwork, why have a group of people working together? Because odds are, the things that you hate doing, somebody else will really enjoy. What's the definition of a disempowered team? Where everybody is doing activities that de-energize them. Suddenly, nobody's got any energy to do anything and the whole team goes to sleep.

I worked with a team about two years ago, and one of the team members said, 'We don't know why, but as a team we're always exhausted.' Turns out that when we looked at the allocation of tasks that had been given to the group members, every person was spending at least 60 per cent of their day doing things that zapped them energetically. Because these activities were contrary to their thinking style they were all exhausted.

Have you really balanced your life so that twice as many tasks you undertake are energizing you as de-energizing you? Perhaps you need to have an activity audit, and rethink about where you put your focus.

You feel good when you're doing things that energize you but there is a catch.

While it is true that you feel tired and at your wit's end when you're spending time doing things that don't energize you, often these are the activities from which you learn the most. Usually the cost of learning is energy. So to keep your energy high you need to make sure that you balance the amount of learning in your life with energizing activities.

It is exactly the same with people. Some boost and some exhaust. My advice is to become aware of those that exhaust and make sure that your time with them is rationed. Sometimes, if for all that investment of energy there is no, or little return you may need to audit them out of your life for a while. Nothing sucks energy like a zapped person looking to you for their reason for living. Actively manage your amount of contact with them or pay the price.

HERE'S HOW TO BOOST YOUR P1 AND P2 FUNCTIONS

Here's another interesting thought. Different times of the day give rise to different kinds of energy. For example, if you are able to get up early and do some exercise, that exercise will increase your willpower. (Your P1 and P2 scores will increase.) If you have a big task ahead of you that's going to require a lot of energy, then consider preparing yourself energetically by getting up early in the morning. Get your pulse going, have a walk, have a swim. Your profile will actually slightly change and your P1 and P2 functions will increase their dominance.

HERE'S HOW TO BOOST YOUR I1 AND I2 FUNCTIONS

But if you need to be extra sensitive consider waking up later in the day. If you wake up after ten o'clock in the morning your sensitivity will be at a peak. You may not have noticed this, but if you get up late on the weekend you'll feel sluggish. As you interact and watch people you'll tend to pick up their moods and feelings. This is because your P1 and P2 scores will be lower, and your I1 and I2 scores will be higher. That's why Sunday newspapers are so different from the rest of the week. The whole human race sleeps in on Sundays and this turns up their I2 scores! They buy papers that feature families, children and animals.

HERE'S HOW TO BOOST YOUR C2 VISION

If you're looking to boost your C2 vision, the secret lies in being awake after 11.00 pm. Last year a team of scientists at a university asked me to facilitate a vision session at 7.00 am. I had to explain to them that it wouldn't work. At this time of the day your visions are not going to be very visionary. At this time of day our P1 and P2 are working well and we are all impatient. We haven't got the time or energy to sit about dreaming. We just want to get on with it. Your mind's ability to use its C2 function is at its highest after 11.00 pm.

'What about marijuana? Does that give you visions?' Curiously enough, according to Drug Arm, a major Australian not-for-profit organization that works with drug addicts, marijuana shatters your ability to have visions for three months. Three months — big cost for a smoke!

And when you have mind-altering chemicals, the visions you do get are usually coming from within you, rather than from without. Mozart and Einstein and many of the people who had stunning visions and revelations all report that these stunning revelations came from outside themselves, not from inside themselves. So 'under the influence of marijuana' you'll see all sorts of interesting subconscious material, all sorts of weird patterns and interesting images but not a groundbreaking vision.

If you are looking to boost your C2, relax, go away for a weekend or spend some time, at night, after dinner, after 11.00 pm and see what happens. (Wine seems to be OK.)

HOW TO BOOST YOUR C1 FUNCTION

Lighten up, relax, don't take it all so seriously and either go somewhere new or build something. The key to boosting your C1 is to engage in practical activities that require your mind to solve problems quickly. Getting into slap-stick comedy is another way to increase your mind's C1 dominance!

MANAGE YOUR ENERGY LEVEL

Take the point of view that you alone are responsible for focusing your energy. Some people call this the meta-position or the 'third person position'. It's as if you helicopter above your life and ask yourself, 'OK, is this person doing the best job he or she can do? How can I now provide guidance to that human being?' (And that human being is you, by the way.) So your job is to lead that human being. 'OK, human being, you're going to need energy this week, so I want to see you up early in the morning.' 'OK, human being, you're going to need a bit of creativity, so I want to see you ...'

USING SUN-TZU'S STRATEGIES TO BOOST YOUR ENERGY

Remember that Sun-Tzu suggested the five strategies for overcoming obstacles. You can use these to break your habitual thinking and behaviors. If necessary these generic strategies can be applied to any task you undertake. Let's review them.

FRONTAL ATTACK

Are you going to employ a frontal attack? So, you could have huge casualties. This is where you simply confront the situation, define the gap and use your energy and focus to blast through the obstacles.

FRAGMENT ATTACK

Are you going to use a fragment attack? In other words, try solving the problem just one fragment at a time. This is where you may start improving your diet by just focusing on breakfast and improving that, rather than overhauling all three or more meals you have every day (much more energy efficient).

FLANKING STRATEGY

Are you going to use a flanking strategy, where you actually kid yourself or almost trick yourself into achieving something? If you are single, for example, and there is somebody you really want to spend time with, you may take up sailing so you can get to know them better. Now if part of your objective is to also learn how to sail this is a good flanking strategy.

Then you have your two positioning strategies: The develop strategy and the defend strategy. If you select the develop strategy the hardest part is to keep yourself committed to it. You need to do what it takes to develop your knowledge or your position so that you are better prepared to hit the problem with one of the attack strategies. Be careful not to just let the whole thing drift.

THE DEFEND STRATEGY

Finally, a burnt-grass, defend strategy is where you decide, 'This is not working. It's time to cut the ties, cut the alliances and get out.' Sometimes you've just got to employ a burnt-grass policy, (a slash-and-burn policy) so you live to fight another day.

So the first thing to realize is that your energy needs to be constantly managed because it is a finite resource. Some will say, 'That seems to me to be a lot of hard work.' Well, it is a lot of hard work, but being a failure is a lot of hard work too, just a different kind of hard work.

THE SEASONS OF LIFE AND HOW THEY AFFECT YOUR ENERGY LEVELS

The second key to personal empowerment is to understand the seasons of your life and how they affect your energy levels. Earlier I talked about the cycle of life

Personal Focus

diagrammatically represented by the BCG matrix. Remember that at any one time you're probably on about six quests simultaneously. (If you're juggling more than six quests, you'll be a bit stressed. If you're juggling fewer than six quests, you'll probably be a bit bored.)

Usually you'll have one major life quest and five other quests that are at less time demanding stages of the cycle. Each of these quests fits somewhere in the BCG. When you start a new project, it falls in the first quadrant or the Question Mark quadrant. At this stage you don't know whether it's going to be successful or not.

Then you increase your energy and focus and push it, push it, push it, push it, and slowly you start getting results. The moment the project starts yielding significant results your Question Mark has become your Rising Star.

THE CYCLE OF LIFE*

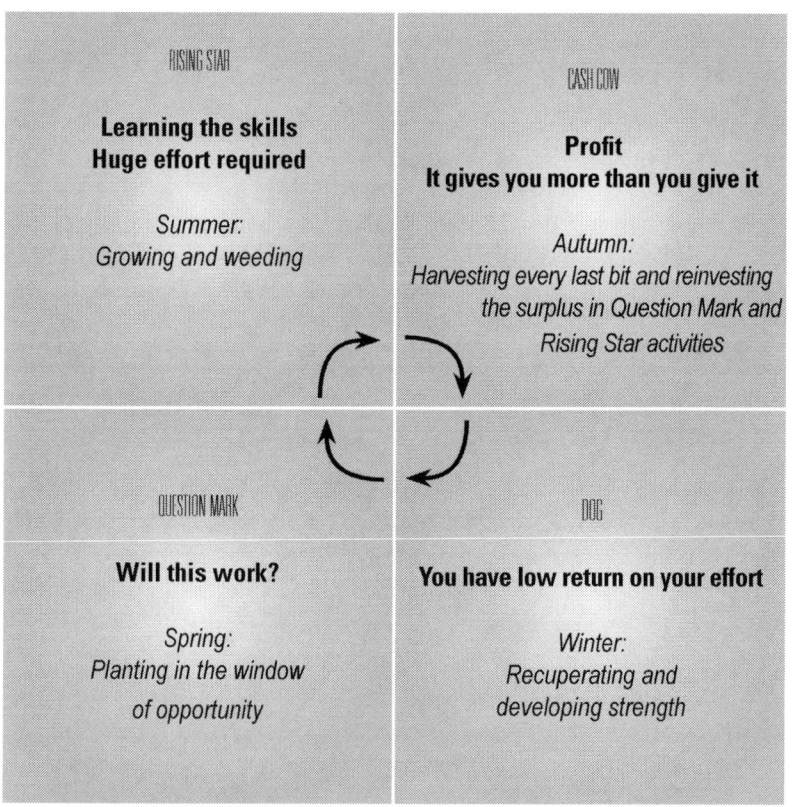

RISING STAR	CASH COW
Learning the skills **Huge effort required** *Summer:* *Growing and weeding*	**Profit** **It gives you more than you give it** *Autumn:* *Harvesting every last bit and reinvesting the surplus in Question Mark and Rising Star activities*
QUESTION MARK	DOG
Will this work? *Spring:* *Planting in the window of opportunity*	**You have low return on your effort** *Winter:* *Recuperating and developing strength*

* Adapted from the BCG matrix.

When the Rising Star yields more energy than is being invested it has reached the Cash Cow phase in the BCG matrix. Then it drops into Dog, where the amount you're getting out of it is line ball with what you're putting into it. And finally it moves into Dog, where you put a heap of energy into completing tasks and you get virtually nothing back in return.

As your tasks track through these four stages, you can predict what's going to happen to your energy level and how you're going to respond to it.

ENERGY IN THE QUESTION MARK PHASE

For example, in the bottom left-hand corner Question Mark phase you'll be drawing primarily on your C1 lateral thinking and C2 thinking functions. Imagine for a moment what this Question Mark time would be like. In this time you'll experience some fantastic emotions including excitement, expectation and optimism with a new lease on life. So when a project is at the beginning, you'll be caught up in those dreams and aspirations and will feel amazingly alive.

But you will also feel incredibly stressed because with every new project comes anxiety. Often anxiety accompanies new Question Mark activities in your life, but remember, as the Maya Lenca people say, anxiety is not to be avoided; it is simply a consequence of your body drawing the energy it needs from the universe to get the activity under way.

If you naturally access your C1 and C2 functions, you will feel most excited about projects in the Question Mark phase, but will you be willing to invest the energy and have the focus to push these projects on to the next Rising Star stage?

ENERGY IN THE RISING STAR PHASE

To create a Star will require sheer willpower, discipline and passion and the help of others to get you there. This means accessing your P2 passion and I2 empathetic functions.

So you can expect that in the second Rising Star stage of a project, you're going to generate a lot of passion and enthusiasm. You will feel powerful as you get in touch with your P2 function. You'll also feel exhausted, and you'll get disappointed when team members fall short of high expectations.

There's lots of fall over, get up, back onto the bike, ride it, fall over, get back on the bike, ride it. The Rising Star phase is a powerful yet challenging part of the cycle.

ENERGY IN THE CASH COW PHASE

Your project then falls into Cash Cow where you start getting returns. This requires the discipline of the P1 and the detail focus of the I1. P1 provides the personal discipline to keep going and I1 provides the know how to do it. But notice there's no C1 or C2 in this phase. Not one bit. So when they're in that Cash Cow people tend to complain that while they are receiving the accolades and the money they've always wanted, they are fundamentally bored and depressed with no energy.

USING THE BCG MATRIX FOR STRATEGIC INSIGHT

If, however, they were to take an integrated view, they would take the money and the energy from the Cash Cow, and invest it in the Rising Star and the Question Mark activities that they are undertaking simultaneously.

Instead, what many tend to do in their careers is throw the baby out with the bath water. A friend of mine was a lawyer who had been stuck in the P1, I1 Cash Cow phase of his career for fourteen years. He had no interest in law any more. He was incredibly bored, yet he made big money at the big end of town. One day he announced, 'I can't stand law any more. It's time to cut my ties and start again.' So he threw away his career and tried, unsuccessfully, to start a vineyard. It was a huge failure and ten years later he is back unhappily practising law to pay back his debts. This is not an integrated approach to managing your life.

An integrated approach would have been for him to keep managing law and to integrate into his life some other new projects that would draw on his C1 and C2 functions.

He would have leveraged the fact that he could have worked from 9 to 5, for a good rate of return to fund some of these other Question Mark and Rising Star activities.

But in using this strategy, be mindful of the fact that unless you challenge yourself in some way the Cash Cow surplus will disappear when the activity becomes a Dog.

Unfortunately there are no parts of your mind that you use in the Dog part of the life-cycle. That's where you don't even really exist. You're not there. Your life is on hold. I'm sure we can all remember parts of our lives like that. This is the phase to recuperate and rest and plan how we can start the whole life cycle again.

WHAT HAPPENS IN THE DOG PHASE?

If you followed the ideal process for making a decision it would involve using all six of your mind's functions. You'd access each one and make sure your decision incorporated insight from each of those points of view. But in practice this is not what generally happens. Usually our most dominant function triggers and then dominates our thought process.

For example, if your most dominant thinking function is P2, your thinking process will be triggered by noticing that something isn't right. But rather than considering the situation by working through our five other functions we tend to first access our memory for thinking of what we may have done in the past on this issue. We want to recall what decisions we may have come to in the past so that we can minimize duplication and speed up our verdict. This storehouse of past decisions is called the unconscious ultimatum.

So you may have decided at age nine that you don't like ice-cream. This decision is then stored so that you don't have to think about it again. Instead, from that day on you know you just go back and retrieve that unconscious ultimatum, 'I don't like ice-cream.'

If someone says, 'Do you like ice-cream?' Without thinking you can respond decisively, 'No, I don't.' But in giving your response you haven't really thought about it at all. You've just recalled a decision that you made as a child.

In Dog, every decision is drawn from the unconscious ultimatum so technically you are brain dead. In many ways you are not even present. You come home from work and someone says, 'What did you do today?'

You say, 'I don't really remember.'

Somebody asks you about your relationship with your husband or wife, and if that relationship is in Dog you won't even be able to recall what you did on the weekend because effectively you weren't even there. It's as if you lived some time ago, but you're not currently in existence. It's the old saying — some people live for fifty years, other people live the same year fifty times. Are you living the same year fifty times?

And if all the activities in your life are in Dog you lose all connection to your feelings and sense of purpose. Now you're not depressed necessarily, but you're not happy either. You've lost all soul (C1 and C2), you've lost all spirit (I1 and I2) and you've lost all willpower (P1 and P2). You're like a robot going through life on automatic pilot.

This doesn't mean that you've got something significantly wrong with your life or that you require some form of major psychotherapy. It doesn't mean anything deep at all, other than the fact that your life is in Dog. It means that **all** your activities in life are in Dog. It means that it's time you started the cycle again.

Personal Focus

APPLYING THE BCG MATRIX TO YOUR RELATIONSHIPS

In what phase, for example, is your principal relationship in life?

Broadly speaking most BCG cycles take about seven years to complete. So if you were married six years ago, odds are you will be moving into the Dog phase next year. Isn't it amazing how often married couples decide to have a family after seven years? This is because it changes all the dynamics of the relationship by putting the couple back into the Question Mark phase.

But you can also do that consciously, by sitting down with your partner and consciously thinking of ways that you can change the dynamics of the relationship such that you have to be in the active process of making fresh decisions every day.

Here's an interesting point. I've spoken to so many people who have one bunch of strategies for courting, and another bunch of strategies for marriage. Successful relationships use many of the courting strategies in marriage.

Another interesting point is that many couples believe that for their entire marriage, as much as possible, they will each remain the same person. If this is the agreement you have in marriage I pity both you and your partner.

In contrast, successful relationships have contracts that require both parties to grow and change. If you know absolutely everything about your partner, that's sad. If you can predict that person 100 per cent, it's time you gave them a wake-up call. If they can predict you too, you're both dead!

The ideal situation is to have a good mix of activities in all four quadrants of the BCG. In manufacturing it's called having a portfolio of products in different phases.

For example, if your relationship is in the Dog phase, it doesn't mean that you have to find a new person. Instead, it means you need to find the new person in the person you're with.

The key is to develop the skill of being able to identify which emotions are related to the cycle and which one is related to the person. People who don't master this skill will sustain relationships until they reach one of the four phases that doesn't sit with them well and then they will end the relationship only to have the next relationship end at exactly the same phase.

So you want a good mix of all these tasks and activities over all four quadrants.

QUESTIONS PEOPLE SOMETIMES ASK

What's wrong with having all six projects in C1, C2?
Answer: You're likely to stress yourself to death.

What's wrong with having all your projects in Rising Star?

Answer: You're going to be a megalomaniac. You're going to be one of those really uptight people who take great pains and give them to others.

Why don't you want all your activities in Cash Cow?

Answer: Well, that's when you go into retirement, and I know some people who are thirty who are retired but there will not be the excitement, passion and energy in life you will want — believe me.

Why don't you want everything in Dog?

Answer: Because then you've got no zest, your life's got no soul, no spirit and you lose all self-respect and willpower to live.

The returns from the Cash Cow phase provide the resources for the C1, C2 in the Question Mark phase and the P2 energy for the Rising Star phase. The Question Mark phase gives the energy and the meaning to your life. The Rising Star phase gives you power and energy in life. The Dog phase gives you time to rest.

How do you know when a C1, C2 Question Mark activity goes into Rising Star?

Answer: The answer lies in the amount of momentum the activity has. Imagine you're pushing a wheel to the top of a hill and suddenly it starts to gather speed by itself. At the point it starts to roll, your project moves into Rising Star. The moment the project starts to get going, people start ringing you and wanting things to happen; or when you have your first small success, you know that your Question Mark has moved to Rising Star. That's when you stop dreaming and start doing.

How do you know when it moves from Rising Star into Cash Cow?

Answer: The simple answer is that for very little effort you start getting compliments, money or return of some nature that you weren't expecting. If we go back to our wheel, Cash Cow is where you can metaphorically put a carriage on the back of the wheel and it still gathers speed as it carries you. Often when we are in the Cash Cow phase we find the sensation of this momentum very strange. The accolades and the awards that come in Cash Cow we crave for in the early stages of the cycle. At these early stages all we want is recognition for all the hard work we are doing. But amazingly when we get there our recognition comes often when we least expect or need it.

Recognition usually comes in the Cash Cow or even in the Dog phase. You see the person get up at the awards and sometimes it's as if they're barely interested in what they're doing, but they're happy to receive it, because they remember how much they wanted it right back at the beginning of the journey.

Personal Focus

The BCG life cycle framework allows you to balance new and old projects and see them all as part of a larger process with its own momentum. Your task is to work with that momentum and invest your energy into the right areas and divest your energy of the right areas.

USE THE PRINCIPLES OF TIME MANAGEMENT TO ENERGIZE YOU

There are two fundamentally different approaches to time. There are 'through time' people and there are 'in time' people. If you're high in P1, as an 'in time' person, your challenge will be to judge what is important versus what is urgent. Because you will tend to do the urgent things instead of the important things. My suggestion to you is get stuck into Covey's book *The Seven Habits of Highly Successful People*. He's developed this great matrix which talks about balancing the important with the urgent.

Conversely, if you're high in P2 you will have a 'through time' paradigm which means that while you will create success you will not be present to enjoy the moment. 'Through time' people always seem to be somewhere else, either in the past or in the future, and often don't successfully apply themselves to the task at hand. The person I recommend you read to solve this bad habit is Anthony Robbins. He has this sensational material on moving towards and moving away from, and being able to create a powerful reward system for yourself to keep yourself motivated and present.

YOUR DESTINY IS SHAPED BY YOUR DECISIONS, SO USE THE NEUROPOWER THINKING TECHNOLOGY TO MAKE POWERFUL DECISIONS

When you're confronted with a problem, discipline yourself to look at it from all six viewpoints, C1 lateral thinking, C2 vision, P1 logic, P2 values and beliefs, I1 information, I2 feelings. Don't get locked into just seeing it from one paradigm. If you have difficulty using some of those functions that are weaker, team up with someone and discuss it with them. Make the commitment to yourself — you are going to look at this problem from all these points of view using all six of your mind's thinking functions.

Start this process with your strongest function and work backwards from your strongest to weakest. By the time you get to your fifth and sixth you may need to team up with someone else.

Look at it from all angles, and you'll be healthily rewarded. A whole chapter of Sun-Tzu's, *The Art of War* is about looking at it from each of these six angles. Know yourself and know the task. Don't just get into an old pattern and keep going around and around and around. This is one way that you can send a wagon down your own rut.

HAVE INSTANT ACCESS TO ALL YOUR THINKING FUNCTIONS WITH THE FOLLOWING EXERCISES

C1 Oracle

To boost your C1 create your own oracle. You can do that by grabbing a dictionary, randomly picking a word and seeing that word as being the answer to your problem. For example, you can ask a question 'What am I going to do about this driveway?' and randomly take a word on one of the pages in the dictionary and try and make a link between that word and a solution. An oracle of this nature is one way of making sure that you look at something in a brand new, fresh way.

C2 Dream board

To enhance your C2 vision create a dream board so that you know where you are going. If you are really keen you can pack up your troubles and head off for a weekend and have a private vision quest.

P1 What is my immediate next step?

When you are confronted with a huge task the P1 question is simply 'but what's the next step?' You've only got to live today, one day at a time, one step at a time.

P2 Why am I doing this and where can I get the most leverage?

To use your P2 function you need to ask yourself the question, 'Is this the right direction and what rewards do I get?' Think through how you can set up an effective self-reward system.

I1 Do I really have enough knowledge in this area?

Often we go through life with the assumption that we've got all the information we need and that we don't need to read books summarizing the wisdom of others. So commit yourself to a reading frenzy on the key areas that you're wanting to move forward on. Become an expert in the area that you want to have as your area of mastery.

And then finally, I2. Keep in touch with your own feelings

Don't ride over your own feelings. Acknowledge them, express them, talk about them and actively find ways that you can convert pain into power through creative expression. Remember that emotion is energy in motion – you need to learn how to identify and use this personal energy in motion.

LEARN FROM THE EXPERIENCES OF OTHER MASTERS — FIND THEIR MASTER STRATEGIES

Become voracious in your search for master strategies. There are fantastic books written just for you. Stephen Covey's *The Seven Habits of Highly Effective People* is particularly good if you're high in P1. You'll feel it feeding your soul. Anthony Robbins' *Awaken the Giant Within* and *Unlimited Power* are fantastic for C2, P2, I2 people. Dr Srully Blotnick's *Area of Mastery* outlines the formulas that took people from being broke into being millionaires. *Optimal Experience* is another book that teaches you about how to totally focus. Jim Rohn has a series of tape sets and books which cover a whole range of areas in terms of life cycles and natural laws.

Think and Grow Rich by Napoleon Hill, *Master Keys to Riches*. *A Whack in the Side of the Head*, which is a short book that gives you exercises for building your C1 lateral thinking function. *Emotional Intelligence* and *Care for the Soul* are very, very good for developing your I2 function.

Personal empowerment is about being able to draw the best out of yourself in the environments that confront you. When you measure how fit a person is, it's not necessarily how fast they can run, or how puffed they are at the end of their journey; it's how quickly they recuperate. The strategies outlined in this book will not make you immune to feeling demoralized, sad, depressed, angry, disappointed, anxious, stressed or fearful but they will give you the ability to quickly diagnose where the problem really is, and what you can do about it.

Mastering this stage doesn't guarantee that it's going to be an easy road, but it guarantees that you can stay on the road that you want to be on, and you'll have the power and the focus and the energy and the insight and the strategy to be able to do it.

Chapter 25 Checklist

1. Give yourself a score out of 10 in terms of how well you manage your energy.
2. Create a BCG matrix for your current projects. How many are in Question Mark, Rising Star, Cash Cow and Dog?
3. Write down what changes need to be made so that you can milk the surplus energy from the Cash Cow, and invest this into the the Question Mark and Rising Star activities.
4. Decide how you will exit the Dog activities.
5. Look at your lifestyle and sleeping patterns and decide if these support or hinder your ability to achieve your objectives. If they hinder them, identify how you will change your sleeping and eating to best support you.
6. Finally, are you making the very best decisions by using all your six thinking functions, or are you becoming tunnel visioned? See just how useful it is to use all six by using this strategy for your next three big decisions.

Personal Focus

A Final Word

As Winston Churchill once said, "This is not the end, it's not even the beginning of the end. It's just the end of the beginning." And this is just the end of the beginning of your new quest of reaching your full potential.

An understanding of the six core thinking functions gives you the ability to more effectively use your mind. An understanding of your gift or leadership style enables you to succeed in life on your own terms. And if you apply the age-old principles outlined in *Personal Focus*, with personal discipline, passion and creativity you will conquer your outer world and gain personal wealth, comfort and outer security.

With your outer world conquered you will be ready to explore a new frontier — your internal world. A world with different challenges, lessons and insights. A world that requires a slightly different map, but the same courage, faith, discipline and creativity you have needed to conquer your external world.

You may be surprised to discover that this will be your next quest.

Personal Focus

Appendix One

Discover Your Strength or Unique Gift

Appendix

THE AWAKENING — UNDERSTANDING THE NATURE OF HUMAN DIFFERENCES

It becomes obvious early in life that everyone is different. We all have a different sense of humor, differing motivations and comfort zones, and differing preferences on everything from the ideal job to the ideal partner in life.

Our differences are complex. Sometimes we agree with a person on one topic and fiercely disagree with that same person on another. Often people we enjoy working with are people we would not invite to our home and vice versa. We can change in an instant – acting and feeling one way around one person yet being completely different with someone else. We can appear fluent, convincing, charming, sincere and powerful in one meeting and yet at the next meeting become inarticulate and appear to lack credibility.

An effective understanding of yourself and others, or having a good working understanding of the system of human differences, enables you to be empowered in any given situation. It gives an insight into what motivates you and how you can best use your natural strengths to succeed.

With an understanding of the NeuroPower Framework of human differences, you can identify activities and people who can dampen your enthusiasm and affect your performance. It will also help you understand the way your mind works. The NeuroPower Framework can explain how decision-making can be a constant internal battle between different poles as you deal with your life's greatest challenges both internally and externally.

You will be able to recognize and understand the conversations you have with yourself, the inner conflicts you experience and the way you ultimately see yourself.

A clear understanding of the system of human differences or types, can explain why some people seem to have boundless energy and others have none at all; why some people appear cold and others warm; why some love to offend and others enjoy being offended; and why some people are refreshingly crazy and others refreshingly sane.

All these variables are determined by just one simple process – the way the mind solves problems.

Every moment of the day we are solving problems in our own unique way. Some people rely mainly on their gut feeling or intuition; others rely on their ability to reason logically and think things through and still others spend most of their decision-making time researching topics and laying the facts out in front of them.

Appendix

Round table of masters

The eight leadership styles of life and their universal gifts

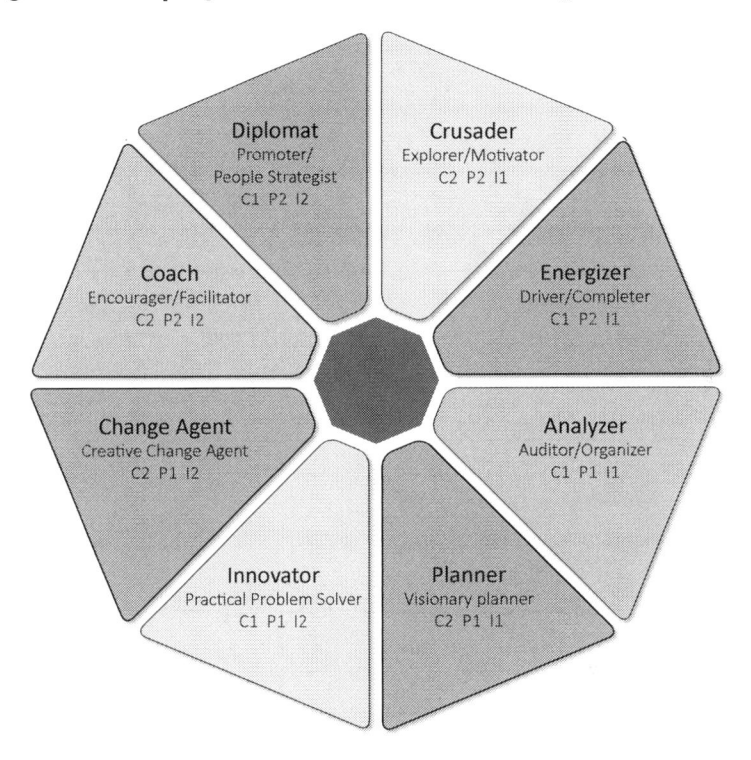

Diplomat
Promoter/
People Strategist
C1 P2 I2

Crusader
Explorer/Motivator
C2 P2 I1

Coach
Encourager/Facilitator
C2 P2 I2

Energizer
Driver/Completer
C1 P2 I1

Change Agent
Creative Change Agent
C2 P1 I2

Analyzer
Auditor/Organizer
C1 P1 I1

Innovator
Practical Problem Solver
C1 P1 I2

Planner
Visionary planner
C2 P1 I1

At any moment of the day whether buying a newspaper, jotting something down, or taking a phone call, you are solving problems.

This system of profiling tracks how you prefer to solve problems. When we interact, we can use the insights from the profile to indicate our natural areas of strength. When using these strengths, you will be fluent. When using the recessive parts of your mind you will be less fluent and may appear insincere and lacking energy.

In much the same way, when you are in a conversation or arguing a point you are most likely to be at your most persuasive when you are using the dominant or preferred parts of your mind.

Many people are using the NeuroPower Framework for understanding human differences to provide vital career guidance or as a guide to team and relationship building.

Appendix

Executives have used it to select sales teams, governments have used it to provide senior public servants with training in crisis management, while educators have consulted the NeuroPower Framework for vital clues in understanding how individuals learn.

Every moment of every day you are solving problems. The eight thinking profiles are based on your approach to solving problems. Every one of us by the age of seven has developed a certain way of approaching the world and solving problems (our thinking profile) and so each of us resembles one of these eight leadership styles.

INTRODUCING THE EIGHT LEADERSHIP STYLES

The eight leadership styles are:
1. The Crusader - C2 P2 I1
2. The Innovator - C1 P1 I2
3. The Diplomat - C1 P2 I2
4. The Coach - C2 P2 I2
5. The Analyzer - C1 P1 I1
6. The Planner - C2 P1 I1
7. The Energizer - C1 P2 I1
8. The Change Agent - C2 P1 I2

The diagram of the round table summarizes each character, their area of mastery and the value they bring to the round table.

Appendix

Appendix Two

Compatibility Matrix

Appendix

Intelligence Compatibility Matrix

= Least Compatible Combination | = Most Compatible Combination

Appendix Three

Capacity Matrix
(Exploring the Mirror)

Appendix

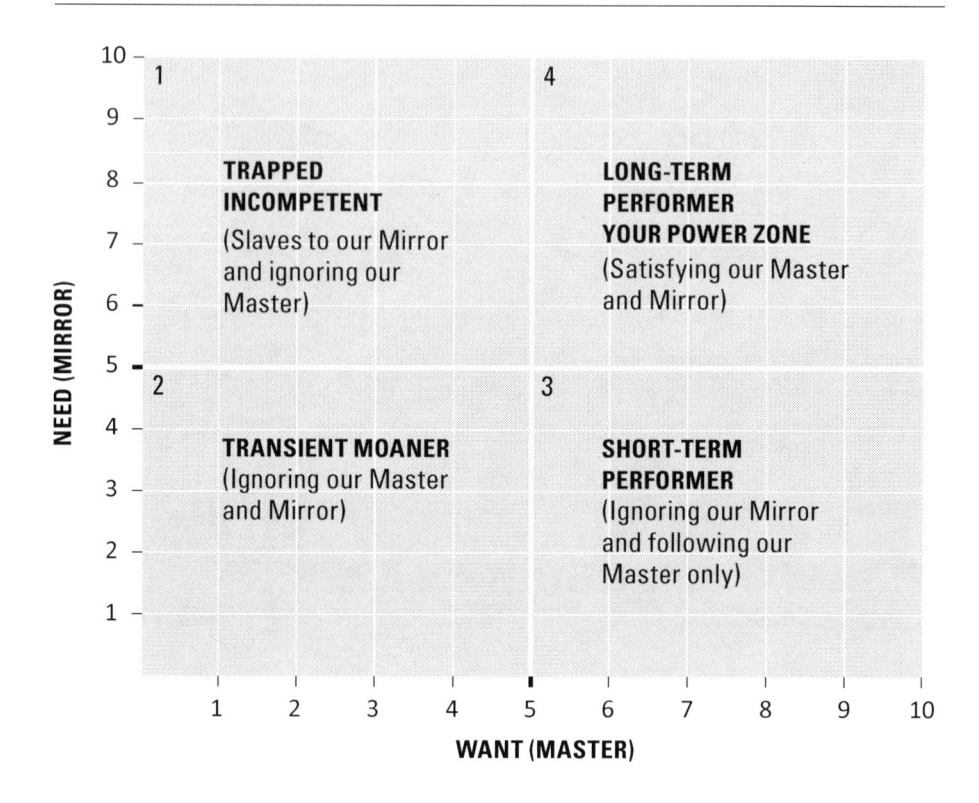

1. TRAPPED INCOMPETENT (Slaves to our Mirror and ignoring our Master)		**4. LONG-TERM PERFORMER YOUR POWER ZONE** (Satisfying our Master and Mirror)
2. TRANSIENT MOANER (Ignoring our Master and Mirror)		**3. SHORT-TERM PERFORMER** (Ignoring our Mirror and following our Master only)

Y-axis: NEED (MIRROR), scale 1–10
X-axis: WANT (MASTER), scale 1–10

THE FOUR QUADRANTS EXPLAINED

1. Trapped Incompetent (slave to our Mirror)

If we are getting what we need but not what we want, we can easily become Trapped Incompetents. This happens because when we are getting what we need the Mirror will refuse to let us move even if the Master finds the job dull and unrewarding. The Master will complain about the job and will refuse to study or improve skills that they don't want to improve. The Master will feel trapped. The Mirror will feel content.

2. Transient Moaner (ignoring our Mirror and Master)

The Transient Moaner is simply an individual who is not getting either what they want or what they need. Both their Master and Mirror are unimpressed. They don't like it on any level; they will feel bored at a Master level and unsatisfied at the Mirror level. They will play politics, try to get fired or simply use the role as a stepping-stone before their real job emerges.

3. Short-term Performer (ignoring our Mirror)

If we are getting what we want — but not what we need — our Master will enthusiastically learn new skills, capabilities, read, attend training and talk highly of the role and organization. Despite all this good press, however, we will move on because our Mirror simply isn't getting what it needs. When asked why they are moving on confusion abounds because the individual can't even understand it themselves.

4. Long-term Performer: your power zone (satisfying our Mirror and Master)

The Long-term Performer is an individual whose Master is getting the challenge, opportunities and role they want and the Mirror is getting all they need. This is the individual's 'power zone'. From here most people get promoted with increased responsibility, money and praise. These people are the organization's leaders and shape the organization's positive culture. In employee terms they are pure gold.

For example:

If my Master is a Coach and my Mirror an Analyzer, and I give the following scores out of 10

Master Coach

Degree to which my Coach is able to create visions and heal: 8/10

Mirror Analyzer

Degree to which my Analyzer has order, security and money: 8/10

8/10 x 8/10 = 64/100 or 64%

In this situation I am running at about 64 per cent capacity. (On average, even the most inspired individual can only maintain an average of about 75 per cent.)

Appendix

Appendix

Appendix Four

Leadership Style Inventory

Appendix

Leadership Style Inventory

TEST INSTRUCTIONS

Following are eight paragraphs that give an overview of each of the Leadership Styles. These are not comprehensive descriptions. Instead, they are written to focus on the main features of the style.

1. Read each of the eight paragraphs and select the **top two** that sound most like you.
2. Make your selection based on the sense of the **whole** paragraph that most sounds like you rather than a sentence here or there or aspects of one.
3. Prioritize the paragraphs.
4. If when you are making your selection you find it difficult to narrow down the field because aspects of all the styles sound like you, consider how others would describe you and use that as a guide.
5. It may also be helpful to make your selection based on how you acted in your early twenties because this is when your Leadership Style is usually at its most strident and obvious.
6. You may also consider having your significant other look at the paragraphs and make a selection granted that they observe your behavior all the time.

© Copyright Peter Burow 2004

Appendix

The Leadership Style Test:
SELECT TWO PARAGRAPHS THAT SOUND MOST LIKE YOU

1. I like to value straightforwardness, honesty and clarity. I dislike conflict and work hard to complete my responsibilities to the highest standard so that it's difficult to blame me if things go wrong. At work I like to know exactly what is expected of me so that I can complete my role to the best of my ability. I strongly believe in personal integrity — which means that I mean what I say and say what I mean. I don't like people who try to deceive or blur the edges of life — I believe they should just tell it as it is. I am not passionate about all things but some issues around justice really fire me up and I can crusade for what is right and true. I am conservative by nature and live in a house I can afford, drive a sensible car and don't pretend I am somebody I am not. I can't stand pretentious or lazy people who try charming their way through life rather than doing what they are supposed to do. People often say that I look stern or angry even when I'm not. When I do relax, there is another side to me. At social gatherings at the end of a week or project, I don't mind a drink or two and can party and mingle with the best of them. People are often amazed at the difference between the two sides of my personality — my serious side and my party side. By and large, however, I take life pretty seriously. I like to do my best and I resent people that want an easy life and don't do their fair share.

2. People see me as solid, relaxed and reliable. I calm people down when they are emotionally hurting and have an easy way about me. I don't really plan for the future or worry about things as many do. I take each day as it comes and deal with things as they arise. I live in the now. This means that while everyone is too busy to care, I am the one who walks beside people when they are going through a bad patch. I like problem-solving and can keep working at something until I nut it out. At work it's the little things that people ask me to help them with — things that I know nothing about, but seem to work out somehow anyway. My family is very important to me, and so is relaxing and having a laugh with friends. I am practical and prefer to take a hands-on approach to life. Every now and then I wonder what I'm doing with my life and can get a little disappointed with what I have achieved. I also have an internal critic that sits in my head and constantly tells me how I am falling short. I am even-tempered but every now and then people push me too far and if I snap they get to see the wrath of a patient person – which sometimes even amazes me. The only down side with going with the flow is that I find it difficult to set, and discipline myself to follow, my own agendas and priorities.

© Copyright Peter Burow 2004

3. I am friendly, relationship-centered and ambitious. I like others to like me and work hard to accommodate their point of view if I am working with them. When there is conflict between two other people I can often build the bridge to bring two different points of view together. I am optimistic and love meeting new people and almost everyone likes meeting me. I enjoy teamwork and discussing issues. I find reading, paperwork and administration difficult although I will do them if I absolutely have to. I seem to see all points of view pretty easily and can sometimes seem to others to be a little indecisive at times if people are at loggerheads and I have to make a call. Good relationships mean a lot to me and I am willing to do what it takes to develop and maintain them.

4. I am a big-picture person. I like to see the vision and work backwards from that. I see the potential in others, in most situations, and often work from this perspective rather than reality. I am sensitive to others and can often see and feel their pain. I am constantly looking to create a better and safer world and put a lot of energy in creating a home and work environment where people feel safe. I can usually tell when people are trying to put on a brave face and somehow seem to be able to see the source of their pain. By nature I look for the best in others and expect them to do the same, although I am constantly amazed at how narrow minded and heartless people seem to be with themselves and others. I like to come up with an exciting or bold plan and then inspire a team to achieve it. I enjoy reading and I find that it settles me down when I am feeling anxious. I love to learn new information and frameworks about success, achievement, and about better understanding myself and others. I am sometimes described by others as having a big personality and it's true that I tend to wear my heart on my sleeve. I love intensity of experience and creating something as close to perfect as possible.

© Copyright Peter Burow 2004

5. I would describe myself as one of life's observers. I like to watch what is happening and make my mind up in my own time. I don't like to be pushed whether at home or at work. I have an excellent memory for details and enjoy collecting information about almost everything. Some people need to talk and make noise for no reason. I like to be quiet and could spend a week by myself if I had interesting books or tasks to complete. If I am by myself with no external stimulus I can get bored. I enjoy creating order out of chaos. I like things to be ordered. They may not always look neat, but I know exactly where everything is and how I can lay my hands on what I need. I like to be self sufficient, financially and emotionally, and structure my life in line with this. I can cope with chaotic situations better than most, and have the ability to break down any situation or problem into parts and deal with each part one at a time.

6. I like to understand my role and responsibilities and once I have that understanding I will perform well. This is true at home and at work. When I don't have a role I feel lost and without purpose. I believe in honor and in the importance of the family. My role as parent, son, daughter, husband or wife is very important to me and I take it very seriously. I believe in actively planning my life and the life of those I love. I can see problems ahead and like to work on solving them months, if not years, ahead. I have a life plan that spans years, if not decades, into the future and I have the discipline and conviction to follow the plan. I enjoy using equipment that is purpose-designed and can often get more performance out of a piece of equipment than others can. I have an off-beat sense of humor which often confuses others so I tend to keep it to myself. I like the structure and discipline that comes with being a part of an organization and don't particularly like those who are more interested in their own glory than the success of the project. I am stable and am able to create stability in teams during periods of intense uncertainty. People who work with me have a sense of certainty.

© Copyright Peter Burow 2004

7. I am spontaneous, quick and energetic. I enjoy getting my teeth into a project and getting it done as quickly as possible. I have a lot more energy than others seem to have and some people say they feel exhausted after they have spent time with me. I enjoy meeting new people and trying new experiences. I believe in the philosophy 'live and let live'. I am intensely loyal to my friends and family and will fight to the death to protect their reputation. I can't stand hypocrites. I don't mind blowing the cover of people who put themselves above the rest of us by asking them difficult questions or turning up the heat in some way. I have a short attention span and get bored very easily so I need to have a few projects on the go at the same time. I don't know why everyone seems to make life so difficult. Life is life. You live it the best you can. I enjoy life overall. What I most enjoy is meeting new people and having new experiences. What is important to me is getting things done quickly, and people that dither around really annoy me — just get on with it! Any action is better than procrastination!

8. I am not easily convinced by bells and whistles. I am amazed at how gullible others seem to be when what is being said is illogical and obviously self-serving. I analyze everything that I see and come to my own conclusions. I'm irritated by loud-mouthed bigots and don't usually waste my energy debating with them unless I feel like an argument, because they can't hear my viewpoint anyway. My home is a pleasant place where my friends and family can relax. I like good food, good wine and good conversation. I have a very good 'bullshit detector' and can see a fraud a mile off. I am practical by nature and like to understand how things will work in practice. At work when new ideas are put forward I am often the one that sees the inconsistency between what is being proposed and the outcomes they are looking for. This irritates people who prefer to live in a make-believe world of ideals and theoretical concepts. I feel betrayed when I have put in the work on a project and somebody else who is more fluent and enthusiastic than I am gets the credit. I am ambitious and like to be acknowledged for my contribution even though I never ask for it. I can think in abstract terms and like discussing philosophical viewpoints. I like to develop systems and practices that ensure the task is completed efficiently and with the minimum of fuss. If I know each team member I am good at placing them in a functional role that best suits their capabilities. Personally I love to learn new capabilities and personally have quite a number of hands-on skills in a range of different disciplines.

© Copyright Peter Burow 2004

Appendix

Now, following the instructions, select your top two choices and note the leadership styles that are used to describe them.

TEST PARAGRAPH

ONE	>>	Crusader
TWO	>>	Innovator
THREE	>>	Diplomat
FOUR	>>	Coach
FIVE	>>	Analyzer
SIX	>>	Planner
SEVEN	>>	Energizer
EIGHT	>>	Change Agent

Make no assumptions at this point about what the names given to each type implies. Now you are ready to look further into each of the eight types before making your final decision.

Your first choice has a 78 per cent chance of being your Master Profile. There is a 40 per cent chance that your second choice is your Mirror.

Appendix

Bibliography

Bardwick, J., 'Peacetime Management and Wartime Leadership' in Hesselbein, Goldsmith, and Beckhard, *The Leader of the Future.*

Blanchard, K., 'Turning the Organizational Pyramid Upside Down' in Hesselbein, Goldsmith, and Beckhard, *The Leader of the Future.*

Blotnick, S., *Getting Rich Your Own Way,* 1st Edition: Jove Publications, 1982.

Bridges, W., 'Leading the De-Jobbed Organizations' in Hesselbein, Goldsmith, and Beckhard, *The Leader of the Future.*

Buckingham, M., and Clifton, D., *Now Discover Your Strengths.* The Free Press, 2001.

Covey, S., 'Three Roles of the Leader in the New Paradigm' in Hesselbein, Goldsmith, and Beckhard, *The Leader of the Future.*

Drucker, P. F., 'Toward the New Organization,' *Leader to Leader 2,* no. 3, 1997.

Fitz-enz, J., Survey. Saratoga Institute 1997.

Handy, C., 'The New Language of Organizing and its Implications for Leaders' in Hesselbein, Goldsmith, and Beckhard, *The Leader of the Future.*

Heskett, J., and Schlesinger, L., 'Leaders Who Shape and Keep Performance-Oriented Culture' in Hesselbein, Goldsmith, and Beckhard, *The Leader of the Future.*

Hill, N., *Think and Grow Rich,* Ballantine Books, 1996.

Kanter, R., 'World-Class Leaders: The Power of Partnering' in *The Leader of the Future,* ed. Hesselbein, F., Goldsmith, M., and Beckhard, R.: Jossey-Bass, 1995.

Kouzes, J., and Posner, B., *The Leadership Challenge: How to Keep Getting Extraordinary Things Done in Organizations* : San Francisco, Jossey-Bass, 1995.

Lombardo, M., and Eichinger, R., 'Learning Agility' working paper, Lominger,

Minneapolis, 1997.

Schein, E., 'Leadership and Organizational Culture' in Hesselbein, Goldsmith and Beckhard, *The Leader of the Future*.

Schiffer, F., *Of Two Minds: The Revolutionary Science of Dual-Brain Psychology*, The Free Press, 1998.

Smallwood, N., Ulrich, D., and Zenger, J., *Results-Based Leadership*, Harvard Business School Pr, 1999.

Stanley, T., *The Millionaire Mind*, Andrews McMeel Publishing, 2001.

Tzu, S., *The Art of War*, Translated by Thomas Cleary: Shambhala, 2004.

Von Oech, R., *A Whack On The Side Of The Head*, 3rd Edition:, 1998.

Yeung and Ready, *Developing Leadership Capabilities of Global Corporations*.

About the Author

Peter Burow

Peter Burow is an expert in leadership development, transformational change management and employee engagement. He is internationally regarded as a trusted advisor and expert facilitator of senior executive teams looking to drive individual, team and organisational performance. Peter has an extensive client list, including international icons such as Emirates Airline, PricewaterhouseCoopers, BHP Billiton, Xerox, Genpact and Ajinomoto.

Peter authored the ground breaking NeuroPower framework, a system which explains human behaviour through the integration of neuroscience, psychology and best practice management theory.

Peter Burow

B.Bus Comm Dip. M.MHH, NS.NLP, AFAIM

Peter is the author of numerous books, Executive Chairman of the NeuroPower Group and a Partner of a number of consulting firms that specialize in applying neuroscience, performance psychology and cultural analysis to the challenges facing leadership teams at all levels of an organization.

Peter is qualified in Business Communications, Neuroeconomics, Neurofeedback, NLP, Integral Coaching and has been awarded an honorary diploma by the Maya-Lenca people of El Salvador for his work in preserving their cultural history.